"This passionate book combines inspired philosophical insight and critical commentary on a range of experiences that constitute transnational yoga. Based on years of participant observation in the United States and India, Miller's intimate understanding of embodied practice provides a new, multivalent understanding of yoga in personal and social experience."

Joseph S. Alter, *author of Yoga in Modern India: The Body between Science and Philosophy*

"Miller's transnational, multi-sited ethnographic research issues a clarion call for more attention to the deeply embodied ways of living and worlding in yoga communities. Including chapters on dietary practices, *mantra* (chants) and *kīrtan* (sacred music), and *prāṇāyāma* (breathing exercises), this wonderfully conceived book is a vital reminder of all that yoga is beyond *āsana* (yoga postures)."

Amanda Lucia, *author of White Utopias: The Religious Exoticism of Transformational Festivals*

Embodying Transnational Yoga

Embodying Transnational Yoga is a refreshingly original, multi-sited ethnography of transnational yoga that obliges us to look beyond postural practice (*āsana*) in modern yoga research.

The book introduces readers to three alternative, understudied categories of transnational yoga practice which include food, music, and breathing. Studying these categories of embodied practice using interdisciplinary methods reveals transformative "engaged alchemies" that have been extensively deployed by contemporary disseminators of yoga. Readers will encounter how South Asian dietary regimens, musical practices, and breathing techniques have been adapted into contemporaneous worlds of yoga practice both within, but also beyond, the Indian Ocean rim.

The book brings the field of Modern Yoga Studies into productive dialogue with the fields of Indian Ocean Studies, Embodiment Studies, Food Studies, Ethnomusicology, and Pollution Studies. It will also be a valuable resource for both scholarly work and for teaching in the fields of Religious Studies, Anthropology, and South Asian Religions.

Christopher Jain Miller is Professor of Jain and Yoga Studies and Vice President of Academic Affairs at Arihanta Institute, San Jose, USA; Visiting Professor at Claremont School of Theology, Los Angeles, USA; and Visiting Researcher at the University of Zürich's Asien-Orient-Institut, Zürich, Switzerland.

Routledge Series on the Indian Ocean and Trans-Asia
Series Editors: **Smriti Srinivas**, *University of California, Davis, USA and* **Neelima Jeychandran**, *Penn State University, USA*

Editorial Advisory Board: **Sunil Amrith**, *Yale University, USA;* **Kumari R. Issur**, *University of Mauritius;* **Pedro Machado**, *Indiana University, USA;* **Dilip M. Menon**, *University of the Witwatersrand, South Africa; and* **Allen F. Roberts**, *University of California-Los Angeles, USA*

This new series brings together the study of Asia, Africa, and Oceania in contemporary times. Focusing on Indian Ocean/Trans-Asian worlds, the series looks at inter-and intra-relations and practices together rather than as separate realms to expand the limits of Indian Ocean and Asian scholarship by including new gateways, trajectories, and conjunctions and disjunctions over land and water. Decentering a coastal/littoral/national approach, it offers a venue for new units of analysis and conceptual frameworks. In addition to exploring new or hidden histories of older cultural connections, this series is also interested in novel methodologies, ethnographies, and historiographies that challenge the spatial and epistemological boundaries of Indian Ocean and Asian Studies. Seeking to unpack the complexities of the rapidly changing Asian/oceanic life-worlds and relationships, we focus on topics including, but not limited to, modern intellectual or material histories, the Anthropocene in Asia, contemporary religious movements, human-nonhuman intimacies, infrastructure and architecture, botanical lives, expressive cultures and media, intangible knowledges and lived histories, forms of embodiment, cultural memory, and landscape practices and ecologies. The series welcomes proposals for edited books and monographs.

Islamic Law in the Indian Ocean World
Texts, Ideas and Practices
Edited by Mahmood Kooria and Sanne Ravensbergen

Devotional Spaces of a Global Saint
Shirdi Sai Baba's Presence
Edited by Smriti Srinivas, Neelima Jeychandran and Allen F. Roberts

Embodying Transnational Yoga
Eating, Singing, and Breathing in Transformation
Christopher Jain Miller

For more information about this series, please visit: www.routledge.com/Routledge-Series-on-the-Indian-Ocean-and-Trans-Asia/book-series/RSIO

Embodying Transnational Yoga

Eating, Singing, and Breathing in Transformation

Christopher Jain Miller

Routledge
Taylor & Francis Group
LONDON AND NEW YORK

First published 2024
by Routledge
4 Park Square, Milton Park, Abingdon, Oxon OX14 4RN

and by Routledge
605 Third Avenue, New York, NY 10158

Routledge is an imprint of the Taylor & Francis Group, an informa business

British Library Cataloguing-in-Publication Data
A catalogue record for this book is available from the British Library

ISBN: 978-1-032-53871-6 (hbk)
ISBN: 978-1-032-53869-3 (pbk)
ISBN: 978-1-003-41403-2 (ebk)

DOI: 10.4324/9781003414032

Typeset in Times New Roman
by SPi Technologies India Pvt Ltd (Straive)

For Valentina

Contents

Figures

Preface

I am a cis-gendered man of Filipino, European, and American descent who was raised in a lower middle-class family in Los Angeles, California. Some would say I am "able-bodied," though the story I will relate to you here intimates that such a stark categorization would erase some of the more deeply personal experiences that led me to yoga, and, eventually, to write this book.

Perhaps I should begin by telling you that my late grandmother, Felice Esteban, born and raised in the Philippines, met my late grandfather, Theodore Miller, while he served in the United States Army during World War II. After the war and a short stint in my grandfather's hometown in Pennsylvania, my grandmother and grandfather moved to Culver City, California, where they remained for the rest of their lives. While I was growing up amidst the alienating disenchantment of the increasingly neoliberal 1980s and 1990s in America, my devotedly Catholic grandmother had fortunately brought with her tales of the supernatural from the Philippines. In addition to the delicious Filipino food she cooked, I recall how much I enjoyed sitting on the couch in my grandparents' living room as a child as she lovingly (and sometimes mischievously) conveyed to me the very real world of ghosts and spirits that she had inhabited in the Philippines, and which she had brought with her to the United States in a form of entangled Catholicism. And while I was sometimes frightened by her occasional story-telling mischief, I also found that her stories introduced shades of experiential variation to our young Catholic lives and imaginations in a world that was otherwise continually demystified, rigid, and disenchanted.

My Catholic elementary school principal and third-grade teacher, Flor Lelis, was also from the Philippines. She augmented my grandmother's enchantment with her own stories of the supernatural in the classroom. In addition to that of Mrs. Lelis, my grandmother's influence would live on, even after she passed away from complications due to pneumonia when I was 16 years old. Grandma died after years of working in difficult, unsafe labor conditions in the textile industry in Los Angeles where she inhaled micro-particles from the fabric she worked with as she hand-tailored clothing for Hollywood's rich and famous.

Though more conservative Catholics in Southern California may have found the superstitious and supernatural world my grandmother and principal inhabited and shared with me problematic, I found its messy nature immensely interesting and very real in its own right. And as I finished high school and went to college, I rediscovered my passion for the spiritual and religious while taking courses in New Testament, Catholic Theology, and Indian Philosophy. The rigid Catholic tradition I was raised in suddenly became much more fluid, fractured, interesting, and diverse than I could ever imagine, and it made much more sense that my Catholic grandmother from the Philippines practiced a different kind of tradition than the one I was raised with outside of her (and Mrs. Lelis's) influence.

Like every human being, I have had many ups and downs and twists and turns in life. My work on the California wildfires in my early twenties presents one particularly dramatic and yet formative event that eventually led me to study and practice yoga. In order to pay the bills in my early twenties after graduating from college, I worked for a logistical company that supported the many firefighters and California inmates who fought the seasonal wildfires in Northern California. I did not realize it until much later, but the challenging context in which we were toiling together daily – which included, among other things, endless work hours, intense physical labor, mental stress, frequent injuries, days without sleep, brutal heat, persistent dehydration, hunger, and the never-ending threat of danger from the fires themselves – would leave their mark on me. So much so that in their traumatic wake I was compelled, like so many others, to search for some solace in mind and body to heal the psychological stress as well as my increasing chronic back pain that resulted from scoliosis. And thus my journey into yoga would begin in my late twenties, where I began to find fragments of the peace I had since been searching for as well as a worldview that seemed to align with the ecological worldview I had developed as a surfer who found solace in the Pacific Ocean almost every day.

This book is very much a reflection upon the systems of yoga into which I have voluntarily implicated my own mind and body. In my ongoing search for peace, I completed a two-year teacher training in yoga in 2012–2013 under the direction of Christopher Chapple at the Hill Street Yoga and Meditation Center in Santa Monica, California, while also completing post-baccalaureate studies in religious studies at California State University Long Beach and, soon thereafter, a masters degree in Comparative Theology with significant support from Tracy Tiemeier and Christopher Chapple wherein I explored the intersection of yoga and surf culture in India. With their encouragement, I eventually explored South Asian religions more closely, made my way into the complexity of yoga and Jain traditions including study at the International School for Jain Studies, and finally, after years of supporting myself as a certified public accountant and yoga studio production manager, received a PhD in the Study of Religion under the direction of my PhD advisor Smriti Srinivas at the University of California, Davis in 2018. During my PhD research, I had the great opportunity to live in an intentional spiritual community based on the yoga teachings of Paramahansa Yogananda on the Big Island of Hawaii, as well as at a yoga therapy center known as Kaivalyadhama just outside of Mumbai in Lonavala, Maharashtra.

For all the support and encouragement I have received from my yoga teachers and academic mentors, my appreciation for yoga and Jain ways of knowing continues to grow. Most recently in early 2021, at the invitation of Mahesh Wadher, President of the Federation of Jain Associations of North America (JAINA), I changed my middle name to "Jain." My newfound commitment to the Jain way of life, along with my longstanding yoga practice, complements the sociological, ethnographic approach in this book. I can say I now occupy a new religious identity that constitutes my lifetime commitment to the legitimacy of fluid, porous religious boundaries as well as to the manifold tensions and opportunities these kinds of identities present for critical academic study and the betterment of society.

I continue to work with the Jain community as JAINA's first non-Indian, non-Jain committee chair member, with its Academic Liaison Committee, and, most recently, as the Vice President of Academic Affairs and Professor of Jain and Yoga Studies at Arihanta Institute where we offer online, graduate-level academic study for those interested in studying Jain and yogic traditions. Invoking the Jain principle of multi-perspectivalism (*anekāntavāda*), I would like to acknowledge that the perspective I share in this book is but one of the countless, innumerable, limited views amidst an ocean of possible limited perspectives. I therefore ask for your forgiveness for any harm or offense that it inadvertently causes you. Micchāmi Dukkaḍaṃ.

Christopher Jain Miller,
Zürich

Acknowledgements

I am grateful to many for their enduring support of my research. First of all, thank you to my PhD advisor, Professor Smriti Srinivas, who has given me a much-needed critical approach to the study of yoga without which this book would not exist. Your untiring encouragement and gentle, yet firm and honest feedback were a rare find in graduate school and you are a lifelong mentor. I thank Smriti also for inviting me to participate in the "Reimagining Indian Ocean Worlds" Mellon Research Initiative at the University of California at Davis as well as for the guidance and feedback of Bettina Ng'weno, Neelima Jeychandran, Nicole Ranganath, and all of the other members of our wonderful interdisciplinary cohort. And, of course, I am deeply grateful for the financial support of the Mellon Foundation for supporting my dissertation research through our research initiative. In retrospect, joining this research cluster was one of the most important career choices I have made.

Thank you also to Christopher Chapple, for encouraging me to pursue a PhD after training me in the techniques of yoga which showed me a better way to be in the world and which helped still my mental fluctuations (*vṛttis*) enough to get this book finished! Thanks likewise to our yoga teacher training cohort at Hill Street Yoga and Meditation Center, who provided their own enduring guidance early in the journey. And thank you also to my mentor Tracy Tiemeier, for introducing me to some of the foundational critical approaches that endure in this book.

I must also thank my academic home, Arihanta Institute, and first and foremost our indefatigable CEO and President Parveen Jain, whose tireless support of my academic work through thick and thin will never be forgotten. Likewise, I thank our co-founders Pramod Patel and Dhanesh Kothari, our many dedicated volunteers and staff, including Bijal Vakil, Kavita Mahendra, Kamlesh Mehta, Sunil Mehta, Shobha Vora, Pramod Khincha, Biren Shah, Narendra Parson, Prem Jain, Raj Shah, Arpit Mehta, the Jain Vegan Initiative's Sunny Jain, Nisha Mehta, Pratik Bhansali, and Tushar Mehta, my academic colleagues Professor Cogen Bohanec and Professor Jonathan Dickstein and all of our faculty colleagues, and of course our graduate students. Without the manifold forms of support and kindness you have all extended to me at

Arihanta Institute, and particularly during the most challenging of times in my life, this book would not have come to completion.

Alongside Arihanta Institute, I am also immensely grateful to my other two academic homes at Claremont School of Theology (CST) and the University of Zürich (UZH). At Claremont School of Theology I extend much gratitude to former president Jeffrey Kuan, current president Bishop Grant Hagiya, Dean of the Faculty Andrew Dreitcer, Associate Dean Yuki Schwartz, Professor Venu Mehta, Board Member Nitin Shah, and Senior Director of Admissions Max Wedel and his admissions team. You all creatively demonstrate the power and potential of progressive, online graduate education and have been an absolute joy to work with as we have collaborated to create our joint online Engaged Jain Studies Masters Degree track. At UZH, I am particularly thankful to Professor Nicolas Martin, Inge Ammering, Tancredi Padova, and my other colleagues at the Asien-Orient-Institut. The collegiality, generosity, and scholarly resources you have shared with me have made the process of researching this book and other research projects streamlined, efficient, and enjoyable.

Writing a book is never done in isolation, and for their feedback, encouragement, and ongoing support I thank all of my other academic colleagues who have, in one way or another, had their hands in my work. Thank you to Amanda Lucia, Anya Foxen, Christa Kuberry, and Jonathan Dickstein for providing extensive and detailed feedback after careful reading of initial drafts of this book. My appreciation also to Joseph Alter for his feedback and encouragement, as well as his own approach to the critical ethnographic and social-historical study of yoga to which this book is deeply indebted. Thank you to Flagg Miller for his early encouragement and resourcefulness during graduate school, many of whose original bibliographic recommendations are cited in this book. And thank you to the anonymous peer reviewer who I will likely never know, but who provided vital feedback on the first draft of this book. I am also indebted to McComas Taylor's online Sanskrit program at Australian National University, which was a lifeline during graduate school to gain crucial knowledge and translation skills in Sanskrit that helped me make my way through all of the yoga texts I encountered during my fieldwork.

Many other colleagues have also, in one way or another, inspired me, collaborated with me, encouraged me, or were just there for me when I needed it most. Huge thanks to Rita Sherma from the Graduate Theological Union and the members of DĀNAM for creating an academic space for the critical and yet constructive study of dharma traditions. Among others I must also thank Andrea Jain, Laura von Ostrowski, Lina Aschenbrenner, Farah Godrej, Timothy Choy, Jeffery Long, Veena Howard, Anand Vaidya, Johannes Beltz, Amy Landau, Steven Vose, Shivani Bothra, Marie-Hélène Gorisse, Eva De Clercq, Tine Vekemans, James Mallinson, David Gordon White, Mark Elmore, Anne Vallely, Johannes Bronkhorst, Atul Shah, Laura Dunn, Alba Rodríguez Juan, Yifan Singharaja, Philip Deslippe, Paul Bramadat, Corinna May Lhoir,

Suzanne Newcombe, Peter Pasedach, Michael Horan, Judith Carlisle, Samantha Griggs, Jasvant Modi, and Hope Bohanec. And to all my colleagues, including Grace Kao who supported me during some of the most difficult times while I was writing this book, I will never forget it. I am also grateful for all of my graduate and undergraduate students past and present, who have challenged me to be my best. I hope that this book will be useful to you, especially since many of you watched its research process unfold.

This book would also not be possible without the generosity and wisdom of all of those who taught me about yoga at each of my field sites. At Yoga Anand Ashram, I extend my thanks to the gentle and kind hearts of Glenn and Theresa James, Maureen Shannon-Chapple, Kathe Jeremiah, Chandni Rodriguez, Salvatore Familia, Steve Crimi, Roy Mitchell, and all of the other generous community members. And of course my sincere gratitude to the legacy of Gurani Anjali without whose yoga teachings and practices my life and worldview would not have been so significantly altered for the better. At Polestar Gardens I give thanks to founders Michael and Ann Gornik for modeling yogic discipline like nobody I have ever seen, Christy Thompson and Vina Ketty for making our stay there so welcoming and comfortable, David Zuhars for all the delicious yogic food, Rich Mills for showing us how the ukulele can be both fun and yogic, Bernadette Sabbath for such a warm welcome and stay, and Trudy, Ray, Denise, and Joe for their joyful friendship. Finally, at Kaivalyadhama, special thanks goes out to CEO Subodh Tiwari, Bernard Britto, Praseeda Menon, the yoga hospital faculty and staff, Rachael Hammerlein, as well as the late Swami Maheshananda for whose eternal yogic wisdom I am deeply indebted.

Special shout-out to my brother Logan for being the best brother a guy can ask for, for all the waves we caught together over the years, and the many more to come, as well as my brother-in-law Dario for all his reliable support over the years. And to all of my friends, old and new, especially Ryan Mills, Karthik Dhandapani, Chuck Hamilton, Deepak Bhansal, Nita Shah, and Adrian Huber. I hold out particular gratitude to my grandfather, Theodore Russell Miller (1923–2017), who passed away while I was in the field, and who will always be in our hearts, as well as my friend, the late Jasmine Lieb (1952–2021), who put me on the mend with her yoga therapy and big healing heart when I hurt my back in graduate school.

For those who I did not explicitly mention here, know that I did not forget you on purpose and deeply appreciate you.

And thank you finally to my wife, Valentina, and our family, for all their patience and steadfast support as I researched and wrote this book. It is, after all, for you.

Note on Transliteration and Names

Sanskrit terms including diacritical marks appear in italics and inside parentheses after the English translation of each word is provided. In selected cases, when doing so is more conducive to the general style of the sentence, the italicized Sanskrit with diacritical marks appears first, followed by the English translation in parenthesis. When common Sanskrit terms are repeated (e.g. "*āsana*," "*prāṇāyāma*"), they often appear with diacritical marks and in italics without parentheses and without repeating the English translation. Sanskrit book titles are rendered in italics with diacritical marks, as are philosophical schools of thought (e.g. "*Yoga-Sūtra*," "*Sāṃkhya-Yoga*").

Some Sanskrit words used commonly in English (e.g. "tantra," "yoga," "mantra") are not italicized and are generally written without diacritical marks unless they form part of a Sanskrit compound.

Informant names, institutional names, and spiritual organizations are rendered without diacritical marks, as are, in most cases, names of songs and chants (e.g. "Gayatri Mantra"). In almost all cases, especially where confidentiality is important, names used in the following chapters are pseudonyms or simply listed as "anonymous."

In quotations of written works, the author's use or disuse of italics and/or diacritical marks in Sanskrit words is maintained. In quotations of interviews, diacritical marks are used for Sanskrit terms for consistency throughout.

Introduction

Engaged Alchemies: New Approaches to the Study of Contemporary Yoga

> I have studied the Sanscrit [sic] texts of Yoga… I believe precisely that at the bottom of all our mystical states there are techniques of the body which we have not studied, but which were perfectly studied by China and India, even in remote periods. This socio-psycho-biological study should be made. I think that there are necessarily biological means of entering into 'communication with God'.
>
> Marcel Mauss, "Techniques of the Body" (Mauss 1973 [1935]: 86–87)[1]

This book is a culmination of the past 15 years during which I practiced, studied, and was employed by yoga teachers, businesses, and traditions in the United States, India, Europe, and other global locations. Based on my training as a critical scholar and a practitioner of yoga traditions, I show how we can expand the definition of contemporary yoga practices for research beyond posture (*āsana*) alone.[2] Postural yoga occupies a central place in the field of Modern Yoga Studies despite the cliché heard in popular yoga culture all over the world which asserts that "yoga is more than just the postures." As an ethnographer, I have taken this cliché seriously. What do practitioners mean by "more than just the postures" or by hashtags like "#thisisyoga" or "#thisisyogatoo"? From a methodological and analytical perspective, how might we most effectively study these other practices? What might they tell us about the history, cultures, and contemporary practices of transnational yoga?

To answer these questions, I focus on three understudied categories of contemporary yoga cultures, including *food*, *music*, and *breathing* practices as understood and performed within three transnational yoga communities: Gurani Anjali's Yoga Anand Ashram on Long Island, New York; Polestar Gardens, an intentional yoga community following the teachings of Paramahansa Yogananda on the Big Island of Hawaii; and Swami Kuvalayananda's Kaivalyadhama Yoga Institute in Lonavala, Maharashtra. I show how the dietary, musical, and breathing practices of three Indian yoga gurus are transformed in their encounters with novel cultural influences, while these disseminators of contemporary yoga and their successors simultaneously implicate their students' bodies into their soteriological yoga systems and in doing so, reshape the broader cultural spaces in which they operate.

DOI: 10.4324/9781003414032-1

The material practices of eating, playing music, and breathing found in the transnational yoga cultures that I studied constitute portable and transposable forms of *engaged alchemy* that have been extensively deployed by contemporary disseminators of yoga (cf. Csordas 2009: 4; cf. Lucas 2013: 166). Borrowing from Tsing's notion of "engaged universals" (Tsing 2005: 8), I use the term *engaged alchemy* to specifically refer to the ways by which transnational disseminators of yoga have adapted dietary practices, music, and breathing techniques within contemporaneous worlds of yoga practice with the intention of producing site-specific instantiations of what they considered to be transformative yoga practice (cf. Augé 1999; Srinivas et al. 2020: 5, 13). Engaging critical insights from the fields of Indian Ocean Studies, Food Studies, Ethnomusicology, and Pollution Studies, I depict how yoga's foodways, musical practices, and breathing techniques have traveled beyond the Indian Ocean rim to become re-rooted, altered, and embodied in ways that reflect specific social concerns, contexts, and spiritual aspirations.

One of the first books I read that inspired the current project was Sumit Sarkar's *Writing Social History* (Sarkar 1997). Writing about the transformation of Ramakrishna's tantric system as it encountered Victorian norms during India's colonial encounters with the British, Sarkar helped me rethink the way we might interpret not only Ramakrishna's teachings, but also those of most other contemporary Indian disseminators of yoga. As Sarkar shows, during the late nineteenth century, Ramakrishna (1836–1886) modified the tantric underpinnings of the yoga practices he disseminated to his middle-class devotees. For instance, though trained in the practices of left-handed tantra (*vāmācāra*) early in his life, he tailored these practices to meet the needs of his colonized *bhadralok*[3] audiences in Bengal by disseminating a right-handed (*dakṣiṇācāra*) approach in their stead (ibid.: 321). Sarkar writes,

> *Coitus reservatus*, the key element in such ritualized sex, could be replaced… in more respectable forms of Tantrism by the mystic union of Shakti and Siva within one's own body through rousing the *kundalini*, or by the sublimation of sex into the childlike love for the mother-goddess.
>
> (ibid.)

According to Sarkar, Ramakrishna's internalization of tantra's transformative practices in such a manner,

> …clearly points towards a contemporary transition. Tantric traditions were being made more respectable through excisions, and at times sought to be suppressed altogether, in bhadralok circles as stricter ideas about gentility developed in the shadow of 'Victorian' norms in the late nineteenth century.
>
> (ibid.: 323)

Working within this Victorian "shadow," but also drawing from a preexisting ascetic "*bhakti* sensibility" that was already reshaping yoga and tantra in early modern North India (Burchett 2019: 169), Ramakrishna's teachings marked a new and critical historical juncture for tantric and yogic practice worldwide. His teachings made "Shakti worship much more respectable and widespread among western-educated middle-class groups" (Sarkar 1997: 334) and would go on to transform the yoga teachings of his influential successors in India and beyond.[4]

Even as the influences of India's Victorian colonizers were reshaping Indian culture in such a manner,[5] so too was the colonial imperium being remade in the image of the colonized. Van der Veer suggests this is true specifically with regard to Ramakrishna's famous successor, Swami Vivekananda, whose influence "impacted a great variety of Western spiritual movements" (van der Veer 2001: 74). While scholars of yoga recognize Vivekananda's rhetorical skill at absorbing other world religions and spiritual traditions including Christianity and Western esotericism into his wider and more accommodating Advaita Vedānta (cf. De Michelis 2005; Albanese 2007; Jain 2015), in this book I explore how he and other disseminators of yoga inflected these Western traditions with transformative yogic logics. In doing so, I suggest that in addition to the yoga texts and linguistic and verbal discourse espoused by yoga's contemporary disseminators, we must turn to the language of the body itself as an accompanying source of ethnographic and historical data.

What Is Yoga?

Several of my colleagues in the field of Yoga Studies have summarized the available evidence regarding yoga's origins and rich history in ways that I will not repeat in the present project (cf. Samuel 2008; Mallinson and Singleton 2017; Newcombe and O'Brien-Kop 2021; Foxen and Kuberry 2021; Sarbacker 2021). My approach augments these studies, inspiring a reconsideration of how we study transnational yoga both ethnographically and historically. I follow the proposition of these scholarly works that yoga is not a monolith (cf. White 2012: 2; Jain 2015: xviii), but rather a multi-dimensional, protean, and ever-changing set of cultural theories and somatic practices, the precise origins of which, though South Asian and developed amidst Buddhist, Jain, Hindu, Sufi, and other influences, are ultimately unknown.

I use the term "yoga" to highlight what yoga gurus and disseminators considered to constitute yoga, which they drew from various texts[6] (cf. von Ostrowski 2022) and practice lineages. I only use the term "modern yoga" throughout this book to situate my work within the field that is known as "Modern Yoga Studies" (cf. De Michelis 2005: 7). Otherwise, I prefer to use the terms "contemporary yoga" or "transnational yoga" to indicate that I am studying yoga traditions that have emerged in the twentieth and twenty-first centuries at the confluence of manifold social and historical flows, frictions, and cultural ideas while acknowledging that the followers of the traditions I study do not necessarily subscribe to Eurocentric conceptions of time, progress, and teleology (cf. Hauser 2013: 16).

Postural yoga practice (*āsana*) has, and continues to receive, focused attention in Modern Yoga Studies (cf. Sjoman and Kṛṣṇarāja 1996; De Michelis 1995, 2005; Singleton 2010; Foxen 2017). At each of my field sites, posture was indeed, to varying degrees, a subordinate and yet integral component of yoga practice. Though I move beyond postural yoga, my object of study is what Singleton refers to as "transnational anglophone yoga," which he distinguishes from "modern yoga" to emphasize the cross-border flows and exchanges that have been "*transmitted in a dialogical relationship between India and the West through the medium of English*" (Singleton 2010: 10; emphasis in original). I follow Singleton here, although my data is not limited to textual and linguistic English discourse alone (ibid.). Additionally, I consider contemporary forms of "soteriological yoga" (Jain 2015: 49–56) and "contemporary yoga philosophy" (von Ostrowski Forthcoming: 1) along with the "repertoire"(s) (Srinivas 2014: 270) of practices within these yoga systems used to achieve embodied transformation.

Though I am sensitive to community voices, I do not debate whether particular forms of yoga are authentic/inauthentic, traditional/modern, good/bad, or right/wrong (cf. Lucia 2020: 69–98; Jain 2015: 102–215). Thinking within these (colonial) binaries restricts our ability to see the multi-layered complexity of contemporary yoga cultures and what their practices are purported to achieve. Some yoga purists may find it "inauthentic," for example, that the *kīrtan* (Sanskrit: *kīrtana*) community that I spent time with in Hawaii has incorporated the ukulele into their meditative ensemble (the subject of Chapter 2). However, once one accepts that yoga cultures have always been changing, the question of whether the addition of the ukulele is "authentic" or "inauthentic" becomes far less interesting than the rich social history that allowed the instrument to enter the ensemble in the first place.

Debating yoga's authenticity would also actually constitute colonizing yoga and supporting certain nationalist, gendered, classist/casteist, and capitalist sentiments. I am very much in favor of what has been called the "decolonization" of yoga, even though many of the leaders in this decolonizing movement continue to reinforce (often unwittingly) colonial binaries in their discourse, activism, and teachings. In this regard, a secondary intention of this book is to help my yoga students, yoga teachers, and those in the decolonizing movement to unravel unacknowledged colonial mental impressions (*saṃskāra*) to which they have become habituated through their study of Orientalist yoga scholarship. My hope is that this book will create a new space for them to continue to appreciate, with a critical eye, the yoga traditions to which they belong.

Modern Yoga Studies

Many influential studies of contemporary yoga – including those considering Ramakrishna and Vivekananda – often emphasize the ways by which Western culture almost unilaterally influenced and domesticated the thought and praxis of contemporary Indian disseminators of yoga. While scholars of modern yoga have undoubtedly recognized a process of bilateral exchange, their research has nevertheless emphasized the ways Western culture – whether in the form of physical culture, harmonialism, gymnastics, dance, esotericism, New Thought, health, or science – has reshaped and domesticated the category of yoga (cf. De Michelis 2005; Albanese 2007; Singleton 2010; Foxen 2020).[7] Following van der Veer, however, I "reject the common assumption – sometimes hidden, sometimes explicit – that the metropole is the center of cultural production, while the periphery only develops derivative, imitative culture" (van der Veer 2001: 3).

In this book, I approach the study of yoga by considering cultural influences on both centripetal *and* centrifugal terms including the flows of yogic influence from India into Western cultures at the level of embodied practice. What I seek to elucidate – and what is at stake here – are potentially occluded "Indian visions of what is possible in the field of human experience" (Alter 2004: 74–75) embedded within contemporaneous worlds of quotidian transnational yoga practice, and which, if we look closely enough, emerge as alternative yoga modernities (Weiss 2019). I present evidence that will encourage us to revisit questions such as, for example, whether or not Ramakrishna's teachings were merely subject to "deodorizing" and "sanitizing" within the constraints of Victorian morality (Urban 2003: 135, 164). Or perhaps, in addition to his student Vivekananda's absorption of the ideological influences of Western esotericism (De Michelis 2005), as well as the Theosophical Society's domestication of his and other Asian teachings (Albanese 2007: 344, 346, 352), what Vivekananda's specific contributions were toward the reshaping of Western spiritual movements. And finally, we can also reexamine postural yoga and try to understand if it is primarily a product of the influence of physical culture and harmonial gymnastics, among other Western influences (Singleton 2010), or perhaps in certain instances part of a wider, more holistic soteriological system.[8]

I draw inspiration from some important scholarly works in the field of Modern Yoga Studies that have demonstrated the reciprocal influences that have taken place during yoga's ongoing and recent historical development. Alter's groundbreaking *Yoga in Modern India* (Alter 2004) demonstrates how "a critical analysis of Yoga's history will show that it is a product of the colonial era" even as yoga can simultaneously "be shown to 'chip away' at the edifice of empire" when we consider the yoga body's situatedness between yoga philosophy and colonial science (ibid.: 26). For example, as Alter demonstrates, Swami Kuvalayanda appropriated the methods and tools of colonial scientific materialism to translate his own yogic vision for humanity into an empirically comprehensible message that eventually "enabled yoga to colonize the West" (ibid.: 106).[9]

In a more recent and equally insightful chapter in *Selling Yoga* that considers transnational yoga outside of India, Jain highlights how Acharya Mahaprajna's *prekṣā dhyāna* (perception meditation) system disseminated by the Jain Terāpanth order adapted many of the popular physical practices found in transnational, modern postural yoga that are not distinctly Jain into its own yoga system in order to attract adherents. Jain also demonstrates how teachers of *prekṣā dhyāna* still maintained many of the transformative ethical, subtle body, and meditation practices Mahaprajna had gleaned from Jain texts and other yoga sources when he created his eclectic system (Jain 2015: 56–65). Even more recently, Foxen convincingly demonstrated how yoga guru Paramahansa Yogananda, whose initial stages of *kriyā-yoga* were clearly a product of his study of Western physical culture and New Thought, still maintained an underlying commitment to implicating his devotees' bodies into the energetics of "*Haṭha* yoga par excellence" (Foxen 2017: 17).

Each of these works point not only to the entangled nature of contemporary yoga culture, but also, more importantly, to the ingenuity of its many teachers to disseminate what they held to be embodied, soteriological yogic truths and experiences, even amidst the influences of their new cultural settings. In this book, I expand upon their insights and draw the field of Modern Yoga Studies into largely unchartered methodological and analytical territory through the ethnographic study of yoga.

Studying Transnational Yoga Cultures

De Michelis suggested long ago that the field of Modern Yoga Studies move into new territory by combining Indological and more nuanced anthropological research methods (De Michelis 2008). Similarly, Newcombe acknowledged that, "The way in which local communities interpret and change modern, transnationalised yoga movements is an area which is only beginning to be considered in modern yoga studies…" (Newcombe 2009: 997). A number of studies have answered these calls, demonstrating the analytical power of contextualizing yoga discourse and philosophy within particular contexts of neoliberal capitalism, health, race, gender, criminal justice, harmonialism, nationalism, and other related categories using well-developed ethnographic and historical methods (Hauser 2013; Jain 2015, 2020; Bevilacqua 2018; Neumann 2019; Lucia 2020; Foxen 2020; Shaw and Kayatz 2021; von Ostrowski 2022; Godrej 2022). My ethnographic study of transnational yoga communities is intended to contribute to this emerging critical ethnographic and historical field.

Botanical Metaphors, Frictions, and Mobilities

Scholars of Modern Yoga Studies have proposed a number of botanical metaphors to attempt to illustrate how forms of contemporary yoga have emerged. Early on, De Michelis described "Modern Yoga" as "the youngest branch of the tree of yoga" which "evolved mainly through the interaction of *Western individuals interested in Indian religions* and a number of more or less *Westernized Indians* over the past 150 years" (De Michelis 2005: 2; emphasis added). This tree metaphor is useful in so far as it suggests that Indian forms of yoga change as they encounter other dominant cultural ideologies and material realities, and yet somehow retain their distinctness as "yoga." De Michelis's research nevertheless predominantly examines how yoga absorbs Western cultural ideologies (cf. Madaio 2017, 5). Writing with regard to Vivekananda, for example, De Michelis claims that, "It was on the basis of the teachings that he was quickly absorbing from his Western cultic entourage that he was to evolve his (occultistic) understanding of (Neo-)Vedanta" (ibid.: 113). Considering van der Veer's two-way "interactional perspective"[10] on history (van der Veer 2001: 8), I turn De Michelis's approach around to instead consider how *Indian individuals interested in Western religions* actually *Indianized Westerners* in ways that have been almost entirely overlooked.

Alter has used the phrase "transnational conjuncture" (Alter 2000: 82) to describe the point where similar ideas or practices from different cultures meet and are absorbed into the cultural categories and broader logics of their corresponding disseminators (cf. Hauser 2018: 519). Along these same lines, more recent botanical metaphors proposed by other scholars of modern yoga which suggest bilateral *and* multilateral cultural connections are more compelling than De Michelis's tree metaphor, which itself seems to suggest unidirectional growth. Consider, for example, Foxen's use of the term to describe the fusion of Western harmonial and Indian yoga cultures, "inosculation," or "the place where two trees, each with their own ancient root system, have entwined so intimately that they have become one" (Foxen 2020: 5). Following this line of thought, Foxen has argued that a significant amount of what is considered "yoga" within transnational postural yoga communities today is actually more genealogically related to Western harmonial traditions, New Thought, and physical culture. For example, Foxen writes,

> ...many white women (for they are overwhelmingly white, and overwhelmingly women) practicing "yoga" in the United States today are actually engaged in something that is only slightly genealogically related to Indian yogic traditions... there is a Western history of practice here that was overwritten by the imported language of yoga, thereby becoming invisible.
>
> (ibid.: 2)

While embracing the bilateral exchanges between Western and Indian cultures, Foxen is still primarily focused on telling the story of a Western history of transmission.

The tree and inosculation metaphors, both of which assume the existence of discrete cultures, methodologically fit into what Hauser has characterized as a "model of linear diffusion" (Hauser 2018: 511). In addition to this linear model for the study of modern yoga, Hauser also characterizes the methods that constitute a "model of global diffusion" which emphasize "*interlinked systems of relations*" (ibid.: 512) and acknowledge "several coexisting and partly blurred transnational yoga cultures as part of a joint yoga world" (ibid.: 513). Strauss and Hoyez subscribed to such a global diffusion model in their studies of transnational Sivananda yoga (Strauss 2005) and therapeutic yoga landscapes (Hoyez 2007). Kuberry and Foxen have more recently engaged the botanical metaphor of "rhizomes" to similarly capture the complexity and messiness of transnational yoga's ongoing transformations and developments globally (Schwind [Kuberry] 2015; Foxen and Kuberry 2021; cf. Deleuze and Guattari 1987: 21). "In a rhizome," they write, "there's no center or core… there is no single definition of yoga, and there is no single yoga tradition, only a web of interconnected nodes" (Foxen and Kuberry 2021: 9). As a result of this rhizomatic growth process, transnational forms of yoga are in substance, "the product of some ingenious grafting and splicing with other ideas and practices that look similar but have different cultural roots" (ibid.: 9). Hauser has similarly invoked the multi-rooted banyan tree to describe the complexity of transnational yoga, which, "absorbed by other plants may, in fact, be the product of multiple distant origins" (Hauser 2013: 11). The botanical metaphors that Hauser, Kuberry, and Foxen propose closely resemble the notion of entanglements, which Bender used to describe how yoga culture is intimately entangled with metaphysical and secular beliefs, practices, and discourses in contemporary Cambridge, Massachusetts (Bender 2010: 24, 90–118). Similarly, Altglas calls our attention to the ways by which an individual's yogic bricolage is always intimately situated within wider social and political contexts outside of which their yoga practice cannot be understood (Altglas 2014).

Though I find all of these metaphors to be useful analytical tools, I add another important metaphor here, "frictions," which has not yet been meaningfully engaged in existing yoga scholarship. Tsing's invocation of the term "friction" (Tsing 2005: 1) helps us understand how the novel cultural constraints yoga disseminators have faced actually became generative forces for contemporary yoga culture. "Cultures are," as Tsing writes, "continually co-produced in the interaction I call 'friction': the awkward, unequal, unstable, and creative qualities of interconnection across difference" (ibid.: 4). Tsing is primarily concerned with the ways by which mobile universals encounter friction and, consequently, are transformed as they travel across different cultural spaces in Indonesia. As homogenizing universals – be they science, neoliberal ideology, or in our case yoga – meet resistance within specific contexts, they become "engaged universals" and, consequently, lose their totalizing influence. According to Tsing,

> Engaged universals travel across difference and are charged and changed by their travels. Through friction, universals become practically effective. Yet they can never fulfill their promises of universality. Even in transcending localities, they don't take over the world. They are limited by the practical necessity of mobilizing adherents. Engaged universals must convince us to pay attention to them. All universals are engaged when considered as practical projects accomplished in a heterogeneous world. (ibid.: 8)

Using Tsing's notion of "engaged universals," I describe the result of the frictions between clashing cultural forces – yogic and otherwise – as *engaged alchemies*, which on the one hand reflect very particular social contexts but also, on the other hand, indicate practitioners' very human urge to transform and transcend these contexts according to yogic universalisms. I use "alchemy" here in its broadest sense and in accordance with its basic definition: "a power or process that changes or transforms something in a mysterious or impressive way."[11] I also draw from a South Asian perspective since the subtle body logics of some yoga systems are understood to enable transformative experiences of embodied alchemy (White 1996; Alter 2005).[12]

At each of my field sites, there were geographical, institutional, and social forces that enabled or constrained the multi-directional movement of people, yoga practices, and their ideas. In this regard, the "mobilities" paradigm is also helpful for conceptualizing engaged alchemies, as it requires us to pay attention to the mobility (and immobility) of people, materials, practices, and other interrelated phenomena throughout global society (Sheller and Urry 2006).[13] The frictions and mobilities paradigms also have a close analogue in the field of Religious Studies: Tweed invokes the terms "crossing" and "dwelling" (Tweed 2006: 24) as well as "confluences" and "flows" (ibid.: 59) to account for the fluid, protean nature of religious practices which also find momentary grounding in particular places.[14] For Tweed, the religious practitioner's *body* is central in the process of crossing and dwelling.[15]

Thus while I conducted standard methods of ethnography including conducting formal and informal interviews, recording lectures and talks, as well as collecting pamphlets, books, and other publications at each of my field sites, I also took into consideration the non-discursive language of the body itself through participation in, and observation of, the dietary, musical, and breathing practices I encountered therein. When ethnographic data collection is otherwise limited to abstract speech and human representational language, the non-linguistic language of the body is marginalized or altogether neglected.[16] This methodology, focusing on both discursive and non-discursive evidence, provided two important insights.

The *first insight* was that the practicing yoga bodies I encountered in the field clearly reflected influences from their wider social contexts. This should come as no surprise, since Mauss famously showed long ago that bodily techniques, whether they relate to everyday tasks such as sitting, bathing, or eating, or instead to specialized pursuits such as athletic activities, are not natural but learned according to a particular cultural logic (Mauss 1973 [1935]). As Bourdieu and Foucault later showed, all bodily practices and resultant dispositions are continually reproduced and, in some cases, coercively reinforced upon individuals to maintain and demonstrate a particular cultural logic through the body itself (Bourdieu 1990; Foucault 1990, 1995).

Sometimes, however, embodied cultural logics can challenge hegemonic discourses and paradigms (Douglas 1996 [1970]; 2001 [1975]; De Certeau 1984).[17] In this regard, it is important to keep in mind that the body, particularly in colonial and post-colonial worlds in India, has always been a site of contestation (c.f. Arnold 1993; Alter 2000). As the epigraph to this chapter indicates, Mauss even conjectured long ago in his famous article (without reference to any specific evidence) that yoga instructs biological techniques for "communication with God" (Mauss 1973 [1935]: 86). Thus the *second insight* I gleaned from the yoga bodies I encountered was how they were clearly harnessing available bodily practices from their local social contexts to produce embodied transformation according to alternative, and allegedly universal, yoga cultural logics gleaned from yoga texts, gurus, and spiritual teachers.

It is beyond the scope (or my ability) of this book to precisely assess how the practices I encountered in my field sites – yogic diet, music, and breathing – affected practitioners' biological systems. I do, however, suggest, following von Ostrowski, that any long-lasting alterations to one's bodily practice undertaken according to a particular yoga system will produce measurable biological effects (von Ostrowski Forthcoming, 7; see also von Ostrowski 2022).[18] Whether these effects lead to "communication with God," however, is up to the interpretations of both my informants and the gurus who undertake the techniques meant to induce them. In each chapter I describe the heteroglossia (Bakhtin 1981: 291) gurus and yoga practitioners themselves used to convey the full soteriological potential of their bodily techniques.[19]

The ways yoga practitioners at my field sites ate, sang, and breathed conveyed important messages regarding their self-understanding of class distinctions, political commitments, racial identities, internalized gender roles, neoliberal aspirations, and much more. At the same time, however, my informants' commitments to these somatic practices also expressed their sincere urges to transcend the worlds that these analytical categories plainly demonstrated they were entangled within – what yoga systems would generally refer to as *saṃsāra*. My immersion in these engaged alchemies at each field site implicated my own scholar-practitioner body into often contradictory epistemes that we can broadly conceive of as "academic" and "yogic." Grappling with the frictions produced between these two ways of knowing has produced the book before you.

Embodying Transnational Yoga

Eating, Singing, and Breathing in Transformation

With limited exception (cf. Wilke and Moebus 2011; Jacobs 2017; Jacobs 2019; Foxen 2020), the lack of detailed attention given to the somatic practices of food, music, and breathing within contemporary transnational yoga communities is surprising, especially due to the fact that when one opens popular yoga texts, spends time in yoga ashrams, or undertakes comprehensive yoga training around the world, three of the primary practical imperatives one often encounters are the necessity to modify one's eating and drinking habits, to re-learn how to breathe, and to engage in various forms of musical or sacred sound practices.[20] I first encountered these categories of yoga practice as they were established at Yoga Anand Ashram (YAA) in Amityville, New York, during my early graduate studies while concurrently attending a two-year yoga teacher training at the Hill Street Yoga and Meditation Center in Santa Monica, California. Hill Street was a non-profit institution founded by Christopher Chapple, a former long-time student at YAA. Here in 2011, for the first time, I was collectively exposed to vegetarianism, breath control (*prāṇāyāma*), and the practice of music and mantra practice in yoga. Because YAA's yoga lineage came from Gurani Anjali, who had moved to New York from Kolkata, I eventually wondered what practices in particular had traveled with her from Kolkata and had taken root in Long Island and then Los Angeles and how these practices were modified as they entered each new location. I had suddenly noticed, for example, that I was seeking vegetarian food at the Santa Monica farmer's market every Sunday after our yoga training with my classmate and friend Karthik. The wider Santa Monica health food culture in which we were undertaking our training was no doubt conducive to practicing the embodied dietary ideology into which I had implicated my own body. Furthermore, as I encountered dietary, musical, and breathing practices in other transnational yoga communities during my intermittent travels to India and time spent working in Hawaii, I often wondered what was "universal" about these practices, given their specificity and unique adaptations within both locations.

During my subsequent field work, I followed these three primary categories of somatic yoga practice – food, music, and breathing – through three individual field sites. The methodology I use in this book thus adopts a transnational, multi-sited (Marcus 1995) approach that has also been used by other ethnographers and anthropologists of transnational yoga to "follow the practice" (Strauss 2005: 93; cf. Jain 2015). Nevertheless, due to the limitations of space, I have chosen in this book to focus on one category for each field site in each chapter. Though unique in expression, what each of these field sites share is the birthing of novel and context-bound forms of engaged alchemy as mobile yoga practice and ideology produce frictions with prevailing countercultural (Chapter 1), tropical (Chapter 2), and necropolitical (Chapter 3) influences.[21]

First, we will meet a female Indian guru, Gurani Anjali, who makes an abrupt move from Bengal to an increasingly urbanizing Long Island, New York in the 1950s. Anjali's foodways reflect those found in many transnational yoga settings wherein dietary modifications usually framed as "*sāttvik*" (pure, true, light; Sanskrit: *sāttvika*) are disseminated alongside other lifestyle reforms, including abstinence from sex, drugs, smoking, and other activities in order to achieve soteriological goals. By engaging scholarship from the field of Food Studies, we will see how Anjali and her yoga ashram community's foodways reflected the predominant American countercuisine ethos but at the same time harnessed this ethos to achieve the goals of Anjali's universal yoga system.

Alongside the preliminary practice of yogic diet, breath control (*prāṇāyāma*) and/or some form of music or sacred sound (*kīrtan/bhajan/mantra*) are frequently deployed in transnational yoga communities as well. Thus in the chapter that follows, we will meet a global network of mobile, middle-class *kriyā-yoga* practitioners in Hawaii, observing how their musical *kīrtan* practice has adapted the ukulele alongside the harmonium into the community ensemble in order to accomplish their guru's universal meditative practice of listening for an internal, unstruck sound. The fields of Ethnomusicology, Historical Musicology, Organology, and allied fields of musicological inquiry help us trace the complicated social histories of the ukulele and harmonium that make this meditative ensemble possible.

Finally, with regard to breathing exercises, we will encounter middle-class city dwellers from Mumbai performing purifying and liberating yogic breath techniques (*prāṇāyāma*) to treat their asthma and other air-pollution-related ailments. They do so at a century-old yoga institute amidst India's polluted air, a consequence of neoliberal capitalism's uneven development dynamics in the Global South. Critical insights from the field of Pollution Studies will help us understand how this tragic, post-colonial situation has emerged.

Taken together, my three field sites in New York, Hawaii, and Maharashtra redraw a multilayered, multi-directional web of relationality between the Indian Ocean and other regions, underscoring centripetal and centrifugal influences that are now operating globally. Instead of beginning in India as most studies of yoga typically do, this book begins on Long Island, moves to Hawaii, and finally *ends* in India. This reverse flow of field sites, not typical in studies of yoga, helps me tell a different story of a globalized, transnational yoga and the ways by which yoga's influence has traveled and rooted itself in other regions beyond that of the Indian Ocean, uniting with the Atlantic and Pacific. Beginning my study outside of India also allows me to show how, "Spaces can be transposed onto others through naming and narration, remembering and sensation" and how "city/home/exile/return are moral projects manifested through embodiment and practice" (Srinivas 2022: 8–9). Ending in India then allows us to see how other global influences encounter friction as they intersect with yogic ideology in South Asia today.

Worlding the Indian Ocean

My engagement with the field of Indian Ocean Studies and the publication of *Reimagining Indian Ocean Worlds* (Srinivas et al. 2020) has significantly influenced the multi-sited approach in this book, compelling me to join the call to rethink the spatial and disciplinary boundaries of the Indian Ocean.[22] Rather than understand the Indian Ocean merely as a geographical and spatial frame of reference, my ethnographic fieldwork intellectually reconfigures the Indian Ocean, "as a space for conceptual/theoretical relationality." In addition to mobilities, "place, placemaking, and quotidian practices" and "new networks of memory and maps in lived experiences" are also explored in this book (ibid.: 13–17). In a decolonial spirit, I do so "without necessarily privileging the West" (ibid.: 12).

Referring to the Indian Ocean's flexible spheres of influence as a "hundred horizons, if not a horizonless infinity" (Bose 2006: 34), Bose once described the Indian Ocean as an "interregional arena" that "was – and, in many ways, continues to be – characterized by specialized flows of capital and labor, skills and services, *ideas and culture*" (ibid.: 3; emphasis added). As Vink has since observed, the Indian Ocean's horizons and boundaries are spatially layered, fuzzy, fluctuating, and not necessarily limited by geographical constraints (Vink 2007: 52–53). It has therefore become imperative, as Vink writes, "...for 'the new thalassology' to disentangle the complex strand of spatial categorizations and explore the permeable inner and outer boundaries of the Indian Ocean world(s)" (ibid.: 60). There is indeed a long history of relationality across the Indian Ocean region (cf. Amrith 2013: 26) that extends outside the ocean's traditional geographic limits. As Prestholdt observes, the boundaries of the Indian Ocean are porous and "remarkably pliant," allowing the Indian Ocean to shape "an ever-increasing number of societies along other shores" *beyond* the ocean's rim (Prestholdt 2020, 25, 28). And, as many scholars have clearly demonstrated, the ocean's influences reach past littoral environments alone and into the hinterlands (cf. Chaudhuri 1985; Ghosh 1993; Samarawickrema 2020; Meek 2020; Srinivas 2022).[23] Considering the Indian Ocean's extra-regional and extra-littoral influences helps us see past nationalist and state-inspired geographical imaginaries and to understand the worlding of Indian Ocean imaginaries globally.

One useful way to consider the extent of the Indian Ocean's boundaries and spheres of influence is to observe human relations facilitated through highly portable transnational religious networks (Prestholdt 2020: 26; Ranganath 2020: 181; Srinivas 2022: 7). How have, for example, "'alternative modernities,' those formations of modernity that have taken shape in an archive of deep and layered existing social and intellectual traditions" made their way into other oceanic worlds in the form of "Religious Universalisms" and "New Textual Circuits" (Hofmeyr 2007: 13, 20–25; cf. Kaur 2023)? Before reaching into other oceanic regions such as those of Europe and the United States, for instance, South Asian yoga texts were already circulating in Southeast Asia (Acri 2021; White 2014: 165). By the late nineteenth century, South Asian texts were also traveling upon preestablished communication routes connecting land and sea between South Asia, Africa, Europe, and North America. These ideas traveled along a network that extended from the Indian Ocean through the Suez Canal, through Mediterranean Europe and eventually across the Atlantic Ocean to the United States via ship travel and the Transatlantic Cable, finally making their way to the Pacific Ocean along the Union Pacific Railroad (Davis 2015: 72–114). These multiple transoceanic routes of yoga connected the Indian Ocean, Mediterranean Sea, Atlantic Ocean, and Pacific Ocean regions and in doing so were already pushing the Indian Ocean's influence far beyond its traditional geographical limits.

Alongside portable transnational religious networks and texts, Indian Ocean influences have also entered into other geographic regions in the form of portable religious *bodily practices*. With regard to dietary practices and the alimentary tract specifically, Meek writes that, "… Indian Ocean worlds exists [sic] as much – and even perhaps more so – through the practices and bodies worlding them than as a physical space whose boundaries could be drawn on a map" (Meek 2020: 199). With the alimentary tract in mind, the field of Food Studies has taken the interdisciplinary methods of Indian Ocean scholars seriously in order to study the distribution of Indian Ocean foodways in the region, thereby, "rescuing taste from the nation," among other things (Leong-Salobir et al. 2016). As Indian Ocean food scholars have repeatedly shown, inter-Asian culinary flows and dietary practices have transcended the borders of nation-states to facilitate the production of Indian Ocean worlds elsewhere (Leong-Salobir et al. 2016: 10–11; cf. Ray 2013; Ray 2015; Hoogervorst 2018: 519; cf. Hoogervorst 2022).[24] Chapter 1 of this book takes this important insight about as far as it will go by showing how Indian Ocean foodways have reached the counterculture in Long Island, New York.

In addition to diet, other bodily practices involving music, instruments, and musicological influences have spread throughout the Indian Ocean. For this reason, scholars in the field of Ethnomusicology have taken an interest in Indian Ocean Studies, citing the limits of Ethnomusicology's area studies paradigm and the vast opportunities an "Indian Ocean ethnomusicology" would open for understanding the transnational distribution of Indian Ocean music (Byl and Sykes 2020: 398; Sykes and Byl 2023). One ethnomusicological opportunity Chapter 2 of this book capitalizes upon is Byl and Syke's suggestion to bring "Western and Eastern Indian Oceanists in music studies" into conversation with one another while balancing between a "scoped-out inventory" and an "intimate ethnography" of musical cultures (ibid.: 402, 409).[25] Because, "Generally speaking the bounds of music lie outside the walls of the archives," I follow "essential clues which indicate the translation between continents and cultures" in musical practice and ensemble creation (Jayasuriya 2008: 136). In doing so I look beyond relationships between communities and nation states alone (Bose 2006: 7), but also far beyond the traditional limits of the Indian Ocean rim as I take us to Hawaii for sacred yoga music in the form of *kīrtan*.

Finally, in addition to eating and singing, everyone must breathe. And yet the polluted air of the Indian Ocean region is making breathing an increasingly dangerous bodily practice, especially when yoga and physical activity are involved. Of particular concern to the Indian Ocean region is a visible atmospheric phenomenon known as (not without controversy, cf. Bhojvaid 2021) the "Asian Brown Cloud,"[26] a seasonal air pollution event that hovers over the Indian Ocean that will continue to have long-lasting adverse effects on the natural environment, the climate, and human health (Ramanathan et al. 2002: 947, 955).[27]

The Asian Brown Cloud became such a concern at the turn of the twenty-first century that Europe, India, and the United States collectively conducted what was known as the "Indian Ocean Experiment" (ibid.: 947). As one highly influential and international scientific study concluded on the subject,

"Unless international control measures are taken, air pollution in the Northern Hemisphere will continue to grow into a global plume across the developed and the developing world" (Lelieveld et al. 2001: 1035). The Asian Brown Cloud and air pollution in the Indian Ocean region are thus global issues in the age of the Anthropocene. Like yoga, the pollution extends significant influence from the Indian Ocean and beyond. And yet, as we will see in Chapter 3, the cloud is a product of the frictions between neoliberal ideology and nationalist economic aspirations as they encounter alternative South Asian ways of knowing the body and its relationship to its environment.

The transnational cultural influences that the chapters in this book trace demonstrate how useful the Indian Ocean can be as an analytical category (cf. Chaudhuri 1985), but also show how we can conceive of *one* global ocean given the vast global connections that bind the world's oceans together today. Indeed, tracing Indian Ocean yogic influence into distant oceanic worlds in the Atlantic and Pacific and then seeing how neoliberal, necropolitical, and nationalist ideas have found ground in the Indian Ocean make it more appropriate to conceive of the world as having one ocean tied together by a plurality of cultural influences. These entangled cultural influences still nonetheless demand – perhaps even more so as this book will show – careful scholarly attention. Such attention reveals how by embodying transnational yoga one embodies manifold contemporaneous cultural and regional influences, but nevertheless in doing so simultaneously worlds the Indian Ocean globally.

Distinct Gurus, Distinct Ways of Knowing

Rather than focusing upon popular gurus or "hyper gurus" (Copeman and Ikegame 2012) of modern yoga (cf. Singleton and Goldberg 2014), each of my field sites was, and continues to be, administered by lesser-known personalities in the yoga world. First, Gurani Anjali (Chapter 1) belongs to the group of "second wave" gurus (Forsthoefel and Humes 2005: 4), who influenced countercultural Americans following the lifting of restrictive immigration legislation in the United States in the 1960s. Next, Polestar Gardens' (Chapter 2) founders are part of a third generation of "homegrown" yoga teachers who grew up on American soil (Gleig and Williamson 2013: 2). Finally, Swami Kuvalayananda (Chapter 3) belongs to the generation of first wave gurus who disseminated yoga outward from India. Though Kaivalyadhama was founded by the somewhat familiar Swami Kuvalayananda (1883–1966) (cf. Alter 2004) and Polestar Gardens traces its origins to the more well-known Swami Paramahansa Yogananda (1893–1952) via Swami Kriyananda's (1926–2013) Ananda Village (est. 1968), both of these communities are currently operated by individuals most readers and scholars have probably never heard of. Yoga Anand Ashram's Gurani Anjali (1935–2001), a little-known and yet truly visionary female yoga teacher, has also remained off the radar for most scholars and yoga practitioners.

Studying each of these somewhat unrecognized but representative figures and the contemporary yoga movements they continue to inspire helps us to more deeply understand the excisions, reformulations, and adaptations that they and other more glamorous and popular transnational yoga gurus have also made to bring their yoga into the globalized present, while also demonstrating how these yoga innovators maintain particular commitments to their soteriological frameworks through specific somatic practices. Perhaps most significantly, these figures and the engaged alchemies they disseminate in the chapters that follow oblige the field of Modern Yoga Studies to expand the definition of what constitutes modern yoga practice and the methodologies used to study it.

Some of my colleagues may object to the simultaneously critical and sympathetic approach I am taking in this book, especially with the recent focus on the intolerable guru abuse that has come to light in many contemporary yoga communities (cf. Miller 2021; Deslippe 2021). In some ways, my book's focus on seemingly universal biological techniques might also seem to support the popular adage often heard in transnational yoga which suggests that we can "separate the teacher from the teachings and practices."[28] I would like to make it clear here that I certainly do not condone guru abuse. I also do not wish to suggest that we can divorce biology, culture, and individual subjects and their practices from one another since an individual's biological techniques are simultaneously social and cultural techniques, as the chapters in this book will make abundantly clear.

In the true spirit of this book's methodologies, however, we must also keep in mind that abuse has been an ongoing two-way interaction. Not only have some yoga gurus been cruelly abusive, but so too has the seemingly objective and universal lens of Yoga Studies itself. It is well known that the field has historical roots in colonialization, appropriation, and racism and today faces an uneasy process of decolonization. Consider, for example, that the *Monier-Williams Sanskrit–English Dictionary*, which remains a vital resource for most all Yoga Studies scholars today, was originally dedicated to British imperialism in India, to support, as Monier-Williams writes in the preface, "all those zealous *men* who have devoted themselves to the social, religious, and intellectual improvement of the natives of *our* Indian Empire" (Monier-Williams 1899: x; emphasis added). The British Empire's historical attempt to erase yogic warrior asceticism and other forms of yoga involving tantric practice in India are glaring examples of this abusive colonial project, as is the colonial endorsement of docile forms of devotional yoga as the only correct and authentic modes of practice (Pinch 2006; White 2009).

Thus while I deeply appreciate – and engage at *extensive* length in this book – critical, evidence-based, scholarly perspectives from multiple academic fields including Modern Yoga Studies, I also recognize that the episteme of the European Enlightenment has shaped these perspectives in ways that have limited our approaches to how we can study and understand contemporary forms of transnational yoga culture. I hope this book will trigger both yoga practitioners and scholars alike to think about their biases, situatedness, and unexamined, deeply held beliefs and approaches to the study of yoga and other religious and philosophical systems in South Asia. Writing it certainly forced me to confront many of my own in a process that continues into the present, and for those interested in understanding my situated and complex perspective as a "scholar-practitioner" (cf. Singleton and Larios 2021) of yoga, please read the preface to this book.

Notes

1 Quote taken from: Mauss, Marcel. 1973 [1935]. "Techniques of the Body." *Economy and Society* 2, no. 1: 70–88 (reprinted by permission of Informa UK Limited, trading as Taylor & Francis Group, www.tandfonline.com).

2 A number of studies in the field of Modern Yoga Studies have beckoned us to move beyond the study of postural yoga alone, considering additional analytical categories such as neoliberalism, therapeutic culture, race, gender, criminal justice, harmonialism, nationalism, and much more (cf. Hauser 2013; Jain 2015, 2020; Bevilacqua 2018; Neumann 2019; Lucia 2020; Foxen 2020; Shaw and Kayatz 2021; von Ostrowski 2022; Godrej 2022).

3 The *bhadralok*, or "gentle folk," were a group of highly educated, middle-class Indian elites in West Bengal and Bangladesh that emerged during India's colonial encounters with the British.

4 As Mallinson has noted, the *Haṭha-Yoga-Pradīpikā* was already internalizing tantric Kaula sexual practices in the fifteenth century (cf. Mallinson 2011: 779–780). There were, therefore, medieval predecessors who enabled Ramakrishna's late nineteenth-century adaptations (cf. Burchett 2019).

5 Following Burchett, I do not reduce the new developments in yoga in colonial India to British influence alone. My book indeed emphasizes, as does Burchett's work in India's early modern context, specific forms of Indian agency involved in the remaking of yoga. As Burchett writes regarding the preexisting "*bhakti* sensibility" (Burchett 2019: 169) influencing yoga in North India (which proved to be highly compatible with Victorian sensibilities), "While the British certainly exaggerated and added new dimensions to a particular view of (and distinction between) bhakti and tantra, the origins of prevalent modern-day North Indian understandings of these two genres of religiosity lie squarely in the early modern flourishing of North India's bhakti movement, circa 1500 to 1700 – well before the British had any significant presence" (ibid.: 12).

6 Von Ostrowski has insightfully deemed the translations of yoga texts into lived embodied practice "Contemporary Yoga Philosophy" (von Ostrowski 2022, Forthcoming).

7 As Hauser also observes with regard to these studies, "by their emphasis on stages of cultural integration they tend to suggest a strict bilateralism and a one-way diffusion that proves delusive to any systematic analysis of multidirectional flows and transnational developments" (Hauser 2013: 9).

8 By posing these questions, I do not mean to undermine the valuable studies that provoke them, which I still use to this day in the classroom to discuss the development of contemporary yoga. Without them, one cannot, for example, understand how a physical posture like *viparīta-karaṇī*, once used as a *mudrā* in *haṭha-yoga* to preserve the semen in the cranial vault of the male practitioner, has come to be used by a population of primarily middle-class female practitioners as a relaxing form of "legs up the wall" therapy. I only intend to point out that these scholarly studies have tended to emphasize the ways that Western cultures have undeniably

constrained, reshaped, and domesticated yoga and yoga texts, even as they acknowledge the dialogical exchange between India and Western agents in the making of contemporary forms of yoga. Instead, I would like to tell the story of contemporary yoga from another, more nuanced perspective.

9 Alter refers to Kuvalayananda's method, which takes the experience of *samādhi* as real (Alter 2004: 98), as "mimetic empiricism" wherein "the properties of *prakṛtic* reality – as opposed to reality as it is governed by natural laws – is subject to the entelechy of rational science" (ibid.: 92). Similarly, Alter observes elsewhere, "…the techniques of yoga that are designed to produce perfection – and about which much has been said in the context of modern medicalization – are what lead to enlightenment" (Alter 2005: 142).

10 Van der Veer's "interactional perspective" on history attempts "to go beyond the national story and get at some of the fragments without losing coherence in the telling of the tale" (Van der Veer 2001: 8).

11 See: https://www.merriam-webster.com/dictionary/alchemy.

12 The concept of engaged alchemies that I use here is also complemented by the notion of what Queen and King refer to as "Engaged Buddhism" (Queen and King 1996: 1), and most specifically the forms of engaged Buddhism which, due to the interpenetration of multiple cultural influences, result in novel forms of Buddhist practice (ibid.: 20). In their study of contemporary manifestations of engaged Buddhism, Queen and King suggest that, "A tradition may be transformed without being betrayed, and heresies may enrich and broaden a cultural heritage while leaving behind those elements – beliefs, practices, institutional forms, public roles – that no longer meet the needs of living communities in a changed world" (ibid.: 31). Like various forms of engaged Buddhism, promoters and practitioners of transnational yoga make excisions, reformulations, and additions to their yoga systems to adapt to the needs of their contemporary social setting, though they do not understand these changes to tradition to be a betrayal, so much as an act of faithfulness, to their yoga traditions.

13 In Sheller and Urry's formulation of mobilities, the fixity underscored in theories of sedentarism and the mobility accentuated in theories of deterritorialisation are understood to be operating in conjunction with one another to produce novel forms of human experience (Sheller and Urry 2006). As they observe, "The new [mobilities] paradigm emphasizes how all mobilities entail specific often highly embedded and immobile infrastructures" (ibid.: 208–210). Sheller and Urry therefore emphasize that the mobilities paradigm combines both the theory of sedentarism and that of post-colonial deterritorialization. Thus the mobilities paradigm, though emphasizing movement, also considers how institutions, structures, blockages, stasis, and constraints both arise from and enable mobility within specific cultural contexts (cf. Hancock and Srinivas 2018).

When considering mobility within the frameworks of movement or stasis, I specifically invoke Urry's notion of "horizontal" mobility/immobility, or the "sense of being 'on the move,' that refers to moving country or continent often in search of a 'better life'…" for those who have the privilege and ability to do so (Urry 2009: 480; cf. Cresswell 2006, 2010, 2012). Likewise, I have in mind Urry's notion of "vertical" mobility/immobility which refers to upward social mobility, or lack thereof (Urry 2009: 480). We will specifically encounter the intersection of horizontal mobilities and vertical immobilities as various social groups converge to create three different yoga communities at my field sites.

14 According to Tweed, "*Religions are confluences of organic-cultural flows that intensify joy and confront suffering by drawing on human and superhuman forces to make homes and cross boundaries*" (Tweed 2006: 54; emphasis in original). Tweed focuses upon movement, relation, and position, challenging static understandings of

religious practice while nevertheless acknowledging that religion allows practitioners "to abide *for a time* in a place, state, or condition" (ibid.: 5, 81; emphasis added).

15 Tweed highlights how the body is intentionally positioned in relation to "the home, the homeland, and the cosmos" (Tweed 2006: 100–101) where it is represented, regulated, and altered in order to construct "collective identity" (ibid.: 101, 11) and to ensure that it is "temporally and spatially" oriented according to a religion's cosmogony (ibid.: 116). Because the body is also central to transnational yoga practice, scholarship on embodiment presents a particularly important theoretical contribution to the methodological approach to the study of yoga that I use in this book.

16 This non-linguistic language provides parallel or perhaps alternative narratives both in the field of anthropology (Comaroff 1985; Srinivas 2001; Downey 2005; Jackson 2013) and in historical ethnographies of body cultures in South Asia (Alter 2000, 2004) and should thus not be overlooked. Put simply, what we *say* does not always express the same message as what we *do*, and it is particularly what yoga people do with their bodies besides speak and write that I wish to consider carefully.

17 This process of socialization thus continuously appropriates bodies, burying ideology into everyday habits (Bourdieu 1990: 188). According to Douglas, because the body is continually engraved with cultural meaning, it serves as an expression of the values of the macrocosmic social world of which it is a part and in some cases challenges these values. The body and its concomitant somatic practices (e.g., diet) thus become the site from which non-verbal data regarding a specific culture and the frictions within it can be derived (Douglas 1996 [1970]; 2001 [1975]). Similarly, like the early work of LeFebvre concerning the connections between the body and space (LeFebvre 1991 [1974]), De Certeau argues that it is indeed necessary to carefully consider the ways by which bodies produce unique social experience through quotidian spatial practices (De Certeau 1984). And as other anthropologists note, the body is where culture is learned and becomes embedded in biology, thereby producing a biocultural subject (Downey 2005; cf. Csordas 1990: 36–37).

Studies concerned with mobility also underscore the semiotic nature of the moving body, emphasizing how "Bodies sense and make sense of the world as they move bodily in and through it, creating discursively mediated sensescapes that signify social taste and distinction, ideology and meaning" (Büscher et al. 2011: 6). The mobile methodology of "shadowing" (Jirón 2011: 37), which involves "not only acknowledging routines, but also entering into practices, into dialogue and interaction in a constant engagement with the people whose lives they constitute," (ibid.) comprises a useful methodological approach for gathering data that is helpful for understanding the cultural logics of particular forms of somatic practice. Similarly, observing habitual bodily movement helps us see how the aggregate of such daily movement might in fact constitute a political practice that makes socio-cultural change possible (Bayat 2010), and furthermore, as Srinivas highlights, seeing "pedestrian-quotidian living" in the form of "the moving and sensory body… that is directed toward some outcome becomes the pathway for understanding place" (Srinivas 2015: 161). Attentiveness to regular, somatic mobilities – both in place and across places – thus provides an entry point into understanding the ways by which bodies themselves produce both cultural meaning and place in ways that augment – or perhaps even defy – discursive hegemonic discourses.

18 As von Ostrowski has shown with regard to postural yoga practices, "practicing certain (cultural) techniques over a longer period inevitably leads to psychophysical and neurological changes" (von Ostrowski Forthcoming: 7; see also von Ostrowski 2022). Von Ostrowski engages Koch's notion of "Body Knowledge" (*Körperwissen*; Koch 2007). As von Ostrowski writes, the concept of "Body Knowledge" can be "used to demarcate implicit psycho-physical changes that emerge from regular yoga practice" (von Ostrowski Forthcoming: 7).

19 Interestingly, Bronkhorst has also shown how the meditative practices found in the *Yoga-Sūtra* potentially reflect what neurologists refer to as "memory reconsolidation," a therapeutic outcome that "can bring about permanent and irreversible changes in the human (and animal) psyche" (Bronkhorst 2022). I thank Johannes Bronkhorst for sharing an early draft of his research in this regard.

20 As White's research suggests, the centrality of breath control (*prāṇāyāma*) and inner sound (*nāḍa*) in pre-modern yoga practice cannot be underestimated (White 1996), and as other anthropological studies of martial arts in South Asia indicate (cf. Alter 1992; Zarrilli 1998), breath control (*prāṇāyāma*) and mantra form a core component of contemporary body cultures built upon yogic models of the body. Finally, with regard to music, following the publication of Joachim-Ernst Berendt's *The World Is Sound: Nada Brahma* (Berendt 1991 [1983]), world music has since provided an entry point into a universal and transformative "Yoga for everybody" accessible to most all members of the transnational yoga community (Wilke and Moebus 2011: 24). As Wilke and Moebus show, Berendt's work represents a contemporary reformulation of the medieval "Sonic Absolute" (*nāda-brahman*) theology of sacred sound found in Sarngadeva's *Saṅgīta-Ratnākara*. Reformulations of yogic theories of sound are common in contemporary transnational yoga on account of the malleability of said theories (Wilke and Moebus 2011). Similarly, in the wake of the "sonic theology" (Beck 1993) of the Radha Soamis and Paramahansa Yogananada (Chapter 2 in this book), a variety of forms of music are included in the transformative transnational practice of the yoga of sound (*nāda-yoga*).

21 Scholars working outside of the field of Yoga Studies have shown how the bodily practices of diet, music, and breathing can play particularly transformative roles within other body cultures in South Asia. For example, Alter shows how physical exercises, dietetics, and celibacy practices are deployed to discipline and transform the North Indian wrestler's body within the context of generalized Hindu and yogic notions of embodiment (Alter 1992: 90). Similarly, in the context of the South Indian martial art known as *kalari*, Zarrilli demonstrates how the practitioner's body, following the principles of both *haṭha* and Patanjalian yoga, undergoes external purification involving massage, exercise, celibacy, dietary modifications, and digestive cleansing; internal purification involving breath control, mantra chanting, and meditation; finally achieving a warrior-like mental state wherein "the body is all eyes" (Zarrilli 1998: 88–89, 201). Other studies have shown how the transformation of bodies in South Indian pilgrimage and festival routes are undergirded by yogic models of the subtle body (Srinivas 2001; Daniel 1984).

22 As someone who is primarily trained in the field of Religious Studies, I also bring to this project my interdisciplinary influence from my participation in the "Reimagining Indian Ocean Worlds" Mellon Research Initiative at the University of California at Davis. The interdisciplinary training I experienced in this research group inspired multiple directions for me to place my contemporary ethnographic research data into conversation with academic fields that reveal, quite strikingly, the broader contexts in which the specific transnational yoga cultures that I study have developed. For further information on the Reimagining Indian Ocean Worlds project, please read the edited volume that emerged from this project: Srinivas, Smriti, Bettina Ng'weno, and Neelima Jeychandran (eds.). 2020. *Reimagining Indian Ocean Worlds*. New York: Routledge.

23 Srinivas's notion of "Spirited Topographies" in Bangalore and other inland cities is particularly relevant here (Srinivas 2022: 7).

24 Hoogervorst shows, for example, how South Asian culinary language and the cooks who brought foodways into other oceanic worlds "transformed the foodscapes of the Indian Ocean" (Hoogervorst 2018: 519). As Hoogervorst also acknowledges,

culinary concepts have extended the boundaries of the Indian Ocean beyond its traditional geographical limits. He writes, "To some extent, the connectivities outlined here also stretched beyond the Indian Ocean, marking a departure from scholarship that sees this geographical space as an integrated world. Ports just beyond its horizon – such as Cape Town in the west and Macau in the east – were significantly influenced by developments initiated in the Indian Ocean, as is clearly reflected in the culinary heritage of these cities" (ibid.: 537). While incorporating Hoogervorst's "language-centric approach" (ibid.: 536), this book moves beyond language alone to demonstrate how discursive Indian Ocean dietary ideology becomes embodied in practice globally.

25 As Byl and Sykes continue, "Inviting local epistemologies to condition historical, cultural, or musical analyses can yield conclusions that are profound, disciplining not just our interpretations but also the assumptions that they are built upon. This is not a fetishization of the emic, but rigorous peer review – that is, if we see our interlocuters as our intellectual peers" (Byl and Sykes 2020: 411).

26 The "Asian Brown Cloud" was named after a preceding cloud of pollution in Denver, Colorado, in the United States known as the "Denver Brown Cloud" (Ramanathan et al. 2002: 954–955).

27 The Asian Brown Cloud is a toxic concoction of pollutants that are both anthropogenic and naturally occurring. Ramanathan et al. describe the contents as follows: "The brownish haze… consists of a mixture of anthropogenic sulphate, nitrate, organics, black carbon, dust and fly ash particles and natural aerosols such as sea salt and mineral dust. The brownish colour is due to the absorption and the scattering of solar radiation by black carbon, soil-derived dust, fly ash and NO2" (Ramanathan et al. 2002: 948).

28 To my knowledge, the gurus I have studied in this book were, thankfully, not involved in the abuse that seems to have plagued the transnational guru movement.

References

Acri, Andrea. 2021. "Yoga and Meditation Traditions in Insular Southeast Asia," in Suzanne Newcombe and Karen O'Brien-Kop (eds.), *Routledge Handbook of Yoga and Meditation Studies*. New York: Routledge: 273–290.

Albanese, Catherine L. 2007. *A Republic of Mind and Spirit: A Cultural History of American Metaphysical Religion*. New Haven: Yale University Press.

Alter, Joseph S. 1992. *The Wrestler's Body: Identity and Ideology in North India*. New Delhi: Munshiram Manoharlal.

Alter, Joseph S. 2000. *Gandhi's Body: Sex, Diet, and the Politics of Nationalism*. Philadelphia: University of Pennsylvania Press.

Alter, Joseph S. 2004. *Yoga in Modern India: The Body Between Science and Philosophy*. Princeton: Princeton University Press.

Alter, Joseph S. 2005. "Modern Medical Yoga: Struggling with a History of Magic, Alchemy and Sex." *Asian Medicine* 1, no. 1: 119–146.

Altglas, Véronique. 2014. *From Yoga to Kabbalah: Religious Exoticism and the Logics of Bricolage*. New York: Oxford University Press.

Amrith, Sunil S. 2013. *Crossing the Bay of Bengal: The Furies of Nature and the Fortunes of Migrants*. Cambridge: Harvard University Press.

Arnold, David. 1993. *Colonizing the Body: State Medicine and Epidemic Disease in Nineteenth-Century India*. Berkeley: University of California Press.

Augé, Marc. 1999. *An Anthropology of Contemporaneous Worlds*. Stanford: Stanford University Press.

Bakhtin, Mikhail Mikhailovich. 1981. *The Dialogic Imagination: Four Essays by M.M. Bakhtin*. Translated by Caryl Emerson and Michael Holquist. Edited by Michael Holquist. Austin: University of Texas Press.
Bayat, Asef. 2010. *Life as Politics: How Ordinary People Change the Middle East*. Stanford: Stanford University Press.
Beck, Guy L. 1993. *Sonic Theology: Hinduism and Sacred Sound*. Columbia: University of South Carolina Press.
Bender, Courtney. 2010. *The New Metaphysicals: Spirituality and the American Religious Imagination*. Chicago: University of Chicago Press.
Berendt, Joachim-Ernst. 1991 [1985]. *The World Is Sound: Nada Brahma: Music and the Landscape of Consciousness*. Rochester: Inner Traditions.
Bevilacqua, Daniela. 2018. "Let the Sādhus Talk. Ascetic understanding of Haṭha Yoga and yogāsanas." *Religions of South Asia* 11, no. 2: 182–206.
Bhojvaid, Vasundhara. 2021. "Hazy Clouds: Making Black Carbon Visible in Climate Science." *Journal of Material Culture* 26, no. 2: 162–177.
Bose, Sugata. 2006. *A Hundred Horizons: The Indian Ocean in the Age of Global Empire*. Cambridge: Harvard University Press.
Bourdieu, Pierre. 1990. *The Logic of Practice*. Stanford: Stanford University Press.
Bronkhorst, Johannes. 2022. "Psychological Transformation in Buddhism and Yoga" paper presented at *the SOAS Center for Yoga Studies*, London, October 5, 2022.
Burchett, Patton E. 2019. *A Genealogy of Devotion: Bhakti, Tantra, Yoga, and Sufism in North India*. New York: Columbia University Press.
Büscher, Monika, John Urry and Katian Witchger, eds. 2011. *Mobile Methods*. New York: Routledge.
Byl, Julia and Jim Sykes. 2020. "Ethnomusicology and the Indian Ocean: On the Politics of Area Studies." *Ethnomusicology* 64, no. 3: 394–421.
Chaudhuri, K.N. 1985. *Trade and Civilisation in the Indian Ocean: An Economic History from the Rise of Islam to 1750*. London: Cambridge University Press.
Comaroff, Jean. 1985. *Body of Power, Spirit of Resistance: The Culture and History of a South African People*. Chicago: University of Chicago Press.
Copeman, Jacob and Aya Ikegame. 2012. *The Guru in South Asia: New Interdisciplinary Perspectives*. London: Routledge.
Cresswell, Tim. 2006. *On the Move: Mobility in the Modern Western World*. New York: Taylor and Francis Group.
Cresswell, Tim. 2010. "Mobilities I: Catching up." *Progress in Human Geography* 35, no. 4: 550–558.
Cresswell, Tim. 2012. "Mobilities II: Still." *Progress in Human Geography* 36, no. 5: 645–653.
Csordas, Thomas J. 1990. "Embodiment as a Paradigm for Anthropology." *Ethos*, 18, no. 1: 5–47.
Csordas, Thomas J. 2009. *Transnational Transcendence: Essays on Religion and Globalization*. Berkeley: University of California Press.
Daniel, E. Valentine. 1984. *Fluid Signs: Being a Person the Tamil Way*. Berkeley: University of California Press.
Davis, Richard. 2015. *The Bhagavad Gita: A Biography*. Princeton: Princeton University Press.
De Certeau, Michel. 1984. *The Practice of Everyday Life*. Berkeley: University of California Press.

De Michelis, Elizabeth. 1995. "Some Comments on the Contemporary Practice of Yoga in the UK, with Particular Reference to British Hatha Yoga Schools." *Journal of Contemporary Religion* 10, no. 3: 243–525.

De Michelis, Elizabeth. 2005. *A History of Modern Yoga: Patañjali and Western Esotericism*. New York: Continuum.

De Michelis, Elizabeth. 2008. "Modern Yoga: History and Forms." In *Yoga in the Modern World: Contemporary Perspectives*, edited by Mark Singleton and Jean Byrne. New York: Routledge: 17–35.

Deleuze, Gilles and Félix Guattari. 1987. *A Thousand Plateaus*. Minneapolis: University of Minnesota Press.

Deslippe, Philip. 2021. "How the Model of Money Laundering Can Help Us Understand Abuse within 3HO," in Christopher Miller (ed.), "Abuse in Yoga and Beyond: Cultural Logics and Pathways for the Future." *Sacred Matters Magazine*. Accessed January 21, 2022. https://sacredmattersmagazine.com/how-the-model-of-money-laundering-can-help-us-understand-abuse-within-3ho/

Douglas, Mary. 1996 [1970]. *Natural Symbols: Explorations in Cosmology*. New York: Routledge.

Douglas, Mary. 2001 [1975]. *Implicit Meanings: Selected Essays in Anthropology*. New York: Routledge.

Downey, Greg. 2005. *Learning Capoeira: Lessons in Cunning from an Afro-Brazilian Art*. New York: Oxford University Press.

Forsthoefel, Thomas A., and Cynthia Ann Humes, eds. 2005. *Gurus in America*. Albany: State University of New York Press.

Foucault, Michel. 1990. *The History of Sexuality Volume 1: An Introduction*, trans. by Robert Hurley. New York: Vintage Books.

Foucault, Michel. 1995. *Discipline and Punish: The Birth of the Prison*. New York: Vintage Books.

Foxen, Anya and Christa Kuberry. 2021. *Is This Yoga? Concepts, Histories, and the Complexities of Modern Practice*. New York: Routledge.

Foxen, Anya P. 2017. *Biography of a Yogi: Paramahansa Yogananda and the Origins of Modern Yoga*. New York: Oxford University Press.

Foxen, Anya P. 2020. *Inhaling Spirit: Harmonialism, Orientalism, and the Western Roots of Modern Yoga*. New York: Oxford University Press.

Ghosh, Amitav. 1993. *In an Antique Land*. New York: Alfred A. Knopf.

Gleig, Ann and Lola Williamson. 2013. *Homegrown Gurus: From Hinduism in America to American Hinduism*. Albany: State University of New York Press.

Godrej, Farah. 2022. *Freedom Inside: Yoga and Meditation in the Carceral State*. New York: Oxford University Press.

Hancock, Mary and Smriti Srinivas. 2018. "Roundtable on Spirited Topographies: Religion and Urban Place-Making: Ordinary Cities and Milieus of Innovation." *Journal of the American Academy of Religion* 86, no. 2: 454–472.

Hauser, Beatrix, ed. 2013. *Yoga Traveling: Bodily Practice in Transcultural Perspective*. New York: Springer.

Hauser, Beatrix. 2018. "Following the Transcultural Circulation of Bodily Practices: Modern Yoga and the Corporeality of Mantras," in Karl Baier, Philipp A. Maas, and Karin Preisendanz (eds.), *Yoga in Transformation*. Vienna: Vienna University Press: 505–528.

Hofmeyr, Isabel. 2007. "The Black Atlantic Meets the Indian Ocean: Forging New Paradigms of Transnationalism for the Global South – Literary and Cultural Perspectives." *Social Dynamics* 33, no. 2: 3–32.

Hoogervorst, Tom. 2018. "Sailors, Tailors, Cooks, and Crooks: On Loanwords and Neglected Lives in Indian Ocean Ports." *Itinerario* 42, no. 3, 516–548.

Hoogervorst, Tom. 2022. "*Qaliyya*: The Connections, Exclusions, and Silences of an Indian Ocean Stew." *Global Food History* 8, no. 2, 106–127.

Hoyez, Anne-Cécile. 2007. "The 'world of yoga': The Production and Reproduction of Therapeutic Landscapes." *Social Science and Medicine* 65: 112–124.

Jackson, Michael. 2013. *Lifeworlds: Essays in Existential Anthropology*. Chicago: The University of Chicago.

Jacobs, Stephen. 2017. "Yoga Jam: Remixing *kīrtan* in the Art of Living." *Journal of Religion and Popular Culture* 29, no. 1: 1–18.

Jacobs, Stephen. 2019. "A Life in Balance: Sattvic Food and the Art of Living Foundation." *Religions* 10, no. 1: 1–16.

Jain, Andrea R. 2015. *Selling Yoga: From Counterculture to Pop Culture*. New York: Oxford University Press.

Jain, Andrea R. 2020. *Peace, Love, Yoga: The Politics of Global Spirituality*. New York: Oxford University Press.

Jayasuriya, Shihan de Silva. 2008. "Indian Oceanic Crossings: Music of the Afro-Asian Diaspora." *African Diaspora* 1, no. 1–2: 135–154.

Jirón, Paola. 2011. "On becoming 'la sombra/the shadow'," in Monika Büscher, John Urry, and Katian Witchger (eds.), *Mobile Methods*. New York: Routledge: 36–53.

Kaur, Inderjit N. 2023. "Making Pilgrimage, Making Home: Sikh Sacred Soundings in Kenya," in Jim Sykes and Julia Byl (eds.), *Sounding the Indian Ocean: Musical Circulations in the Afro-Asiatic Seascape*. Berkeley: University of California Press.

Koch, Anne. 2007. *Körperwissen. Grundlegung einer Religionsaisthetik. Habilitationsschrift, Perspektiven der Religionswissenschaft*. München: Ludwig-Maximilians-Universität München.

Lefebvre, Henri. 1991 [1974]. *The Production of Space*. Massachusetts: Blackwell.

Lelieveld, J., P. J. Crutzen, V. Ramanathan, M. O. Andreae, C. A. M. Brenninkmeijer, T. Campos, G. R. Cass, R. R. Dickerson, H. Fischer, J. A. de Gouw, A. Hansel, A. Jefferson, D. Kley, A. T. J. de Laat, S. Lal, M. G. Lawrence, J. M. Lobert, O. L. Mayol-Bracero, A. P. Mitra, T. Novakov, S. J. Oltmans, K. A. Prather, T. Reiner, H. Rodhe, H. A. Scheeren, D. Sikka, and J. Williams. 2001. "The Indian Ocean Experiment: Widespread Air Pollution from South and Southeast Asia." *Science* 291, no. 5506: 1031–1036.

Leong-Salobir, Cecilia, Krishnendu Ray, and Jaclyn Rohel, eds. 2016. "Introducing a Special Issue on Rescuing Taste from the Nation: Oceans, Borders, and Culinary Flows." *Gastronomica: The Journal of Food and Culture* 16, no. 1: 9–15.

Lucas, Phillip Charles. 2013. "Neo-Advaita in America: Three Representative Teachers," in Ann Gleig and Lola Williamson (eds.), *Homegrown Gurus: From Hinduism in America to American Hinduism*, Albany: State University of New York Press: 163–187.

Lucia, Amanda J. 2020. *White Utopias: The Religious Exoticism of Transformational Festivals*. Oakland: University of California Press.

Madaio, James. 2017. "Rethinking Neo-Vedānta: Swami Vivekananda and the Selective Historiography of Advaita Vedānta." *Religions* 8, no. 6: 101.

Mallinson, James. 2011. "Haṭha Yoga," in Knut A. Jacobsen (ed.), *Brill's Encyclopedia of Hinduism. Vol. 3*. Leiden: Brill. 770–781.

Mallinson, James and Mark Singleton. 2017. *Roots of Yoga*. London: Penguin Classics.

Marcus, George. 1995. "Ethnography in/of the World System: The Emergence of Multi-Sited Ethnography." *Annual Review of Anthropology* 24: 95–117.
Mauss, Marcel. 1973 [1935]. "Techniques of the Body." *Economy and Society* 2, no. 1: 70–88.
Meek, Laura. 2020. "Bibi's *uchungu*: eating, bitterness, and relationality across Indian Ocean worlds," in Smriti Srinivas, Bettina Ng'weno, and Neelima Jeychandran (eds.), *Reimagining Indian Ocean Worlds*. New York: Routledge. 197–211.
Miller, Christopher, ed. 2021. "Abuse in Yoga and Beyond: Cultural Logics and Pathways for the Future." *Sacred Matters Magazine*. Accessed January 21, 2022. https://sacredmattersmagazine.com/ya-introduction/
Monier-Williams, Monier. 1899. *Monier-Williams Sanskrit–English Dictionary*. http://www.sanskrit-lexicon.uni-koeln.de/scans/MWScan/2014/web/webtc2/index.php.
Neumann, David. 2019. *Finding God through Yoga: Paramahansa Yogananda and Modern American Religion in a Global Age*. Chapel Hill: University of North Carolina Press.
Newcombe, Suzanne. 2009. "The Development of Modern Yoga: A Survey of the Field." *Religion Compass* 3, no. 6: 986–1002.
Newcombe, Suzanne and Karen O'Brien-Kop, eds. 2021. *Routledge Handbook of Yoga and Meditation Studies*. New York: Routledge.
Pinch, William R. 2006. *Warrior Ascetics and Indian Empires*. Cambridge: Cambridge University Press.
Prestholdt, Jeremy. 2020. "The ends of the Indian Ocean: notes on boundaries and affinities across time," in Smriti Srinivas, Bettina Ng'weno, and Neelima Jeychandran (eds.), *Reimagining Indian Ocean Worlds*. New York: Routledge. 25–41.
Queen, Christopher S. and Sally B. King, eds. 1996. *Engaged Buddhism: Buddhist Liberation Movements in Asia*. Albany: State University of New York.
Ramanathan, V., P. J. Crutzen, A. P. Mitra and D. Sikka. 2002. "The Indian Ocean Experiment and the Asian Brown Cloud." *Current Science* 83, no. 8: 947–955.
Ranganath, Nicole. 2020. "The ship and the anchor: Shifting cartographies of affinity and belonging among Sikhs in Fiji," in Smriti Srinivas, Bettina Ng'weno, and Neelima Jeychandran (eds.), *Reimagining Indian Ocean Worlds*. New York: Routledge. 180–193.
Ray, Krishnendu. 2013. "Indian Ocean cuisine?: Outline of an argument on the limits of national cultures," in Ruth Morgan, Cecilia Leong-Salobir, and Jeremy Martens (eds.), *Western Australia in the Indian Ocean World*. Crawley: University of Western Australia Press. 119–131.
Ray, Krishnendu. 2015. "Culinary Spaces and National Cuisines: The Pleasures of an Indian Ocean Cuisine?," in James Farrer (ed.), *The Globalization of Asian Cuisines: Transnational Networks and Culinary Contact Zones*. New York: Palgrave Macmillan: 23–36.
Samarawickrema, Nethra. 2020. "Elsewheres in the Indian Ocean Spatio-temporal: encounters and imaginaries beyond the sea," in Smriti Srinivas, Bettina Ng'weno, and Neelima Jeychandran (eds.) *Reimagining Indian Ocean Worlds*. New York: Routledge: 89–102.
Samuel, Geoffrey. 2008. *The Origins of Yoga and Tantra: Indic Religions to the Thirteenth Century*. Cambridge: Cambridge University Press.
Sarbacker, Stuart Ray. 2021. *Tracing the Path of Yoga: The History and Philosophy of Mind-Body Discipline*. Albany: State University of New York Press.
Sarkar, Sumit. 1997. *Writing Social History*. New York: Oxford University Press.
Schwind, Christa. 2015. "Tracing an American Yoga: Identity and Cross-cultural Transaction," PhD Dissertation, University of Denver.

Shaw, Alison and Ersa S. Kayatz. 2021. "Yoga bodies, yoga minds: contextualising the health discourses and practices of modern postural yoga." *Anthropology and Medicine* 28, no. 3: 279–296.
Sheller, Mimi and John Urry. 2006. "The New Mobilities Paradigm." *Environment and Planning* 38: 207–226.
Singleton, Mark. 2010. *Yoga Body: The Origins of Modern Posture Practice*. New York: Oxford University Press.
Singleton, Mark and Ellen Goldberg, eds. 2014. *Gurus of Modern Yoga*. New York: Oxford University Press.
Singleton, Mark and Borayin Larios. 2021. "The scholar-practitioner of yoga in the western academy," in Suzanne Newcombe and Karen O'Brien-Kop (eds.), *Routledge Handbook of Yoga and Meditation Studies*. New York: Routledge: 37–50.
Sjoman, N. E., and Vaḍeyara Kṛṣṇarāja. 1996. *The Yoga tradition of the Mysore Palace*. New Delhi: Abhinav Publications.
Srinivas, Smriti. 2001. *Landscapes of Urban Memory: The Sacred and the Civic in India's High-tech City*. Minneapolis: University of Minnesota Press.
Srinivas, Smriti. 2014. "Satya Sai Baba and the Repertoire of Yoga," in Mark Singleton and Ellen Goldberg (eds.), *Gurus of Modern Yoga*. New York: Oxford University Press: 261–279.
Srinivas, Smriti. 2015. *A Place for Utopia: Urban Designs from South Asia*. Seattle: University of Washington Press.
Srinivas, Smriti. 2022. "Beyond the Rim: Centering Cities in Indian Ocean Worlds." *Verge: Studies in Global Asias* 8, no. 1: 3–11.
Srinivas, Smriti, Bettina Ng'weno, and Neelima Jeychandran (eds.). 2020. *Reimagining Indian Ocean Worlds*. New York: Routledge.
Strauss, Sarah. 2005. *Positioning Yoga: Balancing Acts Across Cultures* New York: Berg.
Sykes, Jim and Julia Byl (eds.). 2023. *Sounding the Indian Ocean: Musical Circulations in the Afro-Asiatic Seascape*. Berkeley: University of California Press.
Tsing, Anna Lowenhaupt. 2005. *Friction: An Ethnography of Global Connection*. Princeton: Princeton University Press.
Tweed, Thomas A. 2006. *Crossing and Dwelling: A Theory of Religion*. Cambridge: Harvard University Press.
Urban, Hugh. 2003. *Tantra: Sex, Secrecy, Politics, and Power in the Study of Religion*. Berkeley: University of California Press.
Urry, John. 2009. "Mobilities and Social Theory," in Bryan S. Turner (ed.), *The New Blackwell Companion to Social Theory*. Chichester: Blackwell Publishing: 477–495.
van der Veer, Peter. 2001. *Imperial Encounters: Religion and Modernity in India and Britain*. Princeton: Princeton University Press.
Vink, Markus P. M. 2007. "Indian Ocean Studies and the 'new thalassology'." *Journal of Global History* 2, no. 1: 41–62.
von Ostrowski, Laura. 2022. *Ein Text in Bewegung. Das Yogasūtra als Praxiselement im Ashtanga Yoga – einehistorische, religionsästhetische und ethnographische Studie* in: *Open Publishing in the Humanities*. UB München, München: Georg Olms Verlag.
von Ostrowski, Laura. Forthcoming. "Practicing the *Yogasūtra*? An Approach to the Analysis of Contemporary Yoga Philosophy's Somatic Aspects," in Knut Jacobsen and Henriette Hanky (eds.), *Practices of Embodied Reception: Adoptions and Adaptations of South Asian Spiritualities through Performance*.
Weiss, Richard S. 2019. *The Emergence of Modern Hinduism: Religion on the Margins of Colonialism*. Oakland: University of California Press.

White, David Gordon. 1996. *The Alchemical Body: Siddha Traditions in Medieval India*. Chicago: University of Chicago Press.

White, David Gordon. 2009. *Sinister Yogis*. Chicago: University of Chicago Press.

White, David Gordon. 2012. *Yoga in Practice*. Princeton: Princeton University Press.

White, David Gordon. 2014. *The Yoga Sutra of Patanjali: A Biography*. Princeton: Princeton University Press.

Wilke, Annette and Oliver Moebus. 2011. *Sound and Communication: An Aesthetic Cultural History of Sanskrit Hinduism*. Berlin: Walter de Gruyter GmbH and Co. KG.

Zarrilli, Phillip B. 1998. *When the Body Becomes All Eyes: Paradigms, Discourses, and Practices of Power in Kalarippayattu, a South Indian Martial Art*. New York: Oxford University Press.

1 Patanjali and Arjuna meet American Countercuisine

Yogic Diet and Selfless Service at Gurani Anjali's Yoga Anand Ashram, Long Island

The American counterculture marked a period of great social and political transformation. Whether one belonged to the political New Left or the romantic counterculture during this period, foodways became one of the primary material practices for demonstrating one's identity, activism, and ideological commitments. Though countercultural foodways, or what Belasco refers to as "countercuisine" (Belasco 2007), were predominantly shaped by White[1] communities, other racial groups such as the Black Panther Party (cf. Anderson 2005: 137; Broad 2016: 136) constructed and participated in alternative engagements with food that maintained distinctive material practices and cultural logics. The field of Food Studies is uniquely equipped to examine and articulate these and other specific practices and logics that shape distinct foodways, both past and present. Because scholars of Food Studies have largely disregarded South Asian religious foodways in the United States, the current chapter uses tools from the field to consider a particular instantiation of countercuisine at Gurani Anjali's (1935–2001) Yoga Anand Ashram in Amityville on Long Island, New York in the 1970s.

Gurani Anjali's restaurant business, vegetarian dietary practices, and fasting at Yoga Anand Ashram clearly reflected existing forms of food-based social resistance movements popularized in the American counterculture in the 1960s and 1970s that targeted environmental, social, and health food justice concerns. Nevertheless, to argue that Anjali's food establishment and dietary regimen were entirely shaped by this context risks missing precisely how she harnessed the countercuisine movement to implicate her students' bodies within an alternative disciplinary regime connected to her own soteriological model of yoga. In other words, Anjali put the popularity of the American countercuisine to the task of initiating students into the preliminary stages of her yoga system's transformative logic.[2] The frictions between the predominant countercuisine and Anjali's philosophy around yogic diet thereby provide our first instantiation of engaged alchemy.

Anjali's foodways were situated at four critical junctures where the countercuisine ethos encountered elective affinities with some of the paramount metaphysical, ethical, and soteriological underpinnings of her eclectic yoga system.[3]

DOI: 10.4324/9781003414032-2

First, as counterculturalists inverted the meaning of the New Left's assertion that "the personal is political"[4] (cf. Hanisch 2000 [1969]) to indicate that one's personal actions alone constituted powerful forms of liberating political and environmental activism, Anjali simultaneously taught from *Sāṃkhya-Yoga* that each person possessed a higher Self (*puruṣa*), the individual liberation (*kaivalya*) of which from nature (*prakṛti*) could be realized entirely through their own yogic efforts and actions. Although Anjali's yoga system fundamentally sought to liberate the soul from nature according to *Sāṃkhya-Yoga*, however, her devotion to nature allowed her to retain a deep respect for the local environment that sat well with her countercultural devotees who were also seeking a connection and return to nature. In addition to various meditation exercises, these connections to nature were achieved, much as they were in the broader counterculture, through a reformed and seemingly more "natural" vegetarian diet.

Second, as segments of the White counterculture adopted a vegetarian diet as a primary means to raise their consciousness, feel more in harmony with nature, and allay anxieties around health, environmental, and social injustice, students' adoption of a vegetarian diet at Yoga Anand Ashram harnessed these concerns to fulfill the requirement to perform *Sāṃkhya-Yoga*'s ethical practices (*yama* and *niyama*), and most notably non-violence (*ahiṃsā*), to achieve yogic liberation. Nevertheless, and hopefully much to the delight of scholars of Food Studies, the ashram's vegetarian dietary regimen was not always oppressively restrictive. Rather, its vegetarian restaurant menus combined, as did the United States' broader countercuisine movement, the tensions between both hedonistic and ascetic approaches to food (Belasco 2007: 66–67) and thereby resonated with what Rosen refers to as "aesthetic ascetics" (Rosen 2011: 145).

Third, fasting, when coupled with vegetarian diet, aligned with counterculturalists' interest in finding methods for experiencing a natural, alternative, drug-free high. In light of the popularity of LSD and other psychedelic drugs during the counterculture, many gurus espoused yoga as a viable and equally effective method for achieving much-sought-after higher states of consciousness. Within Anjali's yoga system specifically, fasting was understood to purify an individual's mental and emotional afflictions (*kleśa*) in their pursuit of awareness of their higher Self (*puruṣa*) in her *Sāṃkhya-Yoga* system.[5]

Fourth and finally, while those working in the United States' countercuisine "hip enterprise" food establishments were basking in the "romance of service" (Belasco 2007: 94), Anjali taught the concept of *karma-yoga* (the yoga of action) found in the *Bhagavad-Gītā* as well as the more general notion of giving selfless service (*sevā*) to god in order to manage her countercultural workforce. In doing so, she suggested to her more permanent volunteer ashram members that they might achieve liberation while they selflessly worked in the ashram's well-known local vegetarian restaurant, Santosha, or one of the ashram's other establishments.

With these four points of connection in mind, it is important to observe that with the arrival of the late 1960s, Anjali found herself at the beginnings of a period in global history wherein, as Lucia writes, "female asceticism and the public figure of the female guru are becoming significantly more influential both within Hindu ascetic traditions and global Hindu religiosity" (Lucia 2014a: 17). Indeed, as the 1960s moved forward, Anjali's capacity to assume a leadership role in the United States' social landscape increased as "*godwomen*" (Jain 2015: 56) began to serve roles as protectors of the urban middle class from "globalization and other modern social processes" while simultaneously rescuing their devotees from modern disenchantment (ibid.: 50). Counting her among many others, Jain briefly considers Anjali as one of these "*godwomen*" (ibid.: 56), and in this chapter I showcase Anjali's understudied foodways and the contributions they make to the social history of transnational yoga.

Food in the Study of Religion

Despite the remarkable expansion of the study of food and the numerous methodological tools at scholars' fingertips, religious foodways have received only limited attention within the field of Food Studies. As Dallam has noted, "… the connections among religion, food, and eating in America have not yet been studied widely and systematically" (Dallam 2014: xx) even though, as Finch rightly argues in the same volume, religious foodways illuminate "the exceedingly concrete, visceral ways that human beings go about being religious" (Finch 2014: xiii). Part of the reason for this lacuna in Food Studies may be due to the fact that, as Norman observes, "scholarly and popular volumes on food blame 'bad food' on 'Puritanism' in the culture's 'guilt-ridden,' 'sin-obsessed' religious history" (Norman 2012: 410). Nevertheless, as Griffith makes clear in a study of the history of Christian diet in *Born Again Bodies*, religion has played an "indispensable role" in the shaping of American dietary culture and should therefore play a significant role in our ongoing analyses of American foodways (Griffith 2004: 12). The existing work focusing on religion and Food Studies from scholars such as Elizabeth Pérez indeed demonstrates the analytical power that food provides us in the ethnographic study of religion (Pérez 2016).

While studies such as those of Griffith and others (cf. Sack 2000) have been concerned with Christian diet in the United States, other scholars have lamented the fact that contemporary accounts of foodways within Asian (Dallam 2014: xxiii) and, more specifically, Hindu (McClymond 2006: 90) religious communities in the United States are even fewer in number. Such studies would be quite valuable insofar as they might "reveal different understandings of and engagements with food from those of their Western predecessors" (ibid.). For example, within the literature that does exist, Singer provided an early and foundational account of diet at the International Society for Krishna Consciousness (ISKCON) wherein he demonstrated how vegetarian *prasāda* (sacred food) offerings are used to enculturate devotees into a Hindu cultural logic that inverts common American assumptions about the meaning of food and how it ought to be consumed in daily life (Singer 1984). Much more recently, Zeller delivered another similar account of ISKCON's conversion practices insisting that *prasāda* serves as "a powerful symbol of the embodied nature of devotion and worship" (Zeller 2012: 691). As Zeller also shows, ISKCON's free Indian vegetarian food distribution program and promises of an alternative "high" achieved through proper diet and other religious practices (e.g. mantra) found a welcome social environment in the United States' countercultural hotspots in Lower Manhattan and the Haight-Ashbury district in San Francisco where other similar activities were already taking place in the 1970s (ibid.: 688). Like other religious immigrant communities in the United States that sought to recreate their sense worlds from their homeland with food (cf. Orsi 2010: 153), founder Swami Prabhupada used his expertise in Indian cooking to fill ISKCON with the familiar – though for his Western devotees *exotic* – tastes and smells of his home in Bengal (Zeller 2012: 688). Finally, McClymond provides an account of the ways by which Hindu temple foodways are negotiated within the context of Southern culture in Atlanta (McClymond 2006). Engaging the early textual studies of Khare concerning food in Hinduism, McClymond suggests that such entangled foodways maintain a connection to the motherland of India while also providing devotees with the hope of experiencing liberation through a proper, albeit American, Hindu diet (ibid.; see also Khare 1992: 89).

Though the studies mentioned here do not comprise all of the existing literature on Hindu foodways in the United States, they are certainly some of the best-designed and frequently cited projects. As we shall soon see, they also help illuminate the entangled nature of the foodways at Yoga Anand Ashram, the yoga teachings of which were fundamentally grounded in Gurani Anjali's own yogic worldview and yet were deeply influenced by the American counterculture. However, none of these studies consider foodways in yoga communities specifically, and thus this chapter is a contribution to both the fields of Food Studies and Modern Yoga Studies insofar as it enters largely unchartered territory concerned with contemporary yogic foodways.

With limited exception, studies of contemporary yogic foodways are indeed quite scarce. Amanda Lucia's ethnographic consideration of yogic food moralism in *White Utopias* describes the "intersectionality" (Crenshaw 1989, as cited in Lucia 2020: 131) of dietary disciplines, gender, neoliberalism, and White class privilege. Lucia highlights how food preferences signal particular class distinctions, morality, and religious identities within the ascetic ethos of the yogic transformational festival scene (Lucia 2020: 131–133). Notable for this chapter, she also mentions that only 7 percent of American yogis are vegetarian despite yoga's high ethical ideals (ibid.: fn 34, 255–256; cf. Dickstein 2017).

Previous to Lucia's work, Jarow had rightly advised that we ought to study yogic diet within particular cultural contexts in Rosen's *Food for the Soul: Vegetarianism and Yoga Traditions* (Rosen 2011). Nevertheless, Jarow's chapter on this topic is mainly comprised of textual references to diet in Indian philosophy, followed then by some broad and conjectural reflections on contemporary yogic diet (Jarow 2011). Conversely, though not focused on the United States specifically, Jacobs' more recent study of yogic diet takes the transnational foodways of The Art of Living Foundation quite seriously and begins to approach the methodology taken in this chapter (Jacobs 2019). In this study, Jacobs is preoccupied with comparing the dietary practices he witnessed during his fieldwork with yogic and *āyurvedic* texts. Other scholars studying American foodways influenced by Asian religions have adopted a similar approach. For example, in his study of American Buddhist diet, Wilson compares his observations between Buddhist texts and modern praxis and concludes that,

> …in the rise of the mindful-eating movement we can see that mindfulness has become the Buddhist equivalent of Hindu-derived yoga in modern American culture: a religious technique that has been largely stripped of its original religious context, then repackaged as a universal panacea that delivers all sorts of practical benefits, especially ones relating to health issues.
>
> (Wilson 2014: 230)

Though texts are undoubtedly engaged earnestly within many yoga communities and we must consider the influence of these texts seriously, assessing whether or not what one sees on the ground during fieldwork is "correct" according to these texts or a perceived "original" tradition is a rather simplistic approach for understanding what, exactly, one is witnessing. Furthermore, while it is true, as Jacobs says regarding yogic diet, that "the goal of many modern forms of yoga tends to be expressed in terms of health and wellbeing" and that "this re-articulation of yoga in terms of wellbeing is consistent with what can be termed the therapeutic turn of culture" (Jacobs 2019: 2), his rather broad assessment reinforces an artificial binary between therapeutic/modern *versus* soteriological/premodern concerns and also overlooks more site-specific cultural influences shaping the organization's foodways. Contemporary yoga's more general focus on health and wellbeing, in other words, does not necessarily diminish the concomitant soteriological concerns that many yoga communities embrace and seek to achieve through diet. Furthermore, focusing unduly on the influence of health and wellbeing on yogic foodways potentially occludes other significant, site-specific motivating factors surrounding communities' adoption of particular yogic diets.

Studying Yogic Foodways: Semiotic, Historical, and Culturalist Approaches

In this chapter I study yogic foodways at Yoga Anand Ashram using three analytical perspectives inspired by the field of Food Studies: semiotic, historical, and culturalist. From the perspective of semiotics, when considering the internal cultural logics of particular yogic foodways, *what*, *why*, and *how* yoga communities eat tells us a lot about who they think they are or what it is they aspire to achieve. Indeed, building on the work of Lévi-Strauss (Lévi-Strauss 1966), anthropologists suggested early on that food was either a "natural symbol" yielding "an analogy with linguistic form" (Douglas 1996 [1970]; 2001 [1975]: 232), a "system of communication" undergirded by a "veritable grammar" (Barthes 2013 [1961]: 24), or perhaps even a "marvelously plastic kind of collective representation" rich with semiotic value (Appadurai 1981: 494). Though it may no longer be necessary to decipher a "grammar of foods" (Barthes 2013 [1961]: 25), food still compels us to consider, as Mintz wrote long ago, that "what people eat expresses who and what they are, to themselves and to others" (Mintz 1986: 13). And indeed foodways, shaped as they frequently are by social rules concerned with dietary purity and pollution (cf. Douglas 2001 [1975]: 231; Douglas 1984 [1966]) or class taste distinctions (Bourdieu 1984), unmistakably express unique forms of social identity and attendant social boundaries. Regarding these distinctions, Bourdieu once suggested that the body serves as a potent symbolic structure through which "one's taste is displayed" according to a particular class culture (ibid.: 190). And with regard to Hindu cultures specifically, not only does the purity of one's diet serve to display one's caste position (Dumont 1980), but the human alimentary tract itself functions as a "fiercely policed but also a contested and hotly trafficked" boundary (Roy 2010: 24) signaling one's nationalist, gender, and religious identity. Within religious and spiritual groups such as yoga communities, these boundaries and their concomitant social identities are continually reinforced through the collective performance of foodways encouraging commensality and belonging.

While semiotic approaches to the study of foodways in yoga communities may reveal much about how foodways express a community's identity, a historical approach requires us to ask *where* and *when* these foodways are practiced and compels us to look at the material and ideological conditions by which they have been forged. Harris argued early on that food practices (and specifically those in Hindu India) are surely shaped by material forces including a particular society's prevailing economic and environmental context (Harris 1978; cf. Counihan and Esterik 2013: 3). Further, as Anderson reminds us in his biocultural approach to Food Studies more broadly,

> …to paraphrase Marx's observations on history, people construct their foodways, but not in a vacuum; rather, they optimize nutrition given the constraints of income, labor, time, and environment they face, and given the cultural knowledge and practice they bring to the table. 'Cultural construction' is not only not arbitrary; it is enormously influenced by interaction with the world out there. It is comprehensible only when one knows what the constructors know, and understands the limits and possibilities they face.
>
> (Anderson 2005: 244)

To be sure, cultural ideas and practices surrounding food cannot be separated from the contexts out of which they emerge, and thus in addition to deciphering what foodways might tell us about a culture's internal identity, self-understanding, and ideological principles, discerning the wider material and ideological contexts by which yogic foodways are shaped, both historically and contemporaneously, comprises a significant and important research task.

That being said, though advocates of new yogic foodways must inevitably make concessions in order to adapt to the conditions and limitations by which they are surrounded (Madden and Finch 2006: 17), considering everyday cultural practices (de Certeau 1984) prevents us from simply reducing yoga's internal dietary logics to these external forces. In other words, even though the social meanings of particular foodways are of course dependent upon broader historical, social, economic, and political ideas and material realities that we cannot afford to ignore, community members nevertheless repeatedly imbue these same foodways with important new meanings that we can only understand through careful observation within particular social contexts.

Scholars of Food Studies have long recognized these cultural dynamics. Mintz, for example, identified two opposing forces he described as "intensification" and "extensification," both of which influence how food is made available, consumed, and given new meaning by users (Mintz 1986: 152). Mintz writes,

> In "intensification," consumption replicates that practiced by others, usually of a higher social status – also imitates, even emulates... In "intensification," those in power are responsible both for the presence of the new products and, to a degree, for their meanings; with "extensification," those in power may take charge of the availability of the new products, but the new users inform them with meaning.
>
> (ibid.)

Similarly, comparing structuralism and culturalism, Ashley et al. point out that while structuralist accounts of foodways assume that "structures exist prior to their human subjects, profoundly shaping their consciousness of the world and limiting their freedom of action within it... Culturalism, on the other hand, recovers men and women making their own histories" (Ashley et al. 2004: 7, 10). Finally, though Madden and Finch acknowledge the value of Bourdieu's notion of the *habitus*, they invoke Foucault to remind us that foodways,

> ... do not flow only from the top down, from authorities to members. Because social meanings are so deeply embedded in everyday practices, any individual, by virtue of participating within the community's *habitus*, has at his or her disposal the tools and know-how to reshape those practices according to personal tastes and desires.
>
> (Madden and Finch 2006: 12–13)

The methodology used in this chapter follows each of these important and interrelated distinctions, recognizing the dynamic interplay between internal and external cultural logics and the value of applying semiotic, historical, and culturalist analytical perspectives. Particularly interesting in this regard is how Gurani Anjali emerged as a female spiritual leader and produced her ashram's foodways in the conservative social context of counterculture-era Amityville on Long Island, New York.

Amityville's Heritage Meets Urbanization, Immigration, and the American Counterculture

Intending to establish the area on Long Island, New York as a "friendly village," citizens named their village "Amityville" in order to create congeniality among residents following a discordant community meeting in 1840 (Amityville Historical Society 2006: 7). The Amityville Historical Society, founded in 1969 by 30 residents who had developed a deep concern for the rapid socio-economic and religious changes occurring within their beloved community, has since aimed to preserve the village's congenial reputation as well as its predominantly Christian, nationalistic, conservative, and distinctly White-American heritage (Miller 2018: 31). In 2006, the Historical Society published a summary of their interpretation of Amityville's history in a popular book titled *Images of America: Amityville*. Among other things, this popular publication excludes Long Island's rich indigenous history, the village's status in the popular American imagination as the location of the gruesome "Amityville Horror" murders that took place there in 1974, as well as the many Asian religious organizations that had begun to establish themselves there in the 1960s and 1970s.

Images from the United States Geological Survey illustrate Amityville's accelerating development during the 1940s and 1950s, activities that were no doubt precursors to the Historical Society's anxieties in the 1960s. Large expanses of what were formerly open green areas and forest in 1947 have been transformed into "Built-Up Area" by 1954 (see Figure 1.1) (United States Geological Survey 1947, 1954, 1969, 1994). By this time, the railroad is being replaced by the family automobile and, thanks to the Robert Moses Parkway on Long Island, city residents are finding increased access to places such as Amityville which is soon transformed into "a single family home paradise on Long Island."[6] By 1969, as we can see in Figure 1.1, almost all of Amityville, with the exception of several small green patches and a sliver of green space running north from the ocean, had been developed into "Built-Up Area" (United States Geological Survey n.d.: 5).

Amityville's rapid development during the mid-twentieth century reflected broader urbanization trends already taking place in the United States following World War II that local, predominantly Christian conservatives were making efforts to contain. As Orsi shows, during this period intricate highway networks were constructed, leading to the destruction of stable communities

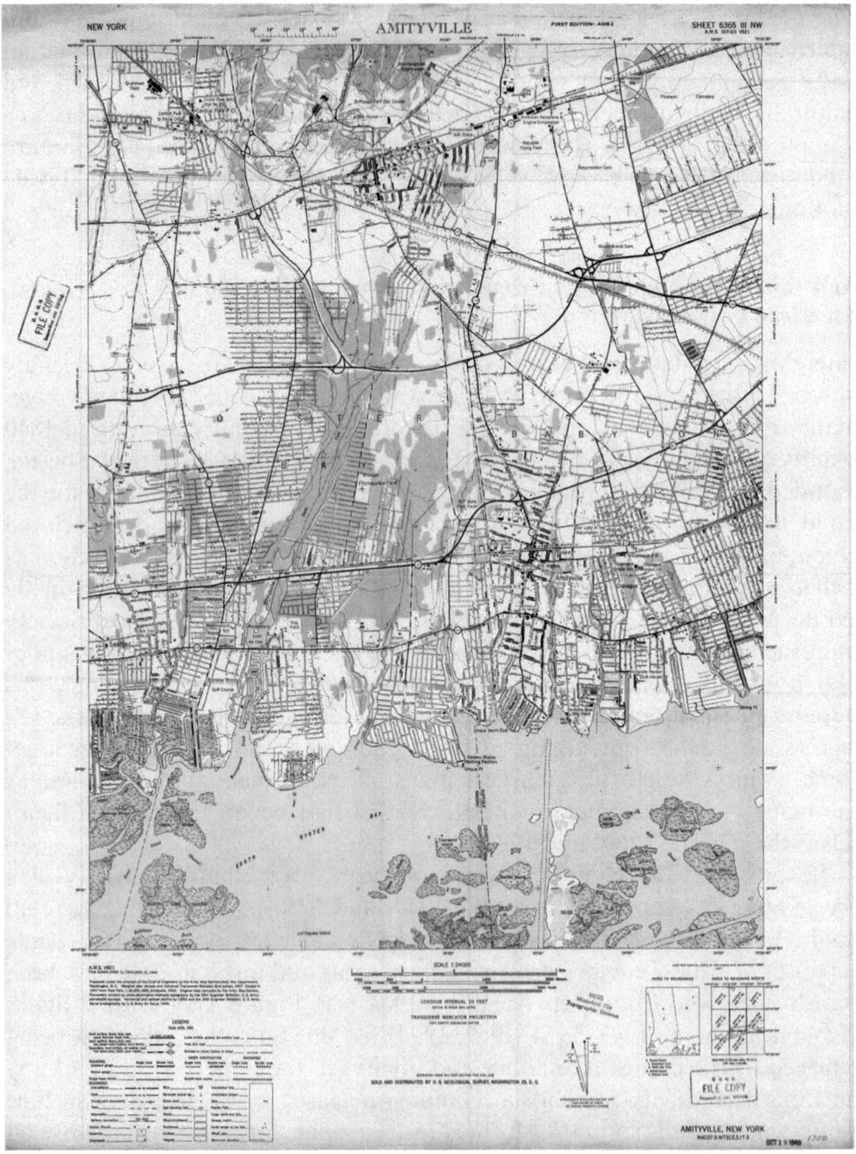

(a)

Figure 1.1 The USGS maps pictured here illustrate Amityville's transformation into "Built-Up Area" indicated by the increasingly dark areas which increase through the years 1947 (a), 1954 (b), 1969 (c), and finally 1994 (d).

Source: United States Geological Survey 1947, 1954, 1969, 1994.

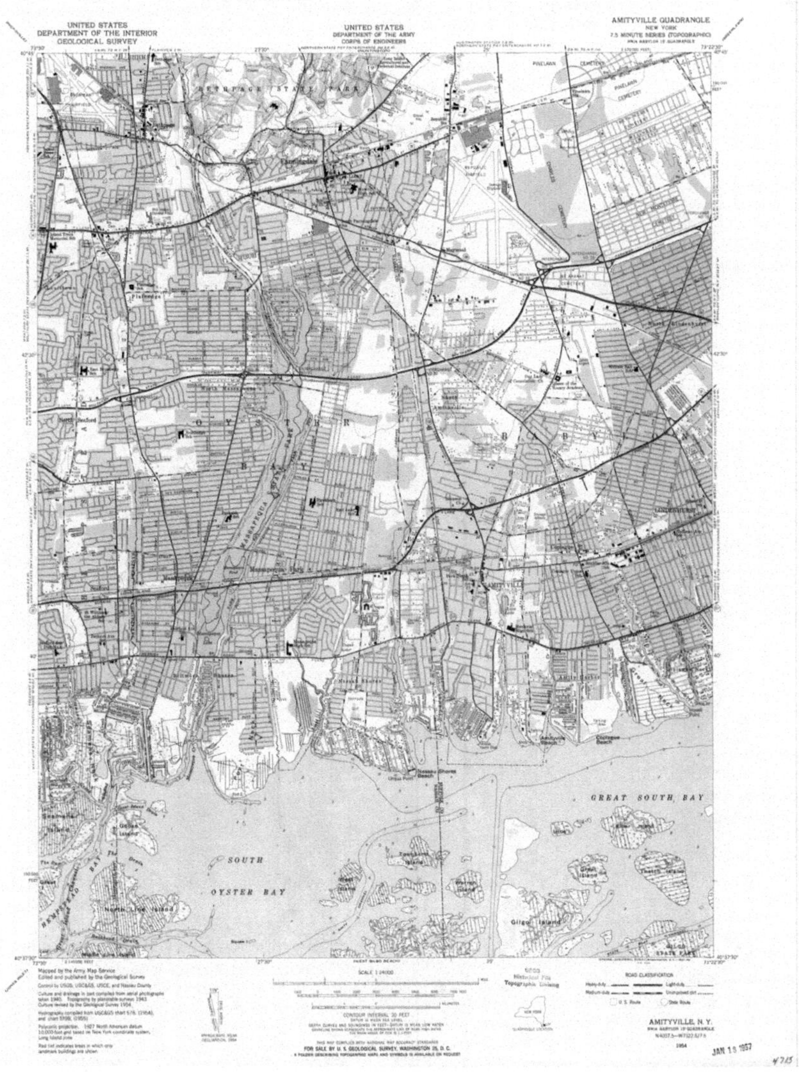

(b)

Figure 1.1 (Cont.).

and sacred places, while 8,000 shopping centers opened across the United States landscape (Orsi 1999: 33–35). In response, Christian reformers had initiated efforts to contain, and in some cases redeem, what they perceived as the morally depraved, "dirty city" (ibid.: 11). As new highways brought city life and consumer culture to Amityville, the various denominations of the village's predominantly Christian community, as the contents found in *Images of America* suggest, undoubtedly found themselves to be part of the "unified action"

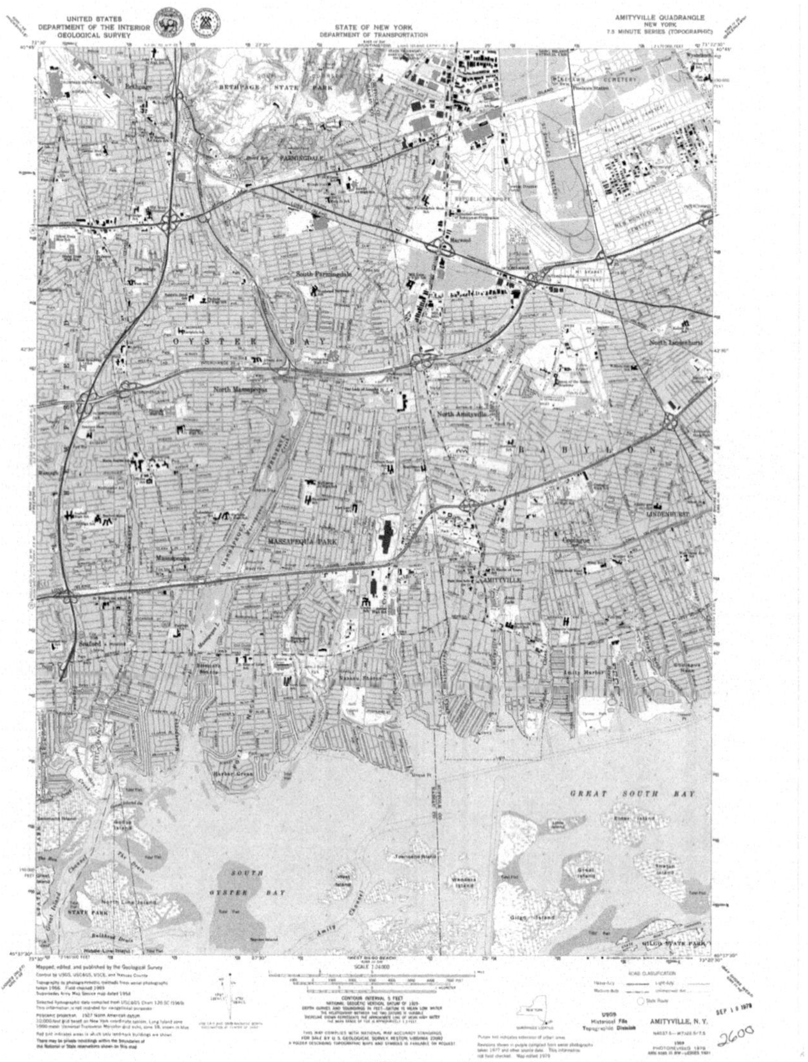

(c)

Figure 1.1 (Cont.).

that "… stretched the resources of individual churches, making cooperation unavoidable and imperative" (ibid.: 24). *Images of America* indeed conveys, although disingenuously, a Christian religious landscape in Amityville. It primarily does so by including picture after picture of religious architecture in the form of churches found throughout the village.

Nevertheless, by the 1960s, Amityville's socio-religious landscape had undergone significant transformation which reflected other broader trends in

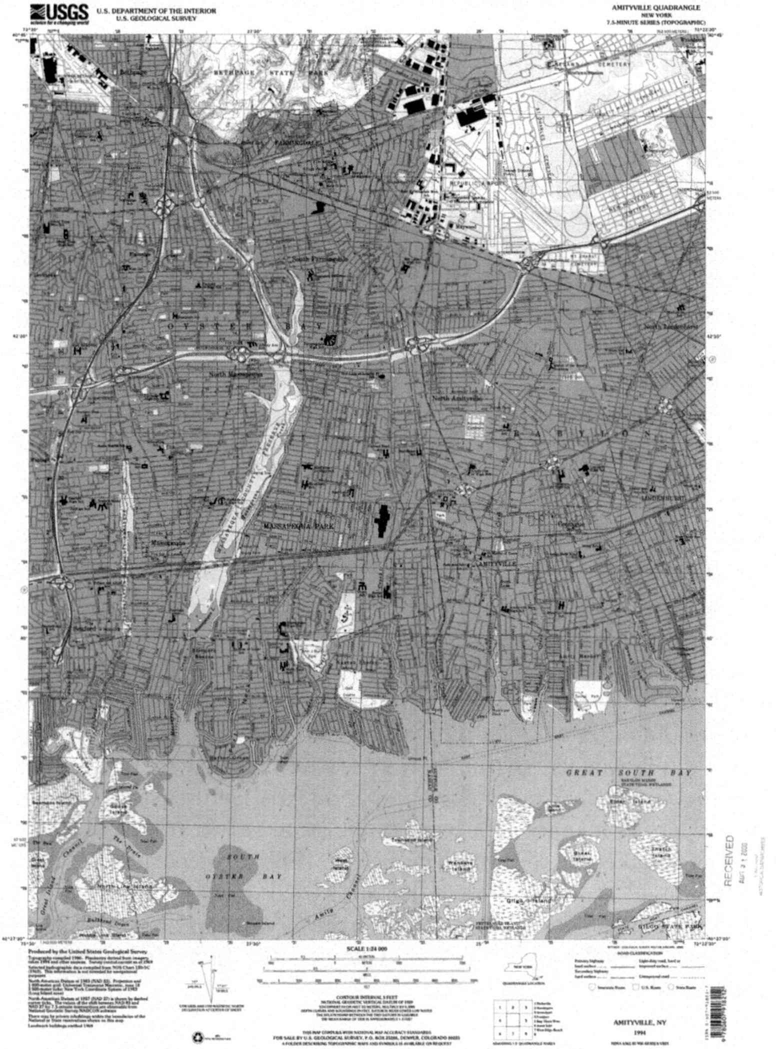

(d)

Figure 1.1 (Cont.).

the United States. Leaning on specious cultural and spiritual authority, as Orsi shows, White Protestants promoted xenophobia and legalized discrimination (ibid.: 29) as 6.5 million African Americans migrated north between 1910 and 1970 (ibid.: 20, 33), while 500,000 Puerto Ricans, many of whom came to New York, immigrated to the United States between 1946 and 1964 (ibid.: 33). Most notably for our purposes here, the year 1965 marked an important moment in the history of American immigration law for Asians, and, as Tweed and Prothero write,

> ...opened a new period in America's encounter with Asian religions... migration emerged as its predominant theme. Almost 40 percent of the new immigrants arrived from Asia, and millions of them practiced an Asian religious tradition... Christians remained the majority, but the cultural landscape of many cities changed... Faced with this new terrain, Americans began to remap the landscape during this period of passages... In the post-1965 period, peoples, artifacts, beliefs, and practices moved back and forth between Asia and America more quickly and more often than ever before... With Asian religions more prominent in American culture, it was difficult at the end of the twentieth century for Christians and Jews to ignore them, although some managed to act as if little had changed... Los Angeles, New York, and Chicago could boast that within their urban boundaries lived representatives of all the major religions.
>
> (Tweed and Prothero 1999: 224–226)

As Forsthoefel and Humes have discussed, an influx of "second wave" Indian gurus and other teachers brought an "alternate universe" to the American religious landscape during this critical period of cultural exchange (Forsthoefel and Humes 2005: 4).

In the wake of pre-established xenophobia and legalized discrimination in the United States, Amityville received the influences of Asian traditions and gurus with ambivalence. By the early 1970s, we find that *Newsday* and several of Long Island's other most popular periodicals featured articles seeking to follow the development of "Eastern" traditions that had arrived in the 1960s as they began to take root in the village (Krown 1972). A 1972 article in *Newsday* titled "Meditate on This: Eastern teachings, say many Long Islanders, have changed their lives" conveys a hesitant attitude toward some of these newly established spiritual groups in Amityville and the Long Island region more generally (ibid.). The article begins,

> Housewives standing on their heads; undergraduates are chanting mantras and there is a Buddhist shrine on the South Shore. Signs of a flourishing Eastern mysticism on Long Island?... No mass movement on the horizon, but Eastern disciplines are attracting more and more Long Islanders. And the most popular seems to be yoga.
>
> (ibid.)

Four years later in 1976, however, another *Newsday* journalist observes the resiliency of three of the area's most prominent "Eastern" traditions, writing,

> The religious belief and practice of the chanting Buddhists of the Nicherin Shoshu Soka Gakkai, the members of the Yoga Anand

> Ashram, the young members of a third organization called Ananda Marga might have been considered outlandishly exotic a decade ago, and given little chance of gaining foothold on Long Island. Yet the Ashram,… Nicherin Shoshu,… and the smaller Ananda Marga group, have shown they have staying power.
>
> (Lahart 1976)

This article also offers some clues with regard to the demographic of these organizations, suggesting diversity with regard to the age, class, and economic backgrounds of their members as well as their ability to provide members with alternative forms of religion and spirituality not available in their local American religious traditions. The author writes,

> The practitioners are not just a bunch of kids. Membership cuts across age, class, and economic lines. What many of the believers have in common, though, is the experience of having become dissatisfied with the religion in which they were raised, turning to an examination of eastern philosophy and religion, trying out one or another of the eastern practices and finally finding what they were looking for.
>
> (ibid.)

Newsday's observations here reflect, as Tweed and Prothero observe more broadly, "the American generation that came of age during the countercultural movements of the sixties…" and which turned "east to find alternatives to the western traditions that had produced, in their judgment, a materialistic and destructive society" (Tweed and Prothero 1999: 244).

With the accelerated development of Amityville's built environment, migration patterns affecting New York, and the village's newfound implications in global consumer culture, residents of Amityville had at least two ways to respond during the critical year of 1969 identified in *Images*. First, for those members wishing to protect what they perceived to be Amityville's heritage, the Amityville Historical Society served as the platform through which the heritage of the White, conservative, Christian majority might be protected and preserved. Alternatively, Americans could take a countercultural turn to the "East" via one of the several new "Eastern" spiritual organizations in the village.

Amityville Turns East

For those wishing to turn to the East, Gurani Anjali brought to the United States a yoga system born of the late colonial yoga Renaissance that took place in Bengal and produced other modern yoga gurus such as Vivekananda and many who followed. Her thought was most influenced by the Brahmo Samaj, Ramakrishna, Vivekananda, Gandhi, Tagore, and Aurobindo (Shannon-Chapple and Chapple 2014: 273, 282–83). Born in Kolkata and given the birth name Anjali Inti, she began her own yoga training at the young age of eight

(Edwards n.d.) and under the direction of a teacher named Krishna, she trained in yoga for seven years (Shannon-Chapple and Chapple 2014: 283).[7] Clearly belonging to India's emerging middle class, during her younger years Anjali was also formally educated in both Western and Eastern philosophy, learned classical Indian dance, and was sent by her father to travel throughout India to visit a number of significant historical and religious sites (ibid.: 283). Living in colonial and post-colonial India before her arrival to the United States, she was surrounded by colonial resistance movements, finding herself most inspired by those that were non-violent. In the United States, she was particularly drawn to the non-violent civil rights movement of Martin Luther King, Jr. (ibid.: 293).

Although a precise date has not been pinpointed, Anjali arrived in the United States sometime in the 1950s[8] approximately one decade earlier than previously proposed (ibid.: 283), and well before the post-1965 influx of guru immigrants from India. An article in the *Massapequa Post* indicates that her father sent her to the United States from India to study in Boston (Edwards n.d.), though she eventually studied nursing at Brooklyn College (Shannon-Chapple and Chapple 2014: 283). In addition to becoming a nurse, Anjali married an American named Hyman Joseph, had three children, and moved to Amityville's neighboring town of Massapequa. Soon thereafter while in her thirties, Shannon-Chapple and Chapple relate, she achieved "a life transforming state of *samādhi*" which prompted her to begin teaching yoga in the attic of her house as well as through an adult education program at Massapequa High School (Shannon-Chapple and Chapple 2014: 283).[9] Anjali found herself further encouraged to teach yoga when a young man who would later become one of her long-time disciples, having seen Anjali for the first time in public, asked her, "Are you from India, can you teach me yoga?"[10] Beyond these accounts, little more is known about Anjali's biographical details because, as many of her former students often told me, she rarely shared them openly.

As a female guru who entered the United States well *before* the influx of Asian immigrants after the United States' 1965 immigration reform, Anjali is rather unique. Nevertheless, and though her biographical details are sparse, the basic account of her life here and her establishment of Yoga Anand Ashram help us understand how her accomplishments were specifically enabled by the United States' shifting social climate in the 1950s, 1960s, and 1970s. She established herself in the United States in the 1950s during a time when female gurus, and guru movements more broadly, were not yet a notable fixture or acceptable social reality in the American cultural landscape. Indra Devi (cf. M. Goldberg 2015) was of course a contemporary of Anjali's during the 1950s, though the countercultural movement that would start to empower more women to take religious leadership roles was yet to begin until the next decade. And though there were some permanent sites of postural yoga practice in New York City, before the middle of the 1960s, yoga was primarily disseminated to the American public in large cities such as New York through a rather loose "Swami Circuit" comprised mainly of itinerant lecturers (Deslippe 2018: 5, 18). This circuit, as Deslippe shows, had laid foundations of the "two

Orientalist forces of repulsion and attraction" that created "strange windows of opportunity for South Asian immigrants" (Deslippe 2016: 110) to be perceived as either threatening or, in Anjali's case, enlightening.

Following the early work of Wallace, who was concerned with identifying "Revitalization Movements," Anjali eventually encountered a "Period of Revitalization" during the late 1960s wherein we find a "deliberate, organized, conscious effort by members of a society to construct a more satisfying culture" (Wallace 1956: 265). Indeed, Love Brown observes a "Period of Revitalization" between 1965 and 1969 in the United States wherein, among other intentional communities, many countercultural yoga communities were established (Love Brown 2002: 163, 165). Not coincidentally, this period overlaps with Anjali's formation of her yoga community in Massapequa in the 1960s as well as with her eventual establishment of Yoga Anand Ashram in Amityville in 1972.

Gurus were a particularly useful catalyst for the formation of communities during the United States' countercultural moment due to a critical shift in the 1960s which continued throughout the 1990s (Kripal 2007: 20).[11] Perhaps the most significant contributing factor to Anjali's capacity to establish a yoga ashram in the conservative town of Amityville arose from yoga's gradual move "from counterculture to pop culture" (Jain 2015: 21). I also found it interesting when I found out that Anjali, "... saw Richard Hittleman teaching yoga on TV and said, 'I can do that,'" to her husband.[12] Anjali's reaction to Richard Hittleman is particularly revealing, as Hittelman had already domesticated postural yoga for American audiences on his popular TV show *Yoga for Health* by 1961 (Gandhi 2009: 103–105), thereby making the practice an acceptable therapeutic self-improvement technique for the masses (Jain 2015: 42) as well as a potentially lucrative career for those in the position to teach it.

However, postural (*āsana*) yoga comprised only one subordinate component of the yoga Anjali disseminated at Yoga Anand Ashram. This, along with the fact that she did not institutionalize her charisma beyond the small nonprofit she formed to create Yoga Anand Ashram, likely accounts for the reasons why she did not eventually achieve the global fame of many of her other guru contemporaries and disseminators of modern postural yoga who mostly strove to cater to individual consumer tastes (Jain 2015: 66) through larger organizations (Newcombe 2014).

Gurani Anjali's Yoga Anand Ashram, established 1972

Though she never achieved the same level of fame as many of her contemporaries, Anjali's curriculum did attract a notable following and her yoga community eventually outgrew the attic space where she originally began her yoga classes in neighboring Massapequa. Her students found a building on Merrick Road in Amityville which they remodeled, and, in the fall of 1972, dedicated as Yoga Anand Ashram (Shannon-Chapple and Chapple 2014: 283) (see Figure 1.2). As we already saw, the ashram was not the only new "Eastern" spiritual organization in town, and as a 1972 article in *Newsday*

Figure 1.2 Yoga Anand Ashram on Merrick Road, which intersects with Broadway just to the south of the Triangle Building and Lauder Museum. The ashram was located on the top floor of the building where we see the ashram's logo. The bottom left floor housed the ashram's vegetarian restaurant, "Santosha." The bottom right housed Amityville's "Modern Methods Exterminating Termite Control".

Source: Yoga Anand Ashram Archives, Amityville, NY.

reports, in addition to the Ananda Marga and Soka Gakkai groups nearby, a Transcendental Meditation center belonging to the followers of Maharishi Mahesh Yogi could be found only a half of a mile away (Krown 1972).

Besides watching Richard Hittleman and attaining the state of *samādhi*, Anjali's motivations for founding the ashram were made explicit in the non-profit organization's founding mission statement which was posted on the wall inside the ashram:

> I want you to know this day and let it be known to all whom it may concern and remembered hereafter, that I Srimathi Anjali Joseph from Calcutta, India [and] now a citizen of the United States, burning with the desires and visions of the Rishis and Sages, felt the fire of compassion stir within my heart, and being moved by the force which is within all, without which nothing would be, seeing the ignorance in man, which is the cause of misunderstanding and confusion; knowing that nothing is

> impossible to the individual who cares about life and living, seeing the need for knowledge, wisdom and understanding in the eyes and hearing it through the voices of many, saw fit to teach Yoga, which is a way of life, a science, a philosophy, and to some a religion, brought into existence Yoga Anand Ashram, Self-Realization Center… *You have chosen of your own free will to serve and be of service, to uphold the dignity of man through the teaching of Patanjali's Yoga as taught by me in this Ashram.*
>
> (Joseph 1974, emphasis added)

From an organizational standpoint, Anjali's mission statement emphasizes her desire to lead individuals to liberation, or "Self-Realization," through a relationship of mutual reciprocity and selfless service (cf. Klepinger 2022) via her interpretation of the teachings of Patanjali's *Yoga-Sūtra*. The *Yoga-Sūtra* and its accompanying *Sāṃkhya* metaphysics, collectively referred to as the *Sāṃkhya-Yoga* tradition, required at the ashram that practitioners, through their individual efforts and Anjali's teachings, acquire the spiritual knowledge (*jñāna*) of the fundamental freedom of their pure, higher Self (*puruṣa*) from the mind, body, and world (collectively known as *prakṛti*, often simply translated as "nature"). In addition to drawing her authority from Patanjali's *Yoga-Sūtra* (ca. 500 CE) and Ishvarakrishna's *Sāṃkhya-Kārikā* (ca. 400 CE), Anjali drew her authority from other yoga texts that were also canonized during the Indian middle class's colonial encounter with the British including, most notably, the *Bhagavad-Gītā* (ca. 300 BCE to 600 CE) (Singleton 2008; Maas 2013; White 2014; Davis 2014).

Along with the ashram's foodways, which I will turn to momentarily, Anjali deployed a comprehensive combination of yoga's ethical and moral observances (*yama* and *niyama*), postures (*āsana*), breath control (*prāṇāyāma*), somatic practices concerned with the four directions, meditations on the elements, and seasonal festivals. Individually and collectively, these practices also served as conducive tools for addressing the health, social, and environmental concerns of her countercultural milieu. Anjali taught deep reverence for nature (*prakṛti*) which emphasized the presence of the great goddess in the world. Classes often ended with the community chanting the Devi Mantra[13] together, while the *tattva-dhāraṇās*, or concentration exercises on the increasingly subtle categories of existence in *Sāṃkhya* philosophy, comprised one of the foundational techniques for developing a relationship between one's mind, body, and the local environment (cf. Shannon-Chapple and Chapple 2014: 286). These practices were also based upon Anjali's yogic logic which proposed that students' progression toward self-realization required an individual, inward turning toward their pure consciousness, though without ever losing sight of the importance and reality of the mind, body, and world in the process. Because Anjali was trained in *Sāṃkhya-Yoga* in Kolkata in her youth (cf. Jacobsen 2018) and several of her students studied Sanskrit and Indian philosophy at one of the nearby universities, the community collectively produced a rather elaborate schema to explain the *Sāṃkhya-Yoga* system (see Figure 1.3a and b).

In addition to daily elemental concentration techniques, sunrise meditations and seasonal festivals were also a centerpiece in the ashram's annual calendar.

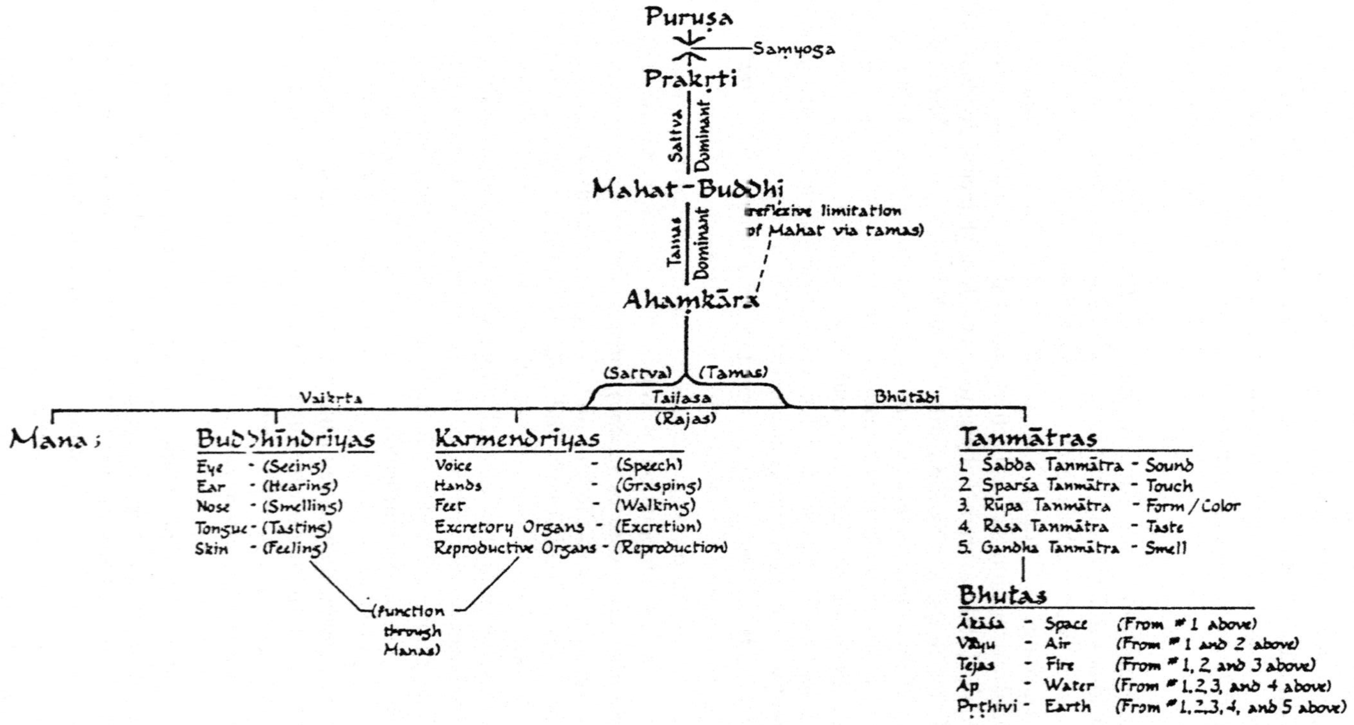

(a)

Figure 1.3 (a) Diagram of *Sāṃkhya* philosophy used in YAA's *Sāṃkhya* course. This diagram illustrates *prakṛti's* process of emergence (*pariṇāma*) into individual embodied experience from the unmanifest (*avyakta*) state to the manifest (*vyakta*) which occurs due to the conjunction (*saṃyoga*) of one's higher Self (*puruṣa*) and nature (*prakṛti*).

Source: Yoga Anand Ashram Archives, Amityville, NY.

Interior (Yogic) Directed Habit of Mind

5 Sense Objects (gross elements)
- **Earth**
- **Water**
- **Fire**
- **Air**
- **Space**

↓

5 Sense Objects (subtle elements, *tanmātras*)

↓

Mind-Organ (*manas*)

↓

I-Sense (*ahaṃkāra,* I-maker or *asmitā,* I-am-ness)

↓

Intellect (*buddhi*)
The Nexus of the Manifest (the experienced), The Unmanifest or Source (*prakṛti*) and Consciousness (*puruṣa*)

(b)

Figure 1.3 (Cont.) (b) Diagram of *Sāṃkhya* philosophy used in YAA's *Sāṃkhya* course. This diagram illustrates manifest nature (*vyakta prakṛti*) as this process is reversed through one's yoga practice to return to the unmanifest (*avyakta prakṛti*) state.

Source: Yoga Anand Ashram Archives, Amityville, NY.

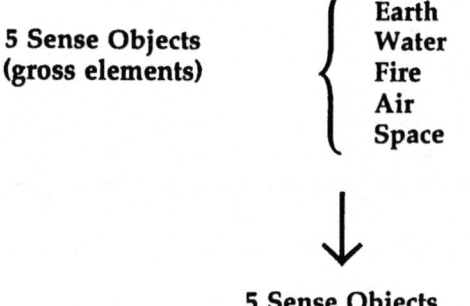

Anjali encouraged students to wake up early in the morning before sunrise to simply observe the sun as it made its way up over the eastern horizon of the Atlantic Ocean, to acknowledge the fullness of day as the sun peaked at midday, and to appreciate the descent of the sun to the West as it set over Long Island's northern hills (Shannon-Chapple and Chapple 2014: 286). In addition to the sunrise meditations, seasonal festivals were used to cater to students' countercultural impulses to be in tune with the rhythms of Amityville and Long Island. Anjali's emphasis on individual responsibility on the path to liberation and her methods for connecting the mind and body with nature to do so were well-received by her countercultural American students who were already seeking to be in harmony with nature and who were committed to the idea that one's personal actions were a demonstration of political activism and the liberation of one's individual freedoms.

Anjali's ability to deploy these exercises in Amityville was further enabled by the broader environmental movement which blossomed within the American counterculture at the time she founded Yoga Anand Ashram. As Rome highlights, three specific social developments during the 1960s gave rise to this national movement (Rome 2003). First, the New Left produced an environmental agenda which made ecological concerns widespread and politically legitimate, sparking public consciousness and criticism of the polluting and overindulgent American lifestyle (ibid.: 25, 528–529). Second, on account of gender expectations concerning care for the household, "the growing discontent of middle-class women" (ibid.: 527) caused an unprecedented number of suburban females who considered local ecologies to be within their domestic domain to join and take self-empowering leadership roles in environmental causes (ibid.: 525, 535–538). Third, "the explosion of student radicalism and countercultural protest" (ibid.: 527) caused "thousands of young suburbanites" to turn "their backs on middle-class life" (ibid.: 543) to challenge environmental destruction. Indeed, environmental destruction became an extremely powerful cause for mobilizing and radicalizing the youth, and many of these students, as Rome observes, "fled to countercultural enclaves in cities" while the hippies "hoped to feel the flow of the seasons, to grow things, to enjoy the beauty of the sunrise, to walk naked" and to acknowledge their "dependence on other people and other creatures" (ibid.: 548) as underground press reports enjoined them to "revere nature" (ibid.: 544).

Shifting gender roles in the United States and citizens' readiness to consume the East thereby provided a platform for Anjali, often called "Guru Ma," to assume a self-empowering leadership role within the context of the environmentally, socially, and health-concerned countercultural movement. Harnessing Americans' longing for simplicity, ecological wholeness, and re-enchantment with nature, her yoga curriculum focused on producing a purified and romantic embodied relationship with the elements, the local landscape, and the seasons in the face of rapid urban growth in Amityville. Her curriculum also provided a forum for the numerous idealistic youth among her devotees – several of whom were undergraduate and graduate students at nearby Stony Brook, Fordham, or Columbia – to authenticate their individual liberties and to enact their countercultural dissent. The ashram's foodways comprised one of the community's most visible material practices in this regard, and illustrate quite well how Anjali understood herself to be translating her yoga teachings within the context of the American counterculture's food justice concerns.

Food Justice: American Countercuisine and Hip Enterprise Movements

Recent voices in the field of Food Studies have urged scholars to consider how particular communities have engaged with or challenged popular food justice reform discourses. In *Eating Right in America*, for example, Biltekoff shows how during the countercultural alternative food movement in the United States, privileged discourse surrounding the control of personal food choices triumphed over calls for structural changes as the key means by which to address environmental, health, and food injustices (Biltekoff 2013: 92). This dominant, consumer-oriented approach to food justice served to protect the insecure White middle class, and the prevailing discourse that suggested personal food choice could be the primary means for creating social change constituted a precursor to the approaching neoliberal ideology and concomitant forms of self-responsibilizing, individualistic subjectivity developed and embraced by the boomers in the 1980s (ibid.). Acknowledging the limits of her broad analysis, however, Biltekoff exhorts us to carefully examine how "people of different racial, cultural, and class backgrounds currently understand and use, or refuse, concepts such as "'good diet,' 'good eater,' and 'eating right' in their everyday lives," as well as to think about how specific communities have historically "adopted, resisted, and contested" dietary reform and have thereby "generated and acted on their own 'truths' about good food" (ibid.: 11, cf. Carter 2021).

Other recent socially-engaged scholarship in Food Studies has challenged consumer-oriented approaches to food justice. Broad highlights how only focusing upon consumer solutions ignores racial and economic constraints (Broad 2016), while Alkon and Guthman critique alternative food movement discourses of the 1970s that were produced by White elites to encourage consumption-based, rather than production-based, activism into the present (Alkon and Guthman 2017). These scholars compel us to consider how (usually racially) marginalized communities have created political change by instead focusing on how they have and continue to confront unjust systems of food *production* rather than consumption alone.

Yoga Anand Ashram's foodways were certainly embedded within countercultural food justice discourses even as they were interpreting those discourses through the prism of Anjali's yoga teachings, and thus have a valuable contribution to make to the conversation regarding food justice in the United States. I suggest that only by reconsidering consumption-based approaches to food justice – privileged and classist as they generally were – during this period can we understand how Gurani Anjali's yogic foodways were both shaped by, and yet channeled the popularity of a predominantly White, middle-class, consumption-oriented, countercultural food justice movement to its own ends. That is to say, as a racial minority and female in the United States, Anjali's ashram foodways may have appeared to conform to the ethos and substance of this alternative food movement taking place throughout the United States. And yet these foodways were one of the key means by which she committed her American students to her own yogic cultural logic grounded primarily in vegetarian diet, fasting, and selfless service in the ashram's restaurant and other establishments. Indeed, alongside the counterculture's undeniable socio-economic, racial, and class realities, Anjali's emphasis on the importance of individual responsibility for achieving yogic liberation through one's individual experience as superior to theory or belief – a dominant view among most all transnational yoga gurus of her time as well as the general counterculture itself – suggests that consumption-focused countercultural foodways were not always primarily serving White countercultural aspirations alone (cf. Anderson 2005: 137 and Broad 2016: 136, regarding food in Black Power movements).[14]

By the time of the ashram's establishment of its vegetarian restaurant in 1977, however, the counterculture had already begun to wane as the United States began to move closer toward neoliberalization in the early 1980s. In this regard, it is important to note that the crucial transition period during which the ashram's restaurant was founded in American history was marked by the maturing of the formerly countercultural baby boomers who were now transitioning toward becoming more firmly established in mainstream political and economic roles in American society. Brooks refers to these maturing individuals who eventually became the vanguard of the new elite political and economic establishment as "Bobos," short for "bourgeois bohemians" (Brooks 2000: 11). As Wilson shows, as these Bobos continued to grow out of the counterculture, they nevertheless continued to capitalize upon, and find themselves magnetized toward, Orientalist conceptions of dietary wellness conveyed through the marketing of holistic Asian cultures and their attendant food products as part of "a pretechnological, changeless existence in which time does not pass" (Wilson 2004: 260). Anjali's restaurant and dietary teachings, grounded as they were in her individualistic yoga philosophy, undoubtedly spoke to and attracted the maturing Bobos as they moved, as Andrea Jain so aptly conveys, "from counterculture to pop culture" (Jain 2015), albeit with their consumption-based, countercultural dietary imaginations fully intact. To fully understand how Anjali's yogic logic intersected with and harnessed the United States' transitioning countercultural foodways, it is first necessary to understand the social and historical dynamics of the American countercuisine and hip enterprise movements.

American Countercuisine and Hip Enterprises

Kauffman defines the years between 1968 and 1974 in the United States as a revolutionary era of "hippie food" wherein a tangible "prospect of dramatic, instantaneous political change felt imminent and food was going to fuel it" (Kauffman 2018: 17). Belasco has described the countercultural food movement that emerged during this period as the "countercuisine," a novel social development which included new foodways aspiring to challenge the political establishment, eliminate famine, protect human health, and save the environment by changing how people ate (Belasco 2007).[15] According to Levenstein, by 1969, activists throughout the United States had begun to take the first concerted steps toward making food and environmental issues political in such a manner (Levenstein 1993: 179). During this time, the notion that individuals could solve these issues through more ethical and well-informed personal food consumption habits was well established according to the popular countercultural logic which viewed one's personal actions as powerful forms of political expression. As Wilson explains,

> Food selection and preparation came to bear a new political significance in light of the warnings of ecological activists about the environmental cost of pesticides, monocropping, resource-wasteful food packaging, and energy-wasteful global food distribution channels... As a concrete and daily fact of life, food provided an outlet for political expression more immediate than other kinds of activism in an era in which leftist politics came to be perceived as beset by endless theorizing and internecine warfare among various activist groups.
>
> (Wilson 2004: 246–247)

The "endless theorizing" to which Wilson refers came from the New Left, a political byproduct of the United States' collapsed Communist party from the 1950s which had fueled early public disenchantment with the nation's food supply and industrial evils (Levenstein 1993: 178, 181).

Through its "large, informal network" the New Left exercised "considerable influence in the nation's elite campuses," although counterculturalists, who were much more inclined to look "to the heart rather than the mind for inspiration," shunned "New Left interest in theory and politics" and instead focused on eating properly in order to return to nature and to promote spiritual growth (ibid.: 178, 180–81). Despite these important distinctions between the intellectually and politically oriented New Left and the more heart-focused and romantically inspired counterculture, by the early to mid-1970s, defeated and disillusioned New Leftists began to turn inward, "seeking salvation through personal betterment and changing lifestyles" (ibid.: 180) in ways that were strikingly similar to those of their romantic countercultural contemporaries. All of this is to say that both groups – which, importantly, comprised Yoga Anand Ashram's membership – shared similar commitments to ideologies of individual self-improvement or spiritual development that were undergirded first and foremost through personal food choices.

Several popular publications provoked new concerns about food and the environment that led to the formation of these new food practices. Perhaps most notable among these was Rachel Carson's early warning in *Silent Spring* regarding the United States' impending environmental and health catastrophes caused by increased pesticide use for agricultural purposes (Carson 2002 [1962]), as well as Frances Moore Lappé's later revelations in *Diet for a Small Planet* concerning the connections between Americans' meat consumption, world hunger, and environmental destruction (Lappé's 1971).[16] Both Carson and Lappé's publications had far-reaching influence in both secular but also, perhaps more interestingly for our purposes here, religious and spiritual circles, which were seeking to change the world through reformed individual food consumption habits. In the early 1960s, George Ohsawa also made a major contribution to this mentality with his "most popular of the counterculture eating regimes, the Zen or Macrobiotic diet" (Levenstein 1993: 178). Practitioners of the Zen macrobiotic diet shared a passion for social transformation through individual diet reform that would, according to one prominent advocate of the movement, spread out through "an ever-widening spiral... of influence" (Kauffman 2018: 84) and clearly reflected the (inverted) countercultural notion that "the personal is political." Though Ohsawa connected his macrobiotic diet with Zen Buddhism, he in fact invented this connection to capitalize on Orientalist fantasies of the East and Asian religions that would surely invest his movement with authenticity (Kauffman 2018: 63; Levenstein 1993: 183). Other self-identified American Buddhists also reformed their food consumption habits, converting to vegetarianism to save the world and its innumerable living beings (Kauffman 2018: 143–146). In addition to Asian religions, American Protestants inspired by Lappé's obsession with ending world hunger initiated a "lifestyle movement" in the 1970s that required a new type of "Protestant asceticism" performed through a significant reduction in one's personal meat consumption or even by adopting the practice of vegetarianism (Sack 2000: 202, 209, 213). Yoga gurus and the countercultural devotees they sought to influence also drew from Carson and Lappé's work, including Gurani Anjali's community at Yoga Anand Ashram.

Due to the United States' concerns surrounding food, health, and environmental justice in the late 1960s and into the 1970s, an emerging countercuisine movement materialized with the establishment of countercultural restaurants and health food stores, all of which had historical precedents. As Miller demonstrates, in the early twentieth-century United States such countercultural enclaves "served as meeting places and discussion spots for natural foods advocates" (Miller 2017: 73). Many of these enclaves were vegetarian and undergirded by religious or spiritual principles. For example, Paramahansa Yogananda's Self-Realization Fellowship opened vegetarian cafés in Southern California (Miller 2017: 146–147; Neumann 2019: 197–198), while Unity Christian Church opened the popular "Unity Inn" vegetarian café in Kansas City (Rapport 2014: 26).

Though he does not closely consider the religious and spiritual influences upon later American countercuisine establishments, Belasco situates similar restaurants and health food stores set up during the late 1960s and 1970s within what he calls the "hip enterprise" movement (Belasco 2007: 94). As he shows, food activists who took part in this movement prioritized human relationships, tasty and healthy food, ecologically friendly diets, ethical business practices, and bare subsistence over profit (ibid.: 94–104). Proprietors of such enterprises also understood themselves to be transforming the United States' infrastructure to provide a more environmentally friendly and educational dietary experience (ibid.: 100). Belasco suggests that within food enterprises espousing such values, "... many early hip food businesses were barely distinguishable from communes and co-ops... The romance of service was especially strong in hip restaurants, which, in effect, attempted to institutionalize the communal culture" (ibid.: 94). One of the key weaknesses that led to the failure of this business model, however, was organization and demographic management, wherein managers had to find a way to, "... balance the often competing needs of men and women, management and labor, control and cooperation, efficiency and experimentation, ideological purity and pragmatic compromise, personal growth and organizational stability..." (ibid.: 105).

Despite these managerial challenges, with low barriers to entry (Miller 2017: 156), an array of hip enterprise restaurants and health food stores flourished during the United States' countercultural period with overlapping and yet unique motivations. Some, such as Alice Waters' "Chez Panisse," combined regional influences and input from the New Left with the French logic of *terroir*, or the "taste of place" and "ability to trace a connection between the symbolic and practical definitions of the earth and the tastes of food and beverage" (Trubek 2008: xv, 130–131). Meanwhile, Odessa Piper's "Ovens of Brittany" in Madison, Wisconsin, combined the influence of *terroir* with her mentor's spiritual teachings from the Theosophical Society (ibid.: 145–146). Norman Paulsen's eclectic Brotherhood of the Sun (est. 1969), a new religious movement, intersected with the organic and natural foods movement in fascinating ways (Hoesly 2019), while the famous Tassajara Zen Center in Carmel, California (est. 1967), established several food businesses grounded in the teachings of Buddhism (Miller 2017: 147).

Thus, like some of their early twentieth-century predecessors, spiritual and religious organizations had a significant influence on the countercuisine that is worthy of our attention. Though we do find occasional references to yoga restaurants and health food stores throughout studies of American countercuisine and the natural and alternative food movements, none of these studies have considered how specific internal yogic logics contributed to the formation of these institutions in great depth. This gap in scholarship is surprising, given that a number of hip enterprise restaurants and health food stores were founded under the influence of yoga gurus and yoga philosophy, including 3HO's Golden Temple restaurant in Los Angeles, the "Sattva" vegan café in San Antonio, the New Riverside Cafe in Minnesota, and Annam Brahma in New York, for example (cf. Miller 2017: 147; Kauffman 2018: 212, 226, 248).

Yogic hip enterprise restaurants and health food stores that opened across the United States during the counterculture were almost universally vegetarian, for both ideological and economic purposes. On the one hand, vegetarianism was and remains today a common dietary practice that signals a community's commitment to the paramount yogic ethical restraint (*yama*) of non-violence (*ahiṃsā*). In this regard, countercultural Europeans and Americans have for centuries turned to India's teachings of non-violence, wherein many Jain, Buddhist, and Hindu philosophies espoused vegetarianism as a spiritual practice aimed at avoiding the unnecessary and immoral violence of animal slaughter (Stuart 2007).[17] On the other hand, however, serving vegetarian food also followed broader strategic economic trends in the hip enterprise movement used to meet the taste preferences of the American higher classes (Levenstein 1993: 222). As menus expanded to satisfy new middle- and upper-class cravings for international and regional foods, using "more starch and less meat" amounted to increased profit margins (ibid.: 234–235), while a commitment to a vegetarian menu also enabled the higher classes to distinguish themselves from "those in the lower orders" who they perceived as "unimaginative" and addicted to "fattening 'junk' foods" (ibid.: 222).

As we will see in what follows, Gurani Anjali's Yoga Anand Ashram clearly reflected the countercuisine and hip enterprise ethos outlined here, capitalizing upon its opportunities and very much shaped by its constraints. Her students' common adoption of a vegetarian diet and intermittent fasting combined with a community-operated vegetarian restaurant set the stage for Amityville's very own countercuisine and hip enterprise movement. Nevertheless, the practices of vegetarianism and intermittent fasting, as well as the restaurant itself, also delicately implicated members' (or even potential members') bodies into the preliminary stages of Anjali's yoga system.

Santosha Vegetarian Dining, Plus…

With the American hip enterprise movement firmly in place, it should now come as no surprise that Gurani Anjali and her ashram devotees opened a health food store, a bookshop, an art gallery, and eventually a vegetarian restaurant of their own in the 1970s. Considering the broader countercuisine movement, it should also come as no surprise that vegetarian diet was one of the primary material practices through which the community expressed its philosophy and identity in all of its establishments and routines including the ashram restaurant, its shared community meals, and in the ritual blessing of sacred food (*prasāda*) during special events.[18] This is certainly not to say that all students, or even Gurani Anjali, were strictly vegetarian. Rather, as several of her former students described to me, vegetarianism was encouraged, practiced intermittently by some, adopted fully by others, though practiced strictly within the ashram establishments as an expression of the yogic principle of *ahiṃsā* as much as was deemed to be practicably possible by each student.[19]

In addition to studying yoga texts, students also learned about and constructed their foodways from other countercultural favorites such as Lappé's *Diet for a Small Planet* (Lappé 1971) and Carson's *Silent Spring* (Carson 2002 [1962]), both of which had been available in the ashram's "Moksha Bookshop and Community Education Center" in the 1970s (and both of which were recommended to me by one of the ashram's members when I indicated my interest in learning more about vegetarian diet). Through this bookshop, the ashram shared various principles of vegetarian diet with the public via its ongoing public lecture programming. Some of the lectures included, for example, "Facts and Fallacies of Vegetarian Nutrition" by Dr. Monroe E. Burton and "Vegetarianism and Detoxification" by Dr. William Rice (Yoga Anand Ashram, n.d.-a). In its street front window, the bookshop also prominently featured books about cooking and family health (see Figure 1.4).

As an immersion in what is still popularly known as "selfless service" (*sevā*) in transnational yoga communities around the world, Anjali assigned volunteer ashram members work to support the organization's day-to-day operations. Labor framed as selfless service provided cost savings while also adapting, as Shannon-Chapple and Chapple suggest, "the style of *gurukula* students providing fuel and labor for the guru and family" within a contemporary context

Figure 1.4 Yoga Anand Ashram's Moksha Bookshop and Community Education Center on Merrick Road down the street from the ashram. Books on "cooking" and "family health" are advertised along with books about "philosophy" in the storefront window.

Source: Yoga Anand Ashram Archives, Amityville, NY.

Figure 1.5 Left: Yoga Anand Ashram members install the Santosha Vegetarian Dining restaurant sign on the ashram building, which it also shared with a pest extermination business. Right: Gurani Anjali (closest to door in yellow sari) inaugurates the restaurant with ashram members.

Source: Yoga Anand Ashram Archives, Amityville, NY.

(Shannon-Chapple and Chapple 2014: 296). As was common in the prevailing hip enterprise movement, Anjali also used selfless service as an opportunity to manage a workforce social space that compelled ashram members to confront social conflict and interpersonal issues while they worked alongside people in whose presence they were uncomfortable. Doing so was understood to purify members of their mental afflictions (*kleśa*) and subtle mental impressions (*saṃskāra*). Most often, as I was informed, these conflicts took place around food preparation and service itself in Santosha, the ashram's local vegetarian restaurant (see Figure 1.5).

Santosha,[20] so-named after Patanjali's fundamental moral observance (*niyama*) of *santoṣa* (contentment), was founded in 1977 following ashram member John Becker's recommendation to Anjali to create a restaurant enterprise. In developing Santosha, Becker was inspired by an eclectic vegetarian restaurant nearby on Long Island known as "Little Easter."[21] Given what we already know about Anjali's yoga as well as the countercuisine and hip enterprise movements, the observations in a 1977 article in the *New York Times* published soon after Santosha's establishment are quite insightful. According to the author, "There are two strictly vegetarian restaurants on [Long] Island, Little Easter in Sea Cliff and Santosha in Amityville" (Fabricant 1977). As the author observes, those who have become vegetarian and frequent these establishments have:

> … been inspired by religious beliefs, such as Hinduism, that forbid taking life, prompted by humanitarian concern for ecology and the balance of foodstuffs on our crowded planet and encouraged by anxiety over the

> modern diet of highly processed, additive-laden foods… Spawned by the 1960's protest movements, members of the still-active counterculture, sporting jeans and sandals, are among its more obvious adherents. However, to judge from the patrons in local vegetarian restaurants, it has been attracting people of every age and social category.
>
> (ibid.)

Thus, despite the decline of the counterculture in the late 1970s, the spirit of the countercuisine and the hip enterprise movements clearly lived on in Amityville as it did elsewhere in the United States (cf. Wilson 2004: 260).

Santosha was situated on the lower left-hand floor in the same building as the ashram itself and eventually replaced the ashram's health food store, "Sakti Sangam"[22] (see Figure 1.6) which, for a period of time before the restaurant was established there, had previously provided the Amityville community with a place to purchase health foods, nutritional supplements, and much more during the height of the American countercultural movement.

Figure 1.6 Sakti Sangam health food store on the bottom floor of the ashram building, run by Yoga Anand Ashram's women's group "Sakti Sangam." The health food store was established prior to the establishment of Santosha, Yoga Anand Ashram's vegetarian restaurant.

Source: Yoga Anand Ashram Archives, Amityville, NY.

The vegetarian restaurant was one of Yoga Anand Ashram's main sources of income and was operated by ashram staff. Once Santosha opened, the hectic work pace and unpredictable nature of the restaurant business compelled community members to work in the company of those with whom they were uncomfortable on a regular basis in order to handle food procurement, preparation, serving, and clean up. Shannon-Chapple and Chapple reflect on their experiences working in the restaurant:

> The somewhat odd assemblage of cooks and servers fell into a cauldron of hustle and bustle, testing everyone's emotional mettle. In the crucible of early mornings and late nights, punctuated with yoga practice and study at both the ashram and for many who were also studying at Fordham, Columbia, or Stony Brook University, the battleground of Kṛṣṇa and Arjuna became the stuff of a living reality…
>
> (Shannon-Chapple and Chapple 2014: 290)

As part of her recruitment efforts for the restaurant labor pool, Anjali took in students from all walks of life, and often much to other students' chagrin. Besides providing an adequate membership base and labor force, the ashram's membership demographic also reflected a countercultural concern for social equality. The workforce incorporated people from a variety of socio-economic backgrounds who "together were faced with finding common cultural ground and linguistic expression in order to serve side by side."[23] While bringing students to a better understanding of their surrounding social milieu, the social composition of the restaurant workforce intentionally produced didactic interpersonal conflict. As community member Bradley King once told me, Anjali did this in order to,

> … create all sorts of uncomfortable social situations to make you realize the source of your annoyance and discomfort… Starting with a life experience, she used *Sāṃkhya-Yoga* to help you get to the seed of a certain situation to figure out how it was created in the first place.[24]

Because *Sāṃkhya-Yoga* posits that one's psyche is laced with subtle mental impressions (*saṃskāra*) which cause mental afflictions (*kleśas*), including ignorance (*avidyā*), egoism (*asmitā*), passion (*rāga*), aversion (*dveṣa*), and attachment to life (*abhiniveśa*), all of which lead only to suffering (*duḥkha*) and the apparent subjugation of one's higher Self (*puruṣa*) within nature (*prakṛti*), it is necessary, as I was often told, to use the practice of austerity (*tapas*) to eliminate these afflictions within oneself in order to achieve liberation. To do so, one had to come to an understanding of how the source of these afflictions and personal discomforts was squarely within one's own psyche and nervous system by tolerating and working through daily social conflict. Anjali's management style, which interpreted interpersonal conflict to be part and parcel of her purifying yogic path, was understood by sincere ashram members to be potentially purifying and liberating if students could endure the approach.[25]

Beyond the *Sāṃkhya-Yoga* system, which was at the core of the ashram's mission statement, Anjali managed the restaurant's workforce by disseminating a contemporary interpretation of the *Bhagavad-Gītā*'s practice of "*karma-yoga*," another ego-purifying yoga practice frequently translated as "selfless service" (and sometimes referred to more broadly as *sevā*) to her students. Padmini, another long-term student of Anjali, recalls that these were her guru's intentions:

> … when the restaurant Santosha was opened, it was used as an opportunity to learn more about karma yoga. There was plenty to do – cleaning the kitchen, cooking, and serving the customers. She said that this was a perfect venue for karma yoga.
>
> (Padmini 2018: 8)[26]

Thus, in addition to eradicating *Sāṃkhya-Yoga*'s afflictions (*kleśas*), Anjali also used Santosha as the grounds for self-purification via *karma-yoga*. Doing so no doubt helped manage a form of organized labor in a manner which was nevertheless quite different from the ancient class (*varṇa*)-based socio-political ideology to which the concept of *karma-yoga* refers in the *Bhagavad-Gītā*. Still, Anjali's *karma-yoga* remained in line with the ashram's mission to lead aspirants to self-realization in so far as it followed the *Gītā*'s broader message which suggests that by renouncing egotistical attachment to the fruits of one's actions, one might achieve liberation (*mokṣa*).

While Anjali drew from the *Bhagavad-Gītā* and *Sāṃkhya-Yoga* traditions to organize her non-profit labor force, her organizational approach here clearly connected with the countercultural virtues of service and voluntarism prevalent in the wider countercultural "hip enterprise" movement taking place in the United States and specifically in New York in the 1960s and 1970s. In order to manage her students' conflicting personalities while overseeing multiple hip enterprises amidst the "romance of service" (Belasco 2007: 94), Anjali's yoga teachings also held out the added promise of spiritual liberation in exchange for participants' willingness to purify and keep their emotions in check while at work. Such promises remain prevalent among many yoga ashram kitchens worldwide today (cf. Lucia 2014b).

While the restaurant and other hip enterprises at Yoga Anand Ashram created (often-uncomfortable) opportunities for liberation among her organization's membership, it also provided a welcoming ambiance for members of the ashram community as well as for members of the wider Amityville and Long Island area to enjoy international cuisine and daily live music (Shannon-Chapple and Chapple 2014: 290). Indeed, like other restaurants and health food stores around the country (cf. Miller 2017: 73), Santosha served as an exciting meeting place wherein ashram members could actively engage the outside community, develop positive community relations, educate patrons about the ecological and health benefits of a vegetarian diet, and, in some cases, recruit new people to join the ashram.

In addition to Little Easter, other yoga community and vegetarian restaurants in the New York area – perhaps most notably Sri Chinmoy's Annam Brahma restaurant in nearby Queens, Moosewood in Ithaca, and ISKCON's well-known vegetarian cuisine used for proselytization – used their food service businesses in a similar manner.[27] For the most part, Yoga Anand Ashram explicitly modeled some of their own customer service practices and recipes in Santosha following these nearby models.[28] Nevertheless, the ashram did not serve the Bengali food Anjali would have been accustomed to from back home as ISKCON did, but rather conformed more closely to standard international countercuisine food familiar to Amityville's American clientele.

The restaurant sign, which read "Santosha Vegetarian Dining," included a tree to suggest that by eating at the establishment, one might get closer to living in harmony with nature, while the word "PLUS…" in the bottom right-hand corner suggested to patrons that vegetarian cuisine was just the first of more experiences to come if one were to become more deeply involved in the yoga ashram and its practices (see Figure 1.7). Non-violence (*ahiṃsā*), which ashram members practiced primarily through varying commitments to vegetarian diet, was, after all, the very first ethical restraint (*yama*) in the eight-limbed path to liberation (*kaivalya*) described in the *Sāṃkhya-Yoga* tradition, which Anjali and the ashram adhered to closely following the organization's mission statement. Thus, in addition to conforming to broader countercuisine dietary trends, the restaurant environment and menu signaled the community's commitment to this paramount yogic virtue. Although simple in the beginning, Santosha's menu selection grew as the years went on, featuring international cuisine and an "award winning carrot cake" dessert "voted 'best on Long Island'" (Yoga Anand Ashram n.d.-b). The menus appear like any other you would find in an American restaurant, except that meat does not make the ingredient list (see Figures 1.7, 1.8a, 1.8b and 1.9).

Santosha's international vegetarian menu[29] absorbed multiple interrelated dietary trends that arose in the 1960s and 1970s within the American countercultural movement. First, the menu selection contained international foods that became particularly popular in 1960s American supermarkets and cookbooks as citizens became increasingly eager to sample foreign cuisine (Lovegren 1995: 220, 244; Levenstein 1993: 234–235). The internationalization of menus, including that of Santosha, was undoubtedly connected to the broader post World-War II ideology of "internationalism" aimed at creating global harmonious relations, which in large part would emerge when all human beings could respect cultural diversity and difference. And yet it is important to acknowledge that within the internationalist movement cultural difference was often sequestered outside the realm of politics so as to not destabilize White hegemony within the global Westphalian political order (Ikenberry 2020; cf. Iriye 1997). Generally speaking, eating foreign foods was an easy way to perform

SANTOSHA
Vegetarian Dining Plus.....
—Fine Vegetarian Foods·Herb Teas·Desserts·Live Entertainment—

Salads

Santosha Salad
Lettuce, Spinach, Zucchini, Carrots, Tomatoes, Cheeses, Sprouts, Bulghur, Apples Sunflower Seeds, Nuts, Peppers, Celery! Your choice of dressing.......... $2.95

Plato's Passion
A fine Greek salad with plenty of Feta Cheese, Lettuce, Peppers, Cucumber, Onions & Greek Olives.
small... $1.95 large.... $3.00

Spinach-Mushroom Salad
Farm fresh Spinach, ripe Tomatoe, raw Mushrooms, Sprouts & hard boiled egg wedges.
small.... $1.50 large..... $2.75

Tabooley
A traditional Mid East salad made with Bulghur Wheat, fresh Parsley, Tomatoes, Scallions and Peppers with a special Olive Oil, Lemon Juice & Mint dressing.
small $1.00 large.... $1.75

Walnut, Avocado & Apple Salad
A delicious blend of chopped Walnuts, Apple, and mashed Avocado with a special dressing served with lettuce, cucumber, green pepper & walnuts...$2.45

Sprout Salad
A mountain of homegrown mixed sprouts, lettuce and Tomatoes...$1.75

Avocado Salad
Fresh Avocado on Lettuce with red ripe Tomatoes and Sprouts $1.95

Caponata Salad
A real Italian salad made with Egg-plant cooked in a Tomatoe sauce with celery, olives & capers. Served w/Bread $2.50

Egg Salad
All natural Egg Salad made with homemade mayonnaise & Sprouts..$1.75

Santosha Specials

Soyburger Platter Our own delicious Soyburger Patty in Pita bread w/melted cheese, Sprouts, Lettuce & Tomatoes. Served w/a tossed salad.$1.95

Cheese, Fruit & Nuts Assorted Cheeses fresh fruits and nuts heaped on our hand crafted, inlaid tile boards. Served w/bread...$3.25

Raw Vegetable Platter Crisp raw vegetables with Homos (chickpea) & Guacamole (Avocado) dips. Served with Pita bread...... $2.50

"Tres Tacos" Three of our delicious vegetarian Tacos served with Tomatoe and Avocado............... $2.00

Curried Lentil Salad & Potatoe Raita Chilled Curried Lentil Salad w/spicy Potatoe Raita served w/Almonds, Cashews, Orange wedges. $3.25

Figure 1.7 Vegetarian menu from Santosha's early days containing some international favorites including "Greek Salad," "Tabooley… A Traditional Mid East salad," "A real Italian Salad," "Tres Tacos," and "Curried Lentil Salad & Potato Raita." Phone numbers have been covered in white at the request of an Ashram member.

Source: Yoga Anand Ashram Archives, Amityville, NY.

Santosha

IS A SANSKRIT WORD FOR

Contentment

INTERNATIONAL VEGETARIAN CUISINE

Come in for a savory and healthy lunch!

Try one of our favorites:

~ Three Bean Chili
~ Shining Sun Sandwich
~ Falafel
~ Walnut Tofu Burger
~ Vegetarian Thali (Indian Platter)

40 Merrick Road, Amityville, NY (516) 598-1787

Lunch Hours: Tues - Fri ~ 11:00 a.m. to 2:00 p.m.

Dinner Hours: Tues - Sat ~ 5:30 p.m. to 10:00 p.m.
Sun ~ 5:00 p.m. to 10:00 p.m.

Signature Entrées

All dinners served with Soup or Salad and Hummus Appetizer ~ $12.95

Quesadillas Ultima
Three flour tortillas with three different fillings. One of refried beans, another of spinach, tofu, and cheese, and lastly, one of vegetables and rice. Served with a spicy salsa.

Eggplant Rollatini
Tender slices of breaded eggplant rolled with a spinach-ricotta filling and baked in marinara sauce. Served with pasta topped with marinara sauce.

Lemon Tempeh Fillets
Tender tempeh fillets broiled in an herb-butter sauce delicately seasoned with lemon and garlic. This delicious, high-protein dish is served with our rice pilaf and steamed vegetables.

7th Dynasty
Fresh garden vegetables, wok stir-fried, with tofu and a touch of ginger and garlic, finished with a dash of tamari. Served over steamed brown rice and topped with grilled cheddar.

Pasta Di Napoli
The original! To prepare this authentic Italian specialty, we begin with pure, delicious olive oil and sauteed garlic, walnuts, and basil. We then add fresh spinach and a dash of pepper. Finally, pasta is gently turned with grated parmesan cheese.

Tofu Scallop Platter
Tender scallops of tofu in a garlic scampi sauce. Served with aramé vegetable melange (a delicious nutty flavored seaweed combined with carrots and onions), steamed broccoli and quinoa (keenwa).

Lentil Burgers
Two high protein lentil-walnut burgers served with steamed veggies and rice. Choice of a mushroom-onion-tamari sauce or a lemon-butter sauce.

Ragin' Cajun Tempeh
Tempeh kickin' with flavor. Finally a new tempeh treat for tempeh lovers! Spicy herbs and seasonings coat the tempeh and are then baked to heat up the flavors. A rice pilaf and steamed vegetables round out the dish. Can be ordered Mild, Medium, Hot, X-Hot or Hotter-n-Hell.

Saffron Cous Cous Africana
This is a traditional African dish. Delicately sauteed veggies are served over semolina couscous and a sauce of ground peanuts, cumin and cayenne. A most intriguing and exquisite blend of flavors. Try this.

Vegetarian Thali (Indian Platter)
This delectable array of Indian staples is enough to please the most discerning palate. It includes dhal (lentil stew), kale sabji (savory greens), sufed channa (chick peas in ~~white~~ savory sauce), basmati rice, chapati, papadam and condiments.

(a)

Figure 1.8 (a) Cover and first page from a more developed international menu at Santosha

Source: Yoga Anand Ashram Archives, Amityville, NY.

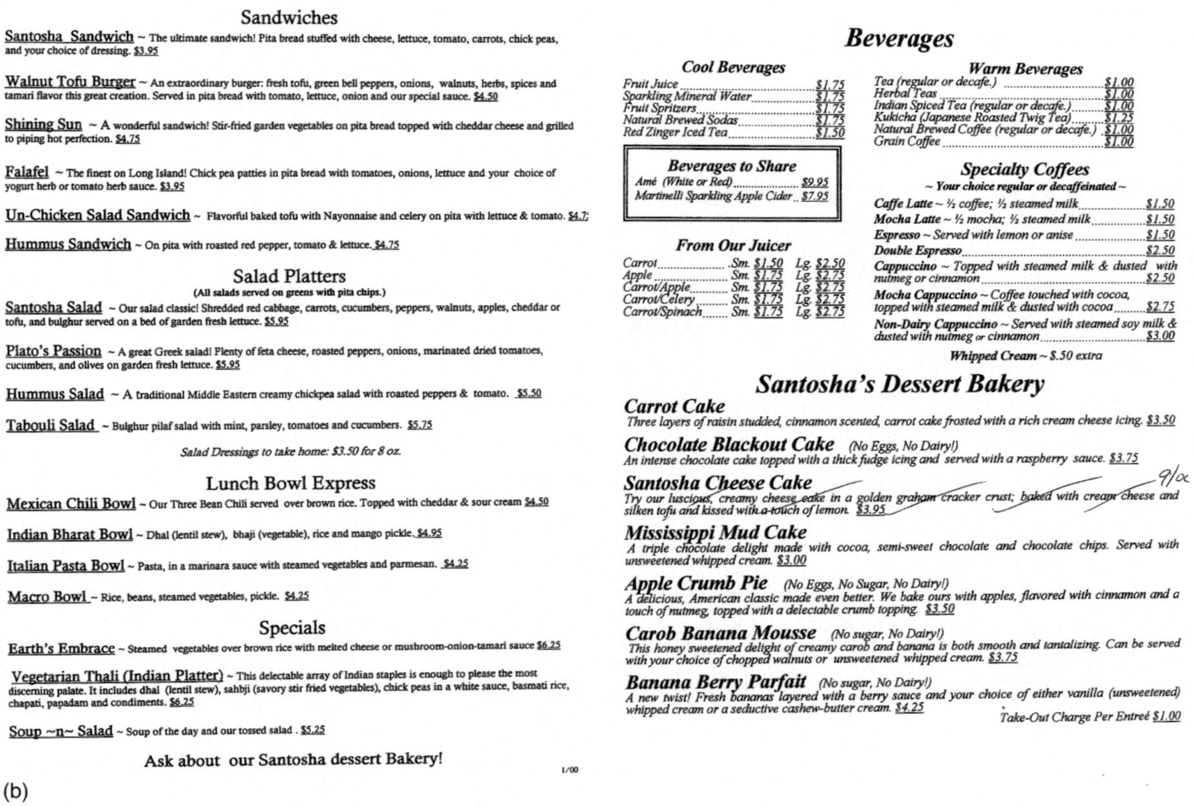

Sandwiches

Santosha Sandwich ~ The ultimate sandwich! Pita bread stuffed with cheese, lettuce, tomato, carrots, chick peas, and your choice of dressing. $3.95

Walnut Tofu Burger ~ An extraordinary burger: fresh tofu, green bell peppers, onions, walnuts, herbs, spices and tamari flavor this great creation. Served in pita bread with tomato, lettuce, onion and our special sauce. $4.50

Shining Sun ~ A wonderful sandwich! Stir-fried garden vegetables on pita bread topped with cheddar cheese and grilled to piping hot perfection. $4.75

Falafel ~ The finest on Long Island! Chick pea patties in pita bread with tomatoes, onions, lettuce and your choice of yogurt herb or tomato herb sauce. $3.95

Un-Chicken Salad Sandwich ~ Flavorful baked tofu with Nayonnaise and celery on pita with lettuce & tomato. $4.7

Hummus Sandwich ~ On pita with roasted red pepper, tomato & lettuce. $4.75

Salad Platters

(All salads served on greens with pita chips.)

Santosha Salad ~ Our salad classic! Shredded red cabbage, carrots, cucumbers, peppers, walnuts, apples, cheddar or tofu, and bulghur served on a bed of garden fresh lettuce. $5.95

Plato's Passion ~ A great Greek salad! Plenty of feta cheese, roasted peppers, onions, marinated dried tomatoes, cucumbers, and olives on garden fresh lettuce. $5.95

Hummus Salad ~ A traditional Middle Eastern creamy chickpea salad with roasted peppers & tomato. $5.50

Tabouli Salad ~ Bulghur pilaf salad with mint, parsley, tomatoes and cucumbers. $5.75

Salad Dressings to take home: $3.50 for 8 oz.

Lunch Bowl Express

Mexican Chili Bowl ~ Our Three Bean Chili served over brown rice. Topped with cheddar & sour cream $4.50

Indian Bharat Bowl ~ Dhal (lentil stew), bhaji (vegetable), rice and mango pickle. $4.95

Italian Pasta Bowl ~ Pasta, in a marinara sauce with steamed vegetables and parmesan. $4.25

Macro Bowl ~ Rice, beans, steamed vegetables, pickle. $4.25

Specials

Earth's Embrace ~ Steamed vegetables over brown rice with melted cheese or mushroom-onion-tamari sauce $6.25

Vegetarian Thali (Indian Platter) ~ This delectable array of Indian staples is enough to please the most discerning palate. It includes dhal (lentil stew), sahbji (savory stir fried vegetables), chick peas in a white sauce, basmati rice, chapati, papadam and condiments. $6.25

Soup ~n~ Salad ~ Soup of the day and our tossed salad . $5.25

Ask about our Santosha dessert Bakery!

1/00

Beverages

Cool Beverages

Fruit Juice	$1.75
Sparkling Mineral Water	$1.75
Fruit Spritzers	$1.75
Natural Brewed Sodas	$1.75
Red Zinger Iced Tea	$1.50

Beverages to Share

Amé (White or Red)	$9.95
Martinelli Sparkling Apple Cider	$7.95

From Our Juicer

Carrot	Sm. $1.50	Lg. $2.50
Apple	Sm. $1.75	Lg. $2.75
Carrot/Apple	Sm. $1.75	Lg. $2.75
Carrot/Celery	Sm. $1.75	Lg. $2.75
Carrot/Spinach	Sm. $1.75	Lg. $2.75

Warm Beverages

Tea (regular or decafe.)	$1.00
Herbal Teas	$1.00
Indian Spiced Tea (regular or decafe.)	$1.00
Kukicha (Japanese Roasted Twig Tea)	$1.25
Natural Brewed Coffee (regular or decafe.)	$1.00
Grain Coffee	$1.00

Specialty Coffees

~ Your choice regular or decaffeinated ~

Caffe Latte ~ ½ coffee; ½ steamed milk	$1.50
Mocha Latte ~ ½ mocha; ½ steamed milk	$1.50
Espresso ~ Served with lemon or anise	$1.50
Double Espresso	$2.50
Cappuccino ~ Topped with steamed milk & dusted with nutmeg or cinnamon	$2.50
Mocha Cappuccino ~ Coffee touched with cocoa, topped with steamed milk & dusted with cocoa	$2.75
Non-Dairy Cappuccino ~ Served with steamed soy milk & dusted with nutmeg or cinnamon	$3.00

Whipped Cream ~ $.50 extra

Santosha's Dessert Bakery

Carrot Cake
Three layers of raisin studded, cinnamon scented, carrot cake frosted with a rich cream cheese icing. $3.50

Chocolate Blackout Cake *(No Eggs, No Dairy!)*
An intense chocolate cake topped with a thick fudge icing and served with a raspberry sauce. $3.75

Santosha Cheese Cake
Try our luscious, creamy cheese cake in a golden graham cracker crust; baked with cream cheese and silken tofu and kissed with a touch of lemon. $3.95

9/00

Mississippi Mud Cake
A triple chocolate delight made with cocoa, semi-sweet chocolate and chocolate chips. Served with unsweetened whipped cream. $3.00

Apple Crumb Pie *(No Eggs, No Sugar, No Dairy!)*
A delicious, American classic made even better. We bake ours with apples, flavored with cinnamon and a touch of nutmeg, topped with a delectable crumb topping. $3.50

Carob Banana Mousse *(No sugar, No Dairy!)*
This honey sweetened delight of creamy carob and banana is both smooth and tantalizing. Can be served with your choice of chopped walnuts or unsweetened whipped cream. $3.75

Banana Berry Parfait *(No sugar, No Dairy!)*
A new twist! Fresh bananas layered with a berry sauce and your choice of either vanilla (unsweetened) whipped cream or a seductive cashew-butter cream. $4.25

Take-Out Charge Per Entreé $1.00

(b)

Figure 1.8 (Cont.). (b) Pages from a more developed international menu at Santosha.

Source: Yoga Anand Ashram Archives, Amityville, NY.

Figure 1.9 Vegetarian ratatouille dish and salad from Yoga Anand Ashram's Santosha restaurant menu.

Source: Author, meal prepared by Maureen Shannon-Chapple and Christopher Chapple, former ashram cooks.

one's commitment to internationalism's ideal of cultural diversity without having to actually engage with members of other cultures, a point to which I will return in the conclusion of this chapter.

Santosha's menu also reflects the broader health food movement which emphasized organic foods and vegetarianism and which arose during the same decade as counterculturalists concerned "about the poisoning of their bodies and the earth by chemical fertilizers and pesticides" and "armed with Rachel Carson's *Silent Spring* and Adelle Davis's *Let's Eat Right to Keep Fit*... set out to do battle with the food establishment" (Lovegren 1995: 258). Nevertheless, as we can see from the ingredient lists on Santosha's menu, the chefs did not sacrifice taste for ethics. For example carrot cake – the ashram's signature award-winning dessert – was in the 1970s Americans' second preferred health food behind only granola (Levenstein 1993: 196) and became a "standard at every health food restaurant" because it was "a high-fat, high-calorie food that was still considered healthy," full of "gooshiness and healthfulness," and therefore "a sure-fire Seventies hit" (Lovegren 1995: 337–338). In this regard, the savory recipes we find on Santosha's menu reflect what Belasco describes as the "two opposing traditions of lightness" (Belasco 2007: 66–67) often reconciled in countercuisine food:

> On the one hand, lightness can suggest a certain bubbly effervescence, hedonism, self-indulgence... On the other hand, when compounded in "enlightenment," "lucidity," or "illumination," light could suggest a transcendent consciousness best attainable through self-sacrifice, abstinence, and renunciation. Ascetic sages had long advised that to see the light, one needed to travel light... But unlike most schemes of dietary simplification, this time there would be no self-mortification, no sacrifice. (ibid.)

As we can see, Santosha's menu absorbed some of the major popular dietary trends of the American countercultural White middle class including, most notably, the desire for international vegetarian foods as well as the inclination to reconcile the "two opposing traditions of lightness" (ibid.). By including savory ingredients and yet abstaining from meat, the menu allowed customers to have their carrot cake, eat it, and yet remain light, so to speak. The starch-based ingredients no doubt saved the organization money, too.

Outside of the restaurant and in daily practice, Anjali found receptivity for vegetarianism among her countercultural students and encouraged it for members of the ashram community. Adopting a vegetarian diet at the ashram again supported, as Chapple recollects from his first encounter with an ashram member who was trying to find cookies made without eggs, the *Yoga-Sūtra*'s first ethical restraint (*yama*) of non-violence (*ahiṃsā*) (Chapple 2005: 27). According to Bradley King, vegetarian diet was the primary means by which Anjali encouraged her students to practice non-violence, mainly due to the fact that it taught students to be increasingly aware that what they ate had wider environmental and social effects.[30] By abstaining from meat, in other words, members of Yoga Anand Ashram were also following a popular (though as already mentioned, inverted) interpretation of the political ideology of the New Left, asserting that the personal was political and that "food was a medium for broader change" (Belasco 2007: 28). Like other countercuisine diets, such as George Ohsawa's macrobiotic diet, members could thus conceivably reduce the violence they inflicted upon other living beings and the planet by merely changing the way they ate. In doing so, they were enacting a quotidian exercise in "Confronting meat eating" as "part of the consciousness-raising-process" (ibid.: 55–56) popularized in books such as Lappé's *Diet for a Small Planet* (Lappé 1971), while also performing the countercultural White middle class's consumption-based approach to food activism that anxiously avoided, as we have seen more broadly, a direct confrontation with structural and production-oriented food injustices (cf. Alkon and Guthman 2017).

In addition to supporting yoga's paramount practice of non-violence (*ahiṃsā*), vegetarianism also helped satisfy the four remaining foundational ethical restraints (*yama*) in the *Yoga-Sūtra*, including that of truthfulness (*satya*), not stealing (*asteya*), sensual restraint (*brahmacarya*), and non-possessiveness (*aparigraha*), as well as the five moral observances (*niyama*) of contentment (*santoṣa*), purity (*śauca*), austerity (*tapas*), self-study (*svādhyāya*), and devotion to god or a higher ideal (*īśvarapraṇidhāna*). A series of articles at Yoga Anand Ashram concerned with the theoretical and practical implications of these ethical restraints (*yamas*) and moral observances (*niyamas*) written by Ashram Assistant Director Yogi Ananda Viraj make these explicit connections between proper diet and yoga practice. For example, in an article titled "The Practice of Śauca," he writes,

> The dietary discipline of avoiding impure food also aims at cultivation of discrimination. An impure body-mind complex which would result from the ingestion of drugs, rotten food, alcohol, chemicals which are synthetically produced, etc. would not be suitable for the extremely subtle task of discriminative discernment between "self" and authentic nature. The brain-mind must be functioning at optimum performance levels in order to concede to the presence of the pure. In the same way that cleanliness and pure diet are not to be taken as mere concepts but practiced, this concession to the presence of the pure is not to be understood as a theory but as a living occupation… The body learns to feel clean; it begins to become sensitive to changes in diet.
>
> (Viraj 1980: 2)

"Pure diet," as we can see here, was understood at Yoga Anand Ashram to have direct implications for one's yoga practice and their experience of the "presence of the pure," by which our author means *puruṣa*, or pure, higher Self. Anjali frequently emphasized the necessity to cultivate a pure and light (*sāttvik*; Sanskrit: *sāttvika*) demeanor in order to be able to reflect this higher Self through one's own corporeality, and eating a pure vegetarian diet as well as abstaining from alcohol and all of the popular drugs of the counterculture were a means through which such a demeanor was understood to be established. In this formulation, Yoga Anand Ashram's recommended dietary guidelines reflected more generally accepted countercultural views held by both meat-eaters and vegetarians alike which espoused "diet as a way to transform consciousness" and "to reintegrate mind and body" (Belasco 2007: 60) as an alternative to some of the other methods found among the dropouts of the counterculture, including the all-too-popular drug LSD. Though less extreme in nature, Yoga Anand Ashram's dietary guidelines also reflected other countercultural dietary regimens such as George Ohsawa's famous brown rice-only diet number seven "which proponents claimed led to the highest stage of enlightenment – a 'natural high'" (Levenstein 1993: 183).

In addition to encouraging a vegetarian diet, Anjali also prescribed abstention from food altogether during weekly community fasting. The practice of fasting was intended to further purify the minds and bodies of participants and was considered a practice of physical and emotional austerity (*tapas*) also capable of attenuating the influence of *Sāṃkhya-Yoga*'s emotional and mental afflictions (*kleśas*) (Shannon-Chapple and Chapple 2014: 291). Referring to the emotional experiences of anger and frustration that ensued during community fasting, Mike Spencer recalls that Anjali "would say you have found the 'eater' when we were fasting."[31] In her book *Ways of Yoga*, Anjali also conveys the practice of abstention from food as a symbolic gesture which silently rejected the community's wider consumer culture and, consequently, encouraged the yogic ethical restraint of non-possessiveness (*aparigraha*):

> Even when you go to the grocery store, look at all those fruits there, look at all those colors. Look at the presence of those apples. Do not rely on your conditioned habit of consuming. Do not be a constant consumer. Our purpose in life is not to consume, but we have become consumers. We have been conditioned to do this, but it is not our nature. Our nature is to give our lives so that others may live through us. Delight in the presence of food. It satisfies you. You do not even have to eat much of it. That is why sages and Yogis eat very little. They constantly enjoy the presence. It satisfies.
>
> We have made the mistake in life of consuming. Use fuel sparingly. Take what you need to survive, so that others can live through you.
>
> (Anjali 1993: 53)

According to Anjali's logic, over-consuming anything, whether it be food, fuel, or something else, is a conditioned behavior diametrically opposed to the practice and soteriological goals of yoga. Like a "pure diet" (Viraj 1980: 2), fasting also allows one to instead "enjoy the presence," by which Anjali again means to imply, as Yogi Ananda Viraj had, the pure, higher Self (*puruṣa*). When considering the countercultural social milieu in which she was teaching, Anjali's yogic fasting theory no doubt sat well with those seeking to live a simpler, drug-free, non-materialistic lifestyle, while Santosha's delicious countercuisine and hip enterprise ethos always provided an outlet for the more indulgent.

Conclusion: Anjali's Yogic Internationalism

As one of her former students conveyed to me, Gurani Anjali was in some ways "counter-countercuisine" and "counter-health foods."[32] What he meant by this is that Anjali was not strictly vegetarian and was not preoccupied with the countercultural health food movement as many of her students were. Instead, she wanted her students to see beyond this social context entirely.[33] Countercuisine and the hip enterprise movements were thus for Anjali not final goals in and of themselves, but merely one central means to reach a yogic goal. What makes Anjali's foodways so unique, therefore, is that she managed an ashram membership that ate and served food reflecting countercultural and internationalist influences while nevertheless maintaining a commitment to her distinct yogic soteriological goals.

We can indeed also situate the ashram's countercuisine within the broader twentieth-century movement known as "internationalism," and more specifically "cultural internationalism," which was a prominent social current of a post-World War II society that was seeking peaceful international relations through cultural exchange across national boundaries. Iriye advocated for the idea of cultural internationalism as an analytical tool for understanding the history of the twentieth century as well as for understanding how we might shape our international futures (Iriye 1997). According to Iriye, internationalism can be "an idea, a movement, or an institution that seeks to reformulate the nature of relations among nations through cross-national cooperation and interchange" (ibid.: 3). Expanding upon this notion, Iriye's "cultural internationalism" comprises "a variety of activities undertaken to link countries and peoples through the exchange of ideas and persons, through scholarly cooperation, or through efforts at facilitating cross-national understanding" which can be shaped by "memory, ideology, emotions, lifestyles, scholarly and artistic works, and other symbols" (ibid.).

It is important to keep in mind that like the counterculture and its predominant foodways, the seemingly innocent and universal truths and aspirations of internationalism more broadly had their roots in White, post-Enlightenment, Euro-American political ideals (Ikenberry 2020: 144). As Ikenberry points out, "[Liberal internationalism] was a creature of the Western and white man's world" (ibid.: 156). Thus while celebrating racial and religious diversity in principle, internationalism also necessarily pushed cultural difference down to the level of civil society and out of the realm of politics in an effort "both to accommodate and transcend this diversity" so that it could not interfere with the ideals of the Westphalian state system and post-World War II, American hegemony (ibid.: 149, 152). With this in mind, Ikenberry asks, "do the principles and ideas of liberal internationalism have wider relevance outside this political formation? Or are they really simply expressions of American and Western values and interests?" (ibid.: 155).

By serving international food in an individualistic countercultural spirit, Yoga Anand Ashram surely accommodated these White internationalist ideals. Nevertheless, following Anjali's own seemingly universal yogic ideology that had been forged in the crucible of her Indian, *bhadralok* spiritual aspirations in her home in Kolkata (cf. Sarkar 1997), her ashram's hip enterprise establishment was also engaged in an ongoing process of translation of a patently somatic yogic internationalism. This yogic internationalism aimed to produce its own kind of transcendent experience and challenged the hegemony of the allegedly transcendent truths of White internationalism at the level of the body itself.

In this process of translation, Anjali performed a uniquely South Asian multilingualism "in the service of a higher unity" wherein nobody lost their unique cultural and linguistic identity (Uberoi and Uberoi 1976: 642) and yet out of which something new could emerge.[34] That something, I suggest, is a form of engaged alchemy produced by the frictions between Anjali's yogic foodways and the White internationalist countercuisine and hip enterprise movement. To varying degrees, her countercultural Amityville students in search of an alternative way of being in the world eagerly embraced her vegetarian countercuisine dietary regimen aimed at embodying non-violence, worked alongside one another in the ashram's uncomfortable restaurant work environment to overcome the effects of the afflictions (*kleśas*), and routinely fasted together in their pursuit to experience, as a result, her yoga's alternative universal and transcendent truth. As I hope we can now appreciate, yogic foodways are an understudied category of contemporary yoga practice quite worthy of further consideration. Yogic foodways are religious identity markers designating group inclusion, can be used as a proselytizing tool, but also serve as a unique avenue for spiritual growth and discipleship for community members as they routinely eat, work, and fast together.

While writing this chapter I found it interesting that while Yoga Anand Ashram's yogic foodways were influenced by countercultural and internationalist values, they also had historical antecedents in the early twentieth-century United States, particularly in the yoga teachings and practices of Paramahansa Yogananda (cf. Neumann 2019: 158–159) who had constructed his own fascinating foodways that were also intended to implicate potential disciples into his own yogic cultural logic (Neumann 2019: 197–198). As interesting as Yogananda's unique foodways most certainly were (cf. Miller 2018), for the sake of variety, we will accompany our meal here at Yoga Anand Ashram with Yogananda's distinctive musical legacy and peculiar practice of internationalism and musical multilingualism in the United States in the chapter that follows.

Notes

1 As Jonathan Kauffman writes, "One of the uncomfortable, even painful, inadequacies of this movement, which became clear to me with each new chapter I researched, was how *white* it was" (Kauffman 2018: 13, emphasis in original).

2 Special thanks to Christopher Chapple, Maureen Shannon-Chapple, Glenn and Theresa James, Kathleen Jeremiah, Chandni Rodriguez, Salvatore Familia, Steve Crimi, Karan Doukas, and all of the other generous members of Yoga Anand Ashram for their support in collecting this research and archival material. You can learn more about Yoga Anand Ashram and Gurani Anjali at guranianjali.org.

3 I borrow the notion of elective affinities from Max Weber, following Löwy who writes,

> Weber does not define it, but one could propose the following definition, based on the Weberian use of the notion: elective affinity is a process through which two cultural forms – religious, intellectual, political or economical – who have certain analogies, intimate kinships or meaning affinities, enter in a relationship of reciprocal attraction and influence, mutual selection, active convergence and mutual reinforcement.
>
> (Löwy 2004; cf. Weber 1992 [1930])

4 The leftist notion that "the personal is political" was popularized by feminist Carol Hanisch and was originally intended to point out that women's individual experiences of oppression were not merely individual women's problems but rather a product of a male-dominated political landscape which itself produced and reinforced the conditions through which women were oppressed. Anticipating the neoliberal forms of subjectivity that would arrive in the 1980s, the American counterculture turned Hanisch's original intention on its head, interpreting "the personal is political" to mean that one's individual actions could have a social and political impact. Through individual reform rather than structural reform, in other words, one might change the world (Hanisch 2000 [1969]).

5 It is important to note here that Anjali was explicitly critical of hallucinogenic substances.

6 Christopher Chapple, in email message to the author, January 2, 2023.

7 Some of the ashram members I spoke with challenged this figure of seven years, suggesting that Anjali trained for a longer period of time.

8 Asha Joseph, in email message to the author, April 7, 2018.

9 This hagiographical account of Anjali's attainment of *samādhi* was challenged by some ashram members, who suggested to me that the timing may have been earlier.

10 Asha Joseph, in recorded phone interview with the author, Davis, California, March 31, 2017.

11 According to Kripal:

> This shift begins in the 1950s, explodes in the '60s, develops in the '70s, and matures in the '80s and '90s. Whereas the reception of Hinduism before 1950, for example, was dominated by a highly ascetic and monastic tradition like Advaita Vedanta, the reception of Hinduism after 1950 was catalyzed largely by charismatic gurus and powerful deities whose 'countercultural' energies were fundamentally Tantric in orientation.
>
> (Kripal 2007: 20)

12 Asha Joseph, in recorded phone interview with the author, Davis, California, March 31, 2017.

13 *yā devī sarva-bhūteṣu*
śakti-rūpeṇa saṃsthitā
namas-tasyai, namas-tasyai
namas-tasyai, namo namaḥ

Anjali's Translation:

"Mother, your power resides in all beings and all forms. I am one with that. I bow to you, I bow to you, I bow to you".

(Anjali n.d.)

14 See for example, Anderson, who points out how, "Black Power activists consciously sought to reevaluate the symbols of African American culture, notably including 'soul food': the old-time food of the impoverished rural South" during the United States' countercultural period (Anderson 2005: 137). Broad also discusses how in the Black Panther Party (BPP), "*food* emerged as a particularly salient and necessary tool for the movement-building capacity of the BPP" (Broad 2016: 136) during the same period.

15 Recent studies of American countercultural food movements such as those contained in Miller's study of natural foods and Kauffman's popular account of the "hippie food" movement have shown that the counterculture's non-conformist ideas surrounding food had a longer transnational history than Belasco's previous research suggests (Miller 2017; Kauffman 2018; Belasco 2007).

16 See, for example, a list of these and other similar publications in Levenstein's *Paradox of Plenty*, where Levenstein shows that by the beginning of the 1970s, "…

mainstream book publishers had begun to turn out New Leftish denunciations of the food industry's depredations on American health" (Levenstein 1993: 179).

17 Though the term "vegetarianism" was coined in the 1840s to denote a countercultural social movement in Europe in 1847, Indian philosophy has played a crucial role in the shaping of Western vegetarianism for the past 400 years (Stuart 2007: xvii, xxiv, xxvi). During Europe's early encounter with India, the ethical precept requiring non-violence (*ahiṃsā*) to all living beings conjured up "stories of Indians living at peace with the animal kingdom" and "imaginatively merged with Christian traditions of prelapsarianism and Puritanism" (ibid.: 39). As Stuart writes, during Europe's colonial encounters with India, "an undertow of cultural influence was flowing back to the European heartland and threatening to overturn its cherished predatory principles" (ibid.: 294). The doctrine of non-violence, which the colonizers witnessed firsthand through Indian vegetarianism, caused "even the most revered figures" to shift from "received traditions of European doctrinal, philosophical, social, and political anthropocentrism towards the Indian philosophy of harmlessness" (ibid.). Many embraced vegetarianism as a result, some even converted to Hinduism.

18 Special thanks to Asha Joseph for emphasizing this point regarding the sacred nature of food at the ashram.

19 John Becker, in discussion with the author, March 25, 2023.

20 For more information about Santosha, please visit: http://guranianjali.org/santosha-vegetarian-restaurant/.

21 John Becker, in discussion with the author, March 25, 2023.

22 For more information about Sakti Sangam, please visit: http://guranianjali.org/shakti-sangam-store/.

23 Bradley King, in email message to the author, January 13, 2023.

24 Bradley King, in recorded phone interview with the author, Davis, California, August 30, 2016.

25 Ibid.

26 Special thanks to Padmini, who gave me permission to quote her memoir. To read her more recent and full work, see *Portals: A Year of Meditation* (Higgins 2015).

27 Kusumita Pedersen, in discussion with the author at Govardhan Eco-Village, Hamrapur, Wada Taluka, Maharashtra, December 12, 2017; Christopher Chapple, in email message to the author, January 2, 2023.

28 Maureen Shannon-Chapple and Christopher Chapple, in discussion with the author at Govardhan Eco-Village, Hamrapur, Wada Taluka, Maharashtra, on December 12, 2017.

29 For more information about Santosha's menus, please visit: http://guranianjali.org/santosha-vegetarian-dining-menus/.

30 Bradley King, in recorded phone interview with the author, Davis, California, August 30, 2016.

31 Mike Spencer, in recorded phone interview with the author, Davis, California, August 28, 2016.

32 John Becker, in discussion with the author, March 27, 2023.

33 Ibid.

34 Here, Uberoi and Uberoi pay tribute to the vision and legacy of the late sociolinguist P.B. Pandit, to whose work we will turn in the next chapter (Uberoi and Uberoi 1976).

References

Alkon, Alison Hope and Julie Guthman, eds. 2017. *The New Food Activism: Opposition, Cooperation, and Collective Action*. Oakland: University of California Press.

Amityville Historical Society, ed. 2006. *Images of America: Amityville*. Charleston: Arcadia Publishing.

Anderson, E.N. 2005. *Everyone Eats: Understanding Food and Culture*. New York: New York University Press.

Anjali, Gurani. 1993. *Ways of Yoga*. Amityville: Vajra Printing and Publishing of Yoga Anand Ashram.

Anjali, Gurani. n.d. *On the Devi Mantra: Oh Great Mother, I am One with You*. Amityville: Yoga Anand Ashram.

Appadurai, Arjun. 1981. "Gastro-politics in Hindu South Asia." *American Ethnologist* 8, no. 3: 494–511.

Ashley, Bob, Joanne Hollows, Steve Jones and Ben Taylor. 2004. *Food and Cultural Studies*. New York: Routledge.

Barthes, Roland. 2013 [1961]. "Toward a Psychosociology of Contemporary Food Consumption," in Carole Counihan and Penny van Esterik (eds.), *Food and Culture: A Reader*. 3rd Edition. New York: Routledge: 23–30.

Belasco, Warren J. 2007. *Appetite for Change: How the Counterculture Took on the Food Industry*. New York: Cornell University Press.

Biltekoff, Charlotte. 2013. *Eating Right in America: The Cultural Politics of Food and Health*. Durham: Duke University Press.

Bourdieu, Pierre. 1984. *Distinction: A Social Critique of the Judgement of Taste*. New York: Routledge.

Broad, Garrett M. 2016. *More than Just Food: Food Justice and Community Change*. Oakland: University of California Press.

Brooks, David. 2000. *Bobos in Paradise; The New Upper Class and How They Got There*. New York: Simon and Schuster.

Carson, Rachel. 2002 [1962]. *Silent Spring*. Boston: Mariner Books.

Carter, Christopher. 2021. *The Spirit of Soul Food: Race, Faith & Food Justice*. Urbana: University of Illinois Press.

Chapple, Christopher Key. 2005. "Raja Yoga and the Guru: Gurani Anjali of Yoga Anand Ashram, Amityville, New York," in Cynthia Ann Humes and Thomas Forsthoefel (eds.), *Gurus in America*. Albany: State University of New York Press: 15–36.

Counihan, Carole and Penny van Esterik, eds. 2013. *Food and Culture: A Reader*. 3rd Edition. New York: Routledge.

Crenshaw, Kimberlé. 1989. "Demarginalizing the Intersection of Race and Sex: A Black Feminist Critique of Antidiscrimination Doctrine, Feminist Theory and Antiracist Politics." *University of Chicago Legal Forum*, no. 1, article 8.

Dallam, Marie W. 2014. "Introduction: Religion, Food, and Eating," in Benjamin E. Zeller, Marie W. Dallam, Reid L. Neilson, and Nora L. Rubel (eds.), *Religion, Food and Eating in North America*. New York: Columbia University Press: xvii–xxxii.

Davis, Richard. 2014. *The Bhagavad Gita: A Biography*. Princeton: Princeton University Press.

De Certeau, Michel. 1984. *The Practice of Everyday Life*. Berkeley: University of California Press.

Deslippe, Philip. 2016. "Rishis and Rebels: The Punjabi Sikh Presence in Early American Yoga." *Journal of Sikh & Punjab Studies* 23, nos. 1 & 2: 93–129.

Deslippe, Philip. 2018. "The Swami Circuit." *Journal of Yoga Studies* 1, no. 1: 5–44.

Dickstein, Jonathan. 2017. "The Strong Case for Vegetarianism in Pātañjala Yoga." *Philosophy East and West* 67, no. 3: 613–628.

Douglas, Mary. 1984 [1966]. *Purity and Danger: An Analysis of Concepts of Pollution and Taboo*. New York: Routledge.

Douglas, Mary. 1996 [1970]. *Natural Symbols: Explorations in Cosmology*. New York: Routledge.

Douglas, Mary. 2001 [1975]. *Implicit Meanings: Selected Essays in Anthropology*. New York: Routledge.

Dumont, Louis. 1980. *Homohierarchicus: The Caste System and Its Implications*. Chicago: University of Chicago Press.

Edwards, Ken. n.d. "And Now a Word from Your Local Guru." *Massapequa Post*.

Fabricant, Florence. 1977. "They'd Rather Eat Tahini." *New York Times*. October 16, 1977.

Finch, Martha L. 2014. "Foreword," in Benjamin E. Zeller, Marie W. Dallam, Reid L. Neilson, and Nora L. Rubel (eds.), *Religion, Food and Eating in North America*. New York: Columbia University Press: xi–xiii.

Forsthoefel, Thomas A., and Cynthia Ann Humes, eds. 2005. *Gurus in America*. Albany: State University of New York Press.

Gandhi, Shreena Niketa Divyakant. 2009. "Translating, Practicing, and Commodifying Yoga in the U.S.," PhD Dissertation, University of Florida. http://etd.fcla.edu/UF/UFE0025157/gandhi_s.pdf.

Goldberg, Michelle. 2015. *The Goddess Pose: The Audacious Life of Indra Devi, The Woman who Helped Bring Yoga to the West*. New York: Alfred A. Knopf.

Griffith, R. Marie. 2004. *Born again bodies: Flesh and spirit in American Christianity*. Berkeley: University of California Press.

Hanisch, Carol. 2000 [1969]. "The Personal is Political," in Barbara A. Crow (ed.), *Radical Feminism: A Documentary Reader*. New York: New York University Press: 113–116.

Harris, Marvin. 1978. "India's Sacred Cow." *Human Nature* 1, no. 2: 28–36.

Higgins, Ann. 2015. *Portals: A Year of Meditation*. Flagstaff: Mountain Lotus Publishing Company.

Hoesly, Dusty. 2019. "Organic Farming as Spiritual Practice and Practical Spirituality at Sunburst Farms." *Nova Religio: The Journal of Alternative and Emergent Religions* 23, no. 1: 60–88.

Ikenberry, John G. 2020. "Liberal Internationalism and Cultural Diversity," in Andrew Phillips and Christian Reus-Smit (eds.), *Culture and Order in World Politics*. Cambridge: Cambridge University Press: 137–158.

Iriye, Akira. 1997. *Cultural Internationalism and World Order*. Baltimore: The Johns Hopkins University Press.

Jacobs, Stephen. 2019. "A Life in Balance: Sattvic Food and the Art of Living Foundation." *Religions* 10, no. 1: 1–16.

Jacobsen, Knut. 2018. *Yoga in Modern Hinduism: Hariharānanda Āraṇya and Sāṃkhyayoga*. New York: Routledge.

Jain, Andrea R. 2015. *Selling Yoga: From Counterculture to Pop Culture*. New York: Oxford University Press.

Jarow, E. H. 2011. "The Yoga of Eating: Food Wars and Their Attendant Ideologies," in Steven J. Rosen (ed.), *Food for the Soul: Vegetarianism and Yoga Traditions*. Santa Barbara: Praeger: 1–20.

Joseph, Anjali. 1974. *Mission Statement*. Amityville: Yoga Anand Ashram.

Kauffman, Jonathan. 2018. *Hippie Food: How Back-to-the-landers, Longhairs, and Revolutionaries Changed the Way We Eat*. New York: William Morrow.

Khare, R.S., ed. 1992: *The Eternal Food: Gastronomic Ideas and Experiences of Hindus and Buddhists*. Albany: State University of New York Press.

Klepinger, Laurah E. 2022. *Transnational Yoga at Work: Spiritual Tourism and its Blind Spots*. Lanham: Lexington.

Kripal, Jeffrey J. 2007. *Esalen: America and the Religion of No Religion*. Chicago: University of Chicago Press.

Krown, Jonathan. 1972. "Meditate on This: Eastern Teachings, Say Many Long Islanders, Have Changed their Lives." *Newsday*, December 10, 1972.

Lahart, Kevin. 1976. "Finding Faith in the East: Long Islanders Search for Peace, Happiness – Even Jobs – in a Variety of Oriental Beliefs." *Newsday*, March 1, 1976.

Lappé, Frances Moore. 1971. *Diet for a Small Planet*. New York: Ballantine.

Levenstein, Harvey. 1993. *Paradox of Plenty: A Social History of Eating in Modern America*. New York: Oxford University Press.

Lévi-Strauss, Claude. 1966. "The Culinary Triangle." *Partisan Review* 33, no. 4: 586–595.

Love Brown, Susan, ed. 2002. *Intentional Community: An Anthropological Perspective*. New York: State University of New York.

Lovegren, Sylvia. 1995. *Fashionable Food: Seven Decades of Food Fads*. Chicago: University of Chicago Press.

Löwy, Michael. 2004. "The Concept of Elective Affinity According to Max Weber." *Archives de Sciences Sociales des Religions* 127, no. 3: 93–103.

Lucia, Amanda J. 2020. *White Utopias: The Religious Exoticism of Transformational Festivals*. Oakland: University of California Press.

Lucia, Amanda J. 2014a. *Reflections of Amma: Devotees in a Global Embrace*. Berkeley: University of California Press.

Lucia, Amanda J. 2014b. "'Give Me Sevā Overtime': Selfless Service and Humanitarianism in Mata Amritanandamayi's Transnational Guru Movement." *History of Religions* 54, no. 2: 88–207.

Maas, Philipp. 2013. "A Concise Historiography of Classical Yoga Philosophy," in Eli Franco (ed.), *Periodization and Historiography of Indian Philosophy*. Vienna: Publications of the De Nobili Research Library: 53–90.

Madden, Etta M. and Martha L. Finch, eds. 2006. *Eating in Eden: Food and American Utopias*. Lincoln: University of Nebraska Press.

McClymond, Kathryn. 2006. "You are Where you Eat: Negotiating Hindu Utopias in Atlanta," in Etta M. Madden and Martha L. Finch (eds.), *Eating in Eden: Food and American Utopias*. Lincoln: University of Nebraska Press: 89–106.

Miller, Christopher Patrick. 2018. "Embodying Transnational Yoga," PhD Dissertation, University of California, Davis.

Miller, Laura J. 2017. *Building Nature's Market: The Business and Politics of Natural Foods*. Chicago: The University of Chicago Press.

Mintz, Sidney W. 1986. *Sweetness and Power: The Place of Sugar in Modern History*. New York: Penguin.

Neumann, David. 2019. *Finding God through Yoga: Paramahansa Yogananda and Modern American Religion in a Global Age*. Chapel Hill: University of North Carolina Press.

Newcombe, Suzanne. 2014. "The Institutionalization of the Yoga Tradition: 'Gurus' B.K.S. Iyengar and Yogini Sunita in Britain," in Mark Singleton and Ellen Goldberg (eds.), *Gurus of Modern Yoga*. New York: Oxford University Press: 147–167.

Norman, Corrie E. 2012. "Food and Religion," in Jeffrey M. Pilcher (ed.), *The Oxford Handbook of Food History*. Oxford Handbooks (Online) accessed July 29, 2022. https://doi.org/10.1093/oxfordhb/9780199729937.013.0023.

Orsi, Robert Anthony. 1999. *Gods of the City: Religion and the American Urban Landscape*. Bloomington: Indiana University Press.

Orsi, Robert Anthony. 2010. *The Madonna of 115th Street. Faith and Community in Italian Harlem, 1880–1950*. 3rd Edition. New Haven: Yale University Press.

Padmini. 2018. "A Memoir of Guru-Ma." Unpublished, viewed May 1, 2018.

Pérez, Elizabeth. 2016. *Religion in the Kitchen: Cooking, Talking, and the Making of Black Atlantic Traditions*. New York: New York University Press.

Rapport, Jeremy. 2014. "Join us! Come, eat!: Vegetarianism in the Formative Period of the Seventh-Day Adventists and the Unity School of Christianity," in Benjamin E. Zeller, Marie W. Dallam, Reid L. Neilson, and Nora L. Rubel (eds.), *Religion, Food and Eating in North America*. New York: Columbia University Press: 23–41.

Rome, Adam. 2003. "'Give Earth a Chance': The Environmental Movement and the Sixties." *The Journal of American History* 90, no. 2: 525–554.

Rosen, Steven J., ed. 2011. *Food for the Soul: Vegetarianism and Yoga Traditions*. Santa Barbara: Praeger.

Roy, Parama. 2010. *Alimentary Tracts: Appetites, Aversions, and the Postcolonial*. Durham: Duke University Press.

Sack, Daniel. 2000. *Whitebread Protestants: Food and Religion in American Culture*. New York: Palgrave.

Sarkar, Sumit. 1997. *Writing Social History*. New York: Oxford University Press.

Shannon-Chapple, Maureen and Christopher Chapple. 2014. "Guru-Centered Education: Gurāṇi Añjali," in Christopher Key Chapple (ed.), *Antonio T. De Nicolás: Poet of Eternal Return*. Los Angeles: Nalanda International: 273–298.

Singer, Eliot. 1984. "Conversion Through Foodways Enculturation: The Meaning of Eating in an American Hindu Sect," in Linda Keller Brown and Kay Mussell (eds.), *Ethnic and Regional Foodways in the United States: The Performance of Group Identity*. Knoxville: University of Tennessee Press: 195–214.

Singleton, Mark. 2008. "The Classical Reveries of Modern Yoga: Patañjali and Constructive Orientalism," in Mark Singleton and Jean Byrne (eds.), *Yoga in the Modern World: Contemporary Perspectives*. New York: Routledge: 77–99.

Stuart, Tristram. 2007. *The Bloodless Revolution: A Cultural History of Vegetarianism from 1600 to Modern Times*. New York: W.W. Norton and Company.

Trubek, Amy B. 2008. *The Taste of Place: A Cultural Journey into Terroir*. Berkeley: University of California Press.

Tweed, Thomas A., and Stephen R. Prothero. 1999. *Asian Religions in America: A Documentary History*. New York: Oxford University Press.

Uberoi, Patricia and J.P.S. Uberoi. 1976. "Towards a New Sociolinguistics: A Memoir of P B Pandit." *Economic and Political Weekly* 11, no. 17: 637–643.

United States Geological Survey. 1947. "Amityville, New York." Accessed December 18, 2022. https://www.yellowmaps.com/usgs/quad/40073f4.htm#ym-viewmap.

United States Geological Survey. 1954. "Amityville, New York." Accessed December 18, 2022. https://www.yellowmaps.com/usgs/quad/40073f4.htm#ym-viewmap.

United States Geological Survey. 1969. "Amityville, New York." Accessed December 18, 2022. https://www.yellowmaps.com/usgs/quad/40073f4.htm#ym-viewmap.

United States Geological Survey. 1994. "Amityville, New York." Accessed December 18, 2022. https://www.yellowmaps.com/usgs/quad/40073f4.htm#ym-viewmap.

United States Geological Survey. n.d. "Topographic Map Symbols." Accessed December 18, 2022. https://pubs.usgs.gov/gip/TopographicMapSymbols/topomapsymbols.pdf.

Viraj, Yogi Ananda. 1980. *The Practice of Śauca*. Amityville: Yoga Anand Ashram.

Wallace, Anthony. 1956. Revitalization Movements. *American Anthropologist* 58, no. 2: 264–281.

Weber, Max. 1992 [1930]. *The Protestant Ethic and the Spirit of Capitalism*. Translated by Talcott Parsons. With an introduction by Anthony Giddens. London: Routledge.

White, David Gordon. 2014. *The Yoga Sutra of Patanjali: A Biography*. Princeton: Princeton University Press.

Wilson, Jeff. 2014. "Mindful Eating: American Buddhists and Worldly Benefits," in Benjamin E. Zeller, Marie W. Dallam, Reid L. Neilson, and Nora L. Rubel (eds.), *Religion, Food and Eating in North America*. New York: Columbia University Press: 214–233.

Wilson, Liz. 2004. "Pass the Tofu, Please: Asian Food for Aging Baby Boomers," in Lucy M. Long (ed.), *Culinary Tourism*. Lexington: University Press of Kentucky: 245–267.

Yoga Anand Ashram. n.d.-a. *List of Lectures Given at Moksha*. Amityville: Yoga Anand Ashram.

Yoga Anand Ashram. n.d.-b. *Dear Friends*. Amityville: Yoga Anand Ashram.

Zeller, Benjamin E. 2012. "Food Practices, Culture, and Social Dynamics in the Hare Krishna Movement," in Carole M. Cusack and Alex Norman (eds.), *Handbook of New Religions and Cultural Production*. Leiden: Brill: 681–704.

2 Yogananda's Sacred Music in Paradise

Ukuleles and the Unstruck Sound at Polestar Gardens, Hawaii

After his arrival to the United States in 1920, Swami Paramahansa Yogananda (1893–1952) enthralled his American audiences with devotional music and chanting which included simple Sanskrit, Hindi, and Bengali chants, Anglicized vernacular songs from India, and other tunes that he himself composed during his lifetime. His popularity among his American devotees led him to establish the Self-Realization Fellowship in 1925, an organization that still initiates practitioners into his *kriyā-yoga* meditation tradition today. Recently, some fascinating scholarship pertaining to Yogananda has been produced (Williamson 2010; Foxen 2017; Goldberg 2018; Neumann 2019), though within this scholarship little attention is given to the influence of his musical practices in the American religious landscape (cf. Srinivas 2008). As Phillip Goldberg observes, "Sacred music became a standard part of Yogananda's repertoire, and his introduction of kirtan to America has been largely underappreciated" (Goldberg 2018: 165). Nevertheless, as Yogananda himself even once admitted, "Chanting is half the battle," and this chapter helps us also understand what the other half of the battle might have been about (Yogananda 1974 [1938]: xviii; Ananda 2016).

I will bring Yogananda's music into focus by examining the function of sacred devotional music (*kīrtan*; Sanskrit: *kīrtana*) in a contemporary independent community devoted to his teachings, Polestar Gardens on the Big Island of Hawaii, where ukuleles, harmoniums, and other instruments and sounds from around the world today form the community's popular ensemble. The contemporary example of Polestar's music brings us beyond Yogananda's Self-Realization Fellowship (SRF), the focus of existing Yogananda scholarship, showing us how his teachings have been reinterpreted outside of the SRF's orthodoxy. As we will see, Polestar's music also gives us clues to understand how Yogananda's lyrics comprised a living form of Indian multilingualism (Pandit 1988) which, while using two or more languages at a time, creatively spoke in a transnational "guru language" (Srinivas 2008: 313) his American audiences could understand. At the same time, Yogananda's music and flexible ensemble had the capacity to communicate the guru's "sonic theology" (Beck 1993) to devotees within a racialized, Protestant early twentieth-century United States (Singh 2020). This theology, as we will see, reconciles the gap between

DOI: 10.4324/9781003414032-3

restless American souls (Schmidt 2005) and their relentless search for god by constructing an indissoluble link between the material manifestation of the divine in audible sacred music and an interior divine sound at the core of every human being. Today, the frictions between Yogananda's musicology and Polestar's novel tropical ensemble produce our next instantiation of engaged alchemy.

Studying Music and Instruments

This chapter follows Laack's call for the secular transdisciplinary study of music and sound in religion (Laack 2015: 230).[1] Rather than focusing on a seemingly bounded or isolated musical culture with an identifiable or authentic provenance (cf. Merriam 1964; Nettl 2015: 64), I consider the mobile musical practices of transnational *kīrtan* as fluid cultural phenomena which, like transnational yoga, are constantly in transformation in the "interstitial spaces" (Bhabha 1994: 56) of particular global contexts. While I take the secular, critical study of religious music quite seriously and inhabit, at least in part, the learned habitus of a scholar of the Western academy, I also recognize my discipline's roots in the European Enlightenment and therefore, as ethnomusicologist Engelhardt writes regarding religion and music, remain "deeply empathetic to the truth claims and lived faith of those who practice" while also being ever "mindful of the epistemological limits" of my scholarly work (Engelhardt 2012: 302–303).

Until recently, scholars of Modern Yoga Studies have neglected to seriously consider the study of sound and music (cf. Laack 2015: 221).[2] The reason for music's neglect, as we also saw with yogic diet, arises primarily from White Protestant influences within the field of Religious Studies that have historically neglected material practices including not only diet, but also music, as comprising what they considered to be religion (ibid.). Within the field of Modern Yoga Studies specifically, little considerable attention has been given to the practice of *kīrtan* in the form of devotional music in transnational yoga, which, like the practice of yogic diet as we saw in the previous chapter, is common within many transnational yoga communities and also within South Asian religions more broadly.[3] Yet Modern Yoga Studies has much to gain from considering music, as has been demonstrated by the cadre of other scholars who are studying the related topic of mantra in South Asian traditions including yoga (cf. Gerety 2021; Gough 2021).

Following van der Linden's study of Indian music's transformation during its encounter with British colonial imperialism and internationalism, I take a "relational approach" (van der Linden 2013: 2) to the historical and ethnographic study of *kīrtan* that considers Indian music from an "internationalist" perspective. With regard to late colonial-era Indian music, internationalism, which we already encountered in its post-World War II context in the previous chapter, was, as van der Linden writes, "the doctrine that the common interests of nations are greater and more important than their differences" (ibid.: 13). Subscribed to by both Indian and Western cultural elites during India's late colonial period, internationalism "drew inspiration from, more than one culture, Western and/or non-Western" (ibid.). Often, Indian and Western internationalists "shared a common front against urban industrial capitalism, the ideology of progress, and sometimes even Western civilization at large," and though internationalists sought "social and intellectual progress," their ideology was in many ways "compatible with imperial politics and tropes" (ibid.: 13–15). Paramahansa Yogananda was one such Indian whose own universal sacred music theory was shaped, at least in great part, by internationalist ideology in his colonial setting in India as well as when he immigrated to the United States.

Nevertheless, similar to the study of foodways in the previous chapter and typical of many studies in Ethnomusicology (cf. Schultz 2013; Rees 2000; Erlmann 1999),[4] I seek to strike a balance between culturalist and hegemonic approaches to the study of music here in order to present a nuanced account of how Yogananda's musical practices were created in the frictions (Tsing 2005) between a number of ideological and material influences, whether they were from India, the West, or, as we shall see, elsewhere. In Yogananda's musicology we will encounter, "a heritage that underlies modern habits of language, religious belief, and musical performance" (Byl and Sykes 2020: 405) from South Asia, though, as we will see, this musicological heritage has nevertheless been simultaneously "transformed by pervasive local traditions" (ibid.: 405) through its encounters with the tropical instrument known as the ukulele. The combination of the ukulele and South Asian musicology in Hawaii pushes a critical insight of Indian Ocean Ethnomusicology to its limits. That is to say, beyond highlighting regional religious musical connections *within* the Indian Ocean (cf. Rasmussen 2016; Byl 2023),[5] this chapter shows how the Indian Ocean's musicological influence has traveled into oceanic regions far beyond the islands of the Indian Ocean (cf. Lorea 2023) via the "island factor" (Alpers 2018: 33).

I do not consider Indian agency in the creation of music to have been completely subsumed by prevailing dominant power structures and discourses in late colonial India (van der Linden 2013: 29). In fact, quite the opposite, as I will consider how Yogananda translated a distinctly Indic "sonic theology" (Beck 1993) into sounds that his American audiences could embrace. Considering Yogananda's interpretation of sacred music is important here because, as Gerety writes,

> Indian religions, which furnish the context for the earliest constructions of yoga, have a long and highly developed history of "thinking sound". This history includes refined metalanguages and sophisticated traditions of critical and philosophical reflection. It also includes ancient sonic ontologies and theologies, elaborate practices of sounding and listening and dynamic auditory cultures. So even as we consider the potential for recent academic scholarship about sound to illuminate yoga, we must also do the reverse: draw on Indian accounts of yoga to illuminate sound.
>
> (Gerety 2021: 503)

Careful consideration of Yogananda's situated assessment of sacred music and sound is crucial here, as it defies mere reduction to his colonial, romantic, and internationalist influences and in fact subsumes these influences to achieve yogic ends. As we will see, he transposed a crucial practical dimension of his *kriyā-yoga* practice onto American soil by accommodating a flexible ensemble and lyrical creativity.

With this in mind, I follow the basic assumption that music and ensembles change as both move through time and into particular contemporaneous social spaces (cf. Bohlman 1989; Brinkmann and Wolff 1999; Reyes 1999; Turino 1999, 2000; Manuel 2000; Olsen 2004; Silverman 2012; Meyers 1999).[6] Thus, to help us understand what we are witnessing in the ethnographic present, I incorporate germane – though certainly not exhaustive – historical details to the extent that they help us comprehend Yogananda's theology, ensemble, and the musical practices he used for converting American devotees to his initiatory method of *kriyā-yoga* in the early twentieth century.

I primarily engage secondary scholarly sources to reconstruct the transnational transmission of Yogananda's *kīrtan* as well as to understand how the particular ensemble at Polestar Gardens came together within the broader history of the two primary instruments used in the community today: the harmonium and the ukulele. As Bates emphasizes, "Even the same instrument, in different sociohistorical contexts, may be implicated in categorically different kinds of relations" (Bates 2012: 364) wherein they become "embroiled in unique stories, trajectories, and sets of social relations" (ibid.: 367). As Dawe has since similarly elaborated, it is important to consider the localization of globally available musical instruments as entangled objects within specific material cultures and social settings (Dawe 2012: 197).[7] It is precisely these entanglements, stories, trajectories, relations, and frictions that I consider in this chapter as I look closely at Polestar's social constructions of the ukulele and the harmonium within the context of their *kīrtan* ensemble and attendant *kriyā-yoga* practice.

Unlike Schultz's study of nationalist forms of *kīrtan* in Maharashtra during which Schultz "didn't want to be associated with American/European spiritual converts to Hinduism who romanticize India" (Schultz 2013: 105), this understudied demographic is the focus of the current chapter. To get to know the *kīrtan* community and practice at Polestar Gardens, I participated in the community's ongoing musical and meditation practices, attended workshops and lectures, and joined the *karma-yoga* program where I worked daily alongside community leaders and participants who maintained the community. The conversations I had with my fellow interns during our daily work hours and breaks illuminated the many opinions and perspectives regarding Polestar's *kīrtan* practice, some of which I share in this chapter.

The social constructions of the harmonium and the ukulele that we will encounter in this chapter are, importantly, dialogical. We will encounter authoritative, hegemonic constructions regarding their meaning through the work and discourse of both Yogananda and contemporary leaders within the

Polestar community. At the same time, however, we will also encounter divergent opinions from those who visit, live in, or work in the community every day. Thus, the stories, beliefs, and discourses surrounding *kīrtan*, the ukulele, and the harmonium are, as we will see, perpetually constituted by heteroglossia (Bakhtin 1981: 291). Rather than having any one meaning or function, a diverse set of voices and historical conditions reveal these instruments' manifold meanings in both the past and the present. While I highlight this range of interpretations and meanings from my time spent at Polestar, I also try not to lose sight of the predominant discourses in Yogananda's sonic theology and how these influence the dominant discourse at Polestar Gardens.

Colonial Encounters: Indian Music, *anāhata-nāda*, and Harmoniums

European and American colonial encounters with cultural arts around the world led to a dramatic transformation of, among other things, the music of the colonized. In these encounters, staunch commitments to musical authenticity and tradition among the colonized and their international allies paradoxically produced new and innovative forms of musical expression as well as novel musical ensembles. Though the harmonium probably seems like an obvious candidate for our consideration here due to its centrality in contemporary transnational *kīrtan* practice, the ukulele, which I consider later in the chapter, does not. Nevertheless, the ukulele has a parallel historical trajectory that is structurally similar to that of the harmonium. When combined with an understanding of Yogananda's colonial, internationalist, and musicological influences, the ukulele's social history will help us appreciate how it finds itself alongside the harmonium in Polestar Gardens' contemporary *kīrtan* practice.

Music in Colonial India

In late colonial India, romantic and colonial Orientalist stereotypes of Indian culture perpetuated by the British and internationalist organizations such as the Theosophical Society created a complicated situation whereby Indian elites were attempting to reconcile the West's punishing rationalism with the newly prevailing romantic notion that India was a land of mysticism and spirituality (cf. Chatterjee 1986; van der Veer 2001). These colonial and romantic stereotypes had a dramatic transformative impact on the creation and public perception of a number of "traditional," "classical," "authentic," and yet "modern" cultural arts including, but not limited to, dance, yoga, and of course music (cf. Singleton 2008). In South India, for example, the ensemble of Carnatic music adopted Europe's violin, which, as Weidman shows, "came to be seen simultaneously as the moderniser of Carnatic music and the preserver of Carnatic Music's authenticity" (Weidman 2006: 14). As Nettl also reminds us, "classical" Carnatic music has also adopted the harmonium, saxophone, clarinet, guitar, and mandolin over the course of the past 200 years (Nettl 2015: 376). In North India, Hindustani music underwent its own changes to define the "classical," while prominent Indian cosmopolitan elites such as the Bengali *bhadralok* who were connected with the Brahmo Samaj and the British East India Company composed other novel forms of music, lyrics, and poetry (in some instances according to styles of Christian congregational singing). One such famous example is the aristocrat Rabindranath Tagore, who, like his fellow *bhadralok*, romanticized, appropriated, translated into English, and disseminated bucolic music from the villages of Bengal in his search for a lost, pre-colonial innocence (van der Linden 2013: 109–111). Altogether, lyrics, repertoires, and, most notably for our purposes, *instruments*, were appropriated, mixed, translated, and socially redefined within elite Indian cosmopolitan social circles. Yogananda was implicated in this process, having lived in Bengal with a father who financially supported his son's work through his employment with the imperialist British (Neumann 2019: 60).

Though these novel and elite cultural expressions were clearly not the only expressions of Indian modernity that arose during India's encounters with British imperialism (cf. Weiss 2019), Indian artistic and somatic expression underwent a dramatic process of transformation to meet middle-class Victorian tastes that had been internalized by high-caste, English-educated, cosmopolitan members of Indian society who were devoted to the process of showcasing Indian culture and religion as respectable and worthy of attention on the international stage.[8] This process has often been referred to as the sanitization or "deodorization" (Urban 2003: 135, 164) of Indian culture, as those who participated in it sought to do away with what Europeans considered primitive and obscene, even if doing so meant appropriating, or even violently erasing, the livelihoods, religious practices, and arts of lower-caste Indian society (cf. Singleton 2008). With regard to music specifically, as van der Linden writes, "the anti-imperial goals of its [Indian] creators, ironically, often overlapped with those of the British civilizing mission" (van der Linden 2013: 5) and the intentions of British folk music scholars who regularly framed Indian music (and at times yogi musicians specifically) as both primitive and quintessentially spiritual (i.e. irrational) (ibid.: 5, 44, 55, 80).

Demonstrating incredible creative ingenuity, however, a number of the new forms of artistic, cultural, and somatic expression that emerged from these elite modernizing projects were eagerly sought after by the romanticizing global middle and upper classes, and particularly among the "restless souls" (Schmidt 2005) of the United States. Broadly speaking, yoga is one such cultural practice that was transformed and disseminated in this manner (cf. Singleton 2010). But more specifically, so too was yoga's music. And what I would therefore like to highlight now are the theological and philosophical underpinnings of Yogananda's yoga music, which though clearly amenable to a Victorian, Protestant ethos, nevertheless maintained roots in a very distinct transformative musicology from thirteenth-century South Asia that helps Yogananda's innovations resist being conceived of as merely sanitized or deodorized.

Yogananda's Musicological Inheritance

As Wilke and Moebus remind us, the Indic landscape of sound "...has always been a performance culture, where the holy literatures are 'sounded out' and embodied, i.e. recited, sung, staged, played and danced" (Wilke and Moebus 2011: 12). One primary type of this "sonic liturgy" (Beck 2012) comes in the form of *kīrtan*, of which there are many musical expressions. Unlike more insular, Hindu nationalist expressions such as *nāradīya-kīrtan* developed in the early twentieth century that preserved particular forms of *kīrtan* within India (Schultz 2013), the internationalist yoga guru Yogananda emerged from the dynamic and productive colonial context described in this section with his harmonium, his *kīrtan*, and some very particular musicological assumptions that he would take to the stage in the early twentieth-century United States.[9]

Yogananda disseminated the music he took to the United States as a universal spiritual practice, a view that was in great part a product of the crucible of India's colonial encounters with the British and other internationalist groups including the Theosophical Society (his guru Sri Yukteswar was a member) seeking to create a worldwide universal brotherhood (cf. van der Linden 2013: 15). But his universal sonic theology was also particularly informed by the Radha Soamis (cf. Juergensmeyer 1991) and their unique strand of South Asian musicology with clear roots in Sarngadeva's thirteenth-century musicological speculations in the *Saṅgīta-Ratnākara* (ca. thirteenth century; Wilke and Moebus 2011: 24, 810). Ultimately, though Yogananda's approach to sacred music was a product of the crucible of British colonialism and internationalism, his music nevertheless entered the American religious landscape with some patently yogic dimensions which, though they may have sounded quite different, nevertheless remained altogether intact at their theoretical core. Indeed, what I found particularly interesting during my research that followed my time at Polestar Gardens was just how closely the practices we undertook in the community still structurally reflected Yogananda's sonic theology from the early twentieth century, and even more so how Yogananda was able to translate this theology – grounded as it was in thirteenth-century South Asian musicology – into the early twentieth-century American musical landscape.

Yogananda's Music in the Early Twentieth-Century United States

While church music satisfied the musically inclined American public in the mid-nineteenth century, the early twentieth-century United States witnessed a dramatic shift in musical tastes, trends, and venues. Within mainstream Protestant traditions, hymnals began to reflect an increasingly ecumenical spirit as they incorporated music from other denominations. As the biggest and wealthiest city in the United States, New York became the country's center of Christian musical activity, sustaining a large concentration of churches as well as a number of prominent educational facilities including the School of Sacred

Music at Union Theological Seminary (est. 1928) (Ogasapian 2007: 228–244). Nevertheless, Ogasapian writes,

> By the late nineteenth century, church music was no longer the primary interest for the musical public or a central activity for many American musicians, performers, and composers... *Concert halls like Carnegie Hall in New York* and Symphony Hall in Boston *displaced churches* that had been the venue for public concerts during much of the nineteenth century.
>
> (ibid.: 229, emphasis added)

Despite the proliferation of churches and the availability of educational opportunities in Christian music in the early twentieth-century United States, both the appeal of church music and the performative site of the church itself lost ground to alternative venues and new styles of world music.

With the shifts from church to concert hall, denominational to ecumenical hymnals, and from church music to world music, the stage had been set for the musically inclined Yogananda to enter the American music scene and Carnegie Hall specifically. Here, he found a critical opportunity for cross-cultural communication and in April 1926, just six years after his arrival to the United States, he capitalized on this opportunity during a public lecture in New York's Carnegie Hall. Yogananda famously recounts the event in the introduction to his songbook *Cosmic Chants*:

> One evening I started to chant "O God Beautiful" and asked the audience, who had never before heard the song, to join me in chanting it. For one hour and twenty-five minutes, the thousands of voices of the entire audience chanted "O God Beautiful" in a divine atmosphere of joyous praise. Even after I had left the stage, the audience sat on, chanting the song. The next day many men and women testified to the God-perception and the healing of body, mind, and soul that had taken place during the sacred chanting, and numerous requests came in to repeat the song at other services.
>
> (Yogananda 1974 [1938]: xiii)

Following this event, and reflecting Ogasapian's aforementioned insights regarding Carnegie Hall (Ogasapian 2007: 229), Yogananda dubbed Carnegie Hall "the musical temple of America" (ibid.). Though Americans were making their way out of the church and into places such as the "temple" of Carnegie Hall for their musical fix, they had clearly not given up their search for soul healing and the divine, providing Yogananda with a valuable venue for cross-cultural communication of his *kriyā-yoga* message. His strategic selection of the English translation of the Sikh song "O God Beautiful" (*e hari sundara*) and his emphasis on "God-perception" and "healing of body, mind, and soul" at Carnegie Hall demonstrate his aptitude for translating Indian music and lyrics into a White, Protestant, and Metaphysical American religious idiom.[10]

We should appreciate Yogananda's skill in musicological cross-cultural communication, given that he had no choice but to tread carefully in the United States. Indeed, as recent scholarship in Modern Yoga Studies has shown, disseminators of yoga in the United States were subjected to Americans' deep-seated racism and xenophobia in the early twentieth century in a variety of ways which required that they deliver their yoga teachings carefully (Singh 2020; Neumann 2019). The treatment of yoga's early disseminators in the United States in such a manner came in the wake of even earlier colonial Orientalist portrayals of yogis in India as filthy charlatans belonging to a degenerate race and religion that only a civilized, Christian British empire could rehabilitate (Pinch 2006; White 2009; Singleton 2010). These imperialist portrayals of yogis combined with Americans' anti-Black racism to create a hostile social environment (or alternatively, as we saw in Chapter 1, an aura of fascination) for the dark-skinned "Hindoo" gurus who came to the United States in the early twentieth century, an environment that persists into the present. As Neumann recently documented, Yogananda himself came close "to being lynched" during his lecture and music tour in the American South in the early twentieth century (Neumann 2019: 13). What is most extraordinary about Yogananda's legacy is that he was able to adapt his music to the tastes of his White audiences in this formidable cultural terrain and convert them to his *kriyā-yoga* tradition.[11]

It is also critical to understand that while sacred music comprises a significant component within Yogananda's *kriyā-yoga* system, it remains only the broadest entry point into his more advanced, silent meditation practice which aims to bring practitioners to the experience of an *internal, unstruck sound* (*anāhata-nāda*). This is what Yogananda meant when he said, "Chanting is half the battle," as we already saw (Yogananda 1974 [1938]: xviii; Ananda 2016). In this way, Yogananda did not understand his creative use of Anglicized, Protestantized music to be heretical to his yoga tradition, but indeed used these forms of music to *augment* his repertoire of communication techniques in order to skillfully deliver his universal sonic theological message to early twentieth-century Americans so that they would become more willing to be initiated into his esoteric and much more expansive *kriyā-yoga* practice.

The "unstruck sound": anāhata-nāda

Yogananda learned how to listen for the "unstruck sound" early in life from the Radha Soamis, founded in India in 1861 by Siv Dayal Singh (1818–1878). Combining Sufi, Sikh, and Hindu influences, the Radha Soamis used devotional singing (*bhajan*) as the gateway toward the practice of listening for an internal, unstruck, divine sound. As Williamson has shown, from a very early age Yogananda (who was then named Mukunda),

> … first learned the meditation techniques of the Radhaswami (Radhasoami) movement, which originated from the Sikh tradition in the late nineteenth century. Their meditation focuses on listening for the inner sound of "aum" and attempting to see an inner divine light. These techniques play a part in many yogic traditions, including the Kriya tradition that Mukunda next learned from his own father in 1906 when he was thirteen.
>
> (Williamson 2010: 70)

Similarly, a biographical account of Yogananda's life provides more details concerning the early influence of the Radha Soami movement upon the yoga guru's sonic spiritual practice:

> Close to home he [Yogananda, then Mukunda] was able to have the company of his elder brother in law Satish Chandra Bashas' brother, Charu Chandra Basa. Charu Baba was an initiate of the well known Radhaswami spiritual path. Charu Baba revealed the mysteries and techniques of that meditation to Mukunda. With intense effort the child-sadhak Mukunda engaged himself in that sadhana with his whole being and in a short time became absorbed in experience of listening in ecstasy to Divine Sound and seeing beatific revelations in Divine Light… That Light remained forever undimmed throughout his entire life, and the profundity of that experience kept him always spiritually aware in many complex situations…
>
> With reverence and discipline he was engaged in practicing the beginning stages of Kriya Yoga that he received from his father. *In later life he held this experience of Sound and Light as complementary to Kriya Yoga.*
>
> (Giri 2004: 155, emphasis added)

As these scholarly and biographical accounts here suggest, listening for the unstruck, inner sound of the sacred syllable "*auṃ*" is a central meditative goal in Yogananda's initiatory practice of *kriyā-yoga* that has connections with practices in other South Asian religious traditions. Gleaned directly from *haṭha-yoga* models of the subtle body (Zapart 2020), this practice still forms a core component of the Radha Soami's *surat-śabd-yoga*, "Word-Yoga for the Soul," into the present (Wilke and Moebus 2011: 895). In Yogananda's system, it is specifically referred to as the "Aum Technique," the theological foundation for which he describes in his famous commentary on the *Bhagavad-Gītā*, oft-quoted at Polestar Gardens:

> … the *Aum* sound vibrates independently of the etheric medium. It is thus referred to as *anahata-nada* (a sound produced otherwise than by being beaten or struck – that is, without detonation) because it manifests

> in the yogi's intuition without striking his eardrum through the medium of ether – as with physical sounds. *Aum*, being a spiritual vibration, is not heard physically, but felt spiritually.
>
> (Yogananda 1999: 614–616)

In group *kriyā-yoga* practice as I have experienced it in several Yogananda-based meditation communities, sacred audible music in the form of *kīrtan* initiates meditation on the internal, unstruck sound wherein one subsequently goes inward into meditation practice following, as Foxen relates, "… a very recognizable *haṭha* yogic character. Energy… is channeled through the *cakras* by way of *prāṇāyāma* and *mantra* practice." "The final goal," Foxen continues, "is to concentrate this energy in the third eye in order to achieve oneness with the effulgent universal sound" (Foxen 2017: 145–146; see also Zapart 2020: 74). Only the initiated, however, are trained in the secret techniques used to accomplish this meditative goal. Critically, listening to and participating in sacred music of any kind, which Yogananda considered to be universal and found in all cultures, serves as the bridge toward having this spiritual experience.[12]

As Wilke and Moebus have demonstrated, the Radha Soami's interlinked musical and meditational practices have their theological roots in Sarngadeva's musicological speculations in the *Saṅgīta-Ratnākara* (Wilke and Moebus 2011). In *Saṅgīta-Ratnākara*, we find the first-known explicit attempt to theologically link external sound in the form of sacred music (i.e., *āhata-nāda*, "struck sound") and the unstruck, internal sound (*anāhata-nāda*) terminating in the impersonal, featureless Absolute (*brahman*). As Wilke and Moebus emphasize, Sarngadeva's medieval "optimistic theology" theorized how sacred devotional music of *any kind* "puts the world under its spell and [at the same time] tears apart the [fetters of] existence" so that the unstruck sound (*anāhata-nāda*) – a phenomenon *beyond* one's mind, body, and emotions – becomes an experience accessible to all (ibid.: 836).

As Wilke and Moebus also show in their extensive book-length chapter, with his innovative theory connecting sacred audible music to an unstruck divine sound within, Sarngadeva laid the foundations for a sense-pleasing musical "Yoga for everybody" (ibid.: 24) that would eventually extend throughout South Asia, including into the canonical *Haṭha-Yoga-Pradīpikā*'s (ca. fifteenth century CE) practice of *nāda-anusaṃdhāna* (investigation of internal sound). As Wilke and Moebus speculate, this practice ultimately found its way into the world of transnational modern yoga as the popular practice of "*nāda-yoga*" (yoga of sound) primarily through the New Age musicological writings of German jazz musician Joachim-Ernst Berendt (1922–2000), in his famous book *Nada Brahma: Die Welt ist Klang* (*Nada-Brahma: The World is Sound*; Berendt 1991 [1985]) (Wilke and Moebus 2011: 809–1041). It is remarkable, however, that Wilke and Moebus and other scholars of yoga have not thoroughly considered the enduring impact of Yogananda's theology of sacred music and internal sound in American yoga practice, influenced as his theology clearly was, as I have shown, by the Radha Soamis as well as Sarngadeva's medieval musicology.

Yogananda's Harmonium: An (in?) Authentic Bridge to the Unstruck Sound

In order to lead practitioners toward the unstruck sound, Yogananda initiated meditation, as his devotees still do today, by singing one of his "Cosmic Chants" (Yogananda 1974 [1938]) often accompanied by his choice instrument, the harmonium. The harmonium was originally a European, Christian invention that could either seemingly destroy what Indian music purists considered "authentic" [13] Indian music, or alternatively, and in a more internationalist spirit such as Yogananda's, give Indian music fully authentic expression. Because the harmonium's contentious social history is largely forgotten both in India and within transnational *kīrtan* communities today, the instrument now primarily serves as a specious symbol of authenticity and tradition.[14] For this reason, and because it was the central instrument in both Yogananda's and eventually Polestar's musical ensemble, its social history is worthy of our attention.

Though first patented in Paris in 1842 as an upright, foot-pumped reed organ (Rahaim 2011: 662), the harmonium had already begun circulating in South Asia at the end of the eighteenth century (Kurt 2009, as cited in Wilke and Moebus 2011: 908 fn 143). Indian musicians had a particularly ambivalent relationship with the instrument, largely on account of the fact that it was of European origin, and no doubt also because it was widely used by Christian navy chaplains and missionaries who found its portability convenient for travel and suitable for accompanying their evangelizing hymn-singing (Rahaim 2011: 662). Nevertheless, in the late nineteenth century, Indian instrument manufacturer Dwarkanath Ghose domesticated the harmonium when he began to make a hand-pumped version of the French foot-pumped model that would become India's homemade standard by 1913.[15] Late colonial Indian musicians thus made the harmonium their own, and, despite its European origins, the instrument was loved by Indians and non-Indians alike because it was easy to learn how to play, portable for travel, affordable, durable, easy to repair, loud for its size, and could hold its tune for long periods of time (Rahaim 2011: 662; van der Linden 2013: 102–103; Lallie 2016: 56). As Purohit also notes, from a performance standpoint it worked well in "bourgeois auditoriums with hundreds of listeners assembled for low per capita admission charges" (Purohit 1988: 895), and would thus work quite well in settings such as, say, Carnegie Hall. For these main reasons, many late colonial period Hindus and Sikhs began to adopt the harmonium into their *kīrtan* ensembles and musical schools with great enthusiasm (van der Linden 2013: 141, 158).

However, although Sikhs apparently "accepted the harmonium without a whim or whimper" (Lallie 2016: 61),[16] the instrument was loathed by some elites such as Rabindranath Tagore and Ananda Coomaraswamy as well as by their romanticist White allies, including Arthur Henry Fox Strangways. These individuals sought to preserve what they perceived as a traditional and authentic Indian musical tradition, and the European-influenced harmonium did not fit into their ideological narratives (van der Linden 2013: 10, 23–25, 158). These and other influential actors who opposed the instrument did so primarily on technical grounds, suggesting that the harmonium was not fit to produce the proper sound for what they considered to be authentic Indian music (Rahaim 2011: 657–661; Lillie 2016: 59) – a critique that other instruments such as the violin (in Carnatic music) did not endure because of their ability to more seamlessly combine with a particular musical system (cf. Weidman 2006). However, with the harmonium, as Rahaim summarizes, "There have been three principal objections… First, that it cannot glide smoothly between discrete notes; second, that its tuning is wrong; third, that it is un-Indian" (Rahaim 2011: 658). Thus, for some Indians and their romantic Orientalist allies, it became important to reject this cultural object in order to establish cultural sovereignty, authenticity, and distinction from the colonial British.

Nevertheless, as Rahaim also writes, "when the distinction between India and the West was not at issue, the harmonium has been seen as paradigmatically Indian" (ibid.: 660). Thus in reality, those holding the negative opinions of the harmonium outlined here could often also be found using the instrument on account of all its attendant practical virtues, and "by the early twentieth century, it had become the accompanist instrument of choice for most Indian musical performers" (Lallie 2016: 56).[17] Yogananda was, of course, among these performers, and he took the harmonium with him to the United States where it would become – and generally remains – the key instrument in his devotees' *kīrtan* and meditation practices.

Polestar Gardens: Puna District's Kīrtan Paradise

Along with the ukulele, the harmonium is the centerpiece of the ensemble at Polestar Gardens where both instruments are used to produce audible sacred music intended to lead *kriyā-yoga* practitioners toward the unstruck, internal sound within. Polestar Gardens was originally founded in 1998 in Sonoma, California by Michael and Ann Gornik, both former residents of Swami Kriyananda's (1926–2013) Ananda Village in Nevada City, California. Ananda Village (itself a splinter organization of the Self-Realization Fellowship) was founded by Swami Kriyananda in 1968 to manifest what Yogananda referred to as "World Brotherhood Colonies," echoing his guru's internationalist ideology and desire for an international network of spiritual communities grounded in the notion of "simple living and high thinking."[18] I met and became interested in Polestar in 2013 at their Sacred Musical Festival on the Big Island of Hawaii, about which I will say more momentarily, while serving as a certified public accountant at another nonprofit intentional community a few miles down the road.

The Polestar community practices the four yogas popularized in the United States by Swami Vivekananda (1863–1902) and later disseminated in the following generation by their own guru Paramahansa Yogananda. The four yogas are: *karma-yoga* (yoga of action), *bhakti-yoga* (yoga of devotion), *jñāna-yoga* (yoga of knowledge), and *rāja-yoga* (royal yoga). As a part of the community's normal operations, *karma-yoga* is taught as a selfless service initiative wherein participants are trained to complete regular tasks and chores with dedication and without anticipation of personal benefit. This habitual relinquishment of personal reward is concurrently presented according to the principles of *bhakti-yoga* wherein participants are trained to devote the fruits of their labors to the divine in a manner similar to what we encountered at Yoga Anand Ashram in the previous chapter. Furthermore, Polestar also practices *bhakti-yoga* during daily, weekly, and yearly devotional music *kīrtan* events, all of which also play an important role in their *rāja-yoga* practice.

In Yogananda's teachings and at Polestar, the term *rāja-yoga* encapsulates the aforementioned system of four-yogas (*karma*, *bhakti*, *jñāna*, and *rāja* collectively) and also refers to a four-step meditation process I describe below (Energization, Hong Sau, Aum Technique, and *kriyā-yoga*) that aims to lead practitioners toward an experience of objectless and thoughtless meditative absorption (*nirvikalpa samādhi*) in which sacred music plays a critical role. Lastly, *jñāna-yoga* is taught in a weekly study group during which community co-founder Michael Gornik expounds Yogananda's teachings from texts, including the famous *Autobiography of a Yogi* (Yogananda 1946) and Yogananda's *Bhagavad-Gītā* (Yogananda 1999) commentary. During these study groups, the connections between selfless service, sacred music, meditation, and the habit of emotional restraint (*titikṣā*, or "imperturbability") are continually reinforced.

Polestar's situatedness on the Big Island of Hawaii is not coincidental, and there are significant material conditions that make its Puna District a particularly apropos place for the community to be located. Michael and Ann Gornik first learned of Puna from a fellow Yogananda devotee who goes by the name of "Bhakti." Bhakti convinced the Gorniks to take a trip to the Puna area on the Eastern tip of the Big Island of Hawaii to consider moving Polestar there on account of its openness to intentional spiritual communities.[19] Following Bhakti's encouragement, in 2005 the Gorniks moved the community to the Kalapana area of the Puna District to an area popularly known as "Puna Palisades." After a few years, they eventually found a 20-acre piece of land that Michael knew was the right place for Polestar when he stood atop an old broken down vehicle there amidst a tall patch of cane grass and could see the Pacific Ocean off in the distance. The land, as co-founder Ann Gornik once lightheartedly informed me, like "all of the land around here, was under ownership by the Lyman family, the same people who own the Lyman Museum in Hilo."[20] Polestar's main community house and meditation temple were built upon this subdivided, formerly Lyman-owned land, both today overlooking the Pacific Ocean.

The community's presence in Puna indeed has its roots in the 1848 great *Māhele* ("divide"), an archipelago-wide "legal" event wherein Calvinist missionaries from the United States privatized Hawaiian land in order to displace the longstanding communal land management system (*ahupua'a*), effectively taking the land from the native Hawaiians who had lived in areas like Puna for centuries. As a result, a number of foreigners came to own large swaths of land throughout the Hawaiian archipelago. Among these foreigners, the Lyman and Shipman missionary families acquired significant acreage on the East side of Hawaii's Big Island including, for our purposes here, in the Puna District. The intentional communities spotting the landscape in Puna today are not generally concerned about the politics of space or the fact that the land that they occupy in Puna is native Hawaiian land.

Puna ("well-spring"), one of nine districts in Hawaii County (i.e., Hawaii's Big Island), is a rather unique area on the southernmost island in the Hawaiian archipelago (see Figure 2.1). Situated just East of Hawaii Volcanoes National Park and the active Kilauea volcano, Puna lies in several zones designated as prone to eruption and has, over the centuries, received ongoing flows of lava. During one flow in 2014, the district's main town of Pahoa was evacuated but spared at the last moment when the lava decided to stop its destructive march. As a half-mile-wide river of lava made its way to the island's eastern tip during the devastating 2018 lava flow which began as I was writing this chapter, a large section of Puna's southeastern land area, including the community of Polestar Gardens, was forced to evacuate to other parts of the island.

According to an 1884 census, the Puna demographic was still comprised of 95 percent native Hawaiians living at subsistence level as the volcanic land showed little use for foreign investors interested in agriculture and ranching projects (Matsuoka et al. 1996: 19). However, after the United States seized

Figure 2.1 Map of Hawaii's Big Island (left) and the Puna District (highlighted region), as well as its place among all of the Hawaiian Islands (upper right).

Source: Public Domain.

Hawaii in 1898, a sugar cane industry, coffee plantations, and logging and lumber trade were profitably established in the area. Since the fallout of these industries culminating with the closing of the Puna Sugar Company in 1984 (Campbell and Ogburn 1992), Puna and its neighboring Ka'u and Hilo districts have become the most impoverished areas on the Big Island, and among the most impoverished in the state (Healthcare Association of Hawaii 2015). Along with Puna's poverty, the local population is also challenged by drug and alcohol addiction, domestic abuse, high crime rates, and public health issues (Affonso et al. 2007; Consillio 2018). Underscoring the severity of Puna's socioeconomic situation, a 2015 study conducted by the Healthcare Association of Hawaii (HAH) determined the Puna District to be second among its four *statewide* "Highly Impacted Populations" with "High Socioeconomic Need" (Healthcare Association of Hawaii 2015: 5). According to the HAH report, "These highly impacted populations tend to experience poorer health status, higher socioeconomic need, and/or cultural and linguistic barriers" (ibid.).

While those who were born and raised in Puna struggle daily with these issues, those more economically privileged who have moved to the district – usually from the mainland United States – to make the island their new home have become, as I was frequently reminded, obsessively concerned with how to "clean up" the homeless, crime, and drug addiction problems in downtown Pahoa, Puna's central hub and main town. Reflecting these concerns a few months after my departure, a forum titled "Concerned with all of the Front Page Puna Crime Stories? 2018 Community Forum on Crime and Drug Abuse in Puna" was held by state political representatives in the Pahoa community center in the downtown area (Damon Tucker 2017).

In downtown Pahoa, one transparently encounters these two main overlapping social landscapes of Puna which combine to create, to borrow two terms from Hancock and Srinivas, an "*underscape*" subject to "*urban re-fabulation*" at the hands of the mobile American middle class (Hancock and Srinivas 2018: 461–465). A mixture of dilapidated buildings, murals of gods and goddesses, fancy New Age clothing and souvenir stores, expensive restaurants, New Age cafés, cheap Hawaiian fast food, a 7–11 convenience store, a state-run public health clinic, a laundromat, a natural food store, a budget grocery store, and a bar hesitantly coexist (see Figure 2.2). In the fast food joints, 7–11, laundromat, budget grocery store, public health clinic, and bar, one will generally encounter those from the "Highly Impacted Populations" identified in the HAH report who have long called Puna home (Healthcare Association of Hawaii 2015: 5). Meanwhile, in the New Age stores, expensive restaurants, cafés, and natural food store, one can generally expect to meet a predominantly White, middle-class group of mobile, back-to-the-land, self-proclaimed "spiritual but not religious" (SBNR) tourists and transplants from the mainland United States who are very often residing in one of the area's intentional spiritual communities.

Puna's spiritual communities and the SBNRs who inhabit them have their origins in a critical moment in 1958 when the United States declared Hawaii's statehood. At this time, privately held land in Puna owned by missionary families such as the Lymans and Shipmans was subdivided and sold to build

Figure 2.2 Stores on Keaau-Pahoa Road, the main street in downtown Pahoa. Top left: Island Naturals health food store. Top right: "Pahoa Museum" featuring a café and souvenir shop. Bottom Left: "Black Rock," Pahoa's bar behind which is the local laundromat. At the back of the picture with a red roof is "L & L Hawaiian Barbecue," a fast food restaurant. Across the street from these establishments and not pictured is 7–11. Bottom Right: "Pele's Kitchen" (first store on left with hanging sign) organic restaurant.

Source: Author.

suburban communities in reach of the nearest city, Hilo, which was only a short drive away. A number of subdivisions arose during this time period, some of the earliest of which were "Tropic Estates," "Hawaiian Acres," and "Royal Acres." In the 1960s, a development known as "Royal Gardens" promoted its development project in the Kalapana area in Puna as follows:

> Along the southern shores of the Big Island, Hawaii, largest of the Hawaiian chain lies the historic and legendary lands of Kalapana. This site is the setting for Royal Gardens, a fertile area directly adjacent to the Hawai'i Volcano National Park with its spectacular attractions, yet only walking distance away from lovely beach and shore areas. Royal Gardens lots are all one acre in size, making it possible for the owners to have a small orchard or truck garden, or a magnificent garden, as well as a home and a haven for retirement.
>
> (Cooper and Daws 1985: 262)

With the volcano nearby, parcels were cheap and yet they offered those who could afford them a chance to live "off the grid" in paradise. Risk was always part of the deal, however, and the last remaining home in the Royal Gardens subdivision was consumed by lava in March 2012, while the wider Kalapana area, a once-beautiful beach and surfer's paradise, was dramatically transformed by the volcanic flow that began in 1983 (Zennie 2012). As surfers and former residents will often remark, the Kalapana landscape today remains only a tiny fraction of its former self. And as the volcano continues to dramatically transform the landscape amidst the active lava flow that is occurring during the writing of this chapter, Puna's future as a residential area and spiritual tourist destination remains uncertain.

Like the founding of Yoga Anand Ashram in Chapter 1, the 1960s suburbanization of Puna coincided with what Wallace identified more generally as a "Period of Revitalization" wherein we see a "deliberate, organized, conscious effort by members of a society to construct a more satisfying culture" (Wallace 1956: 265). During one such period in the late 1960s and early 1970s, the United States witnessed an explosion in the development of intentional communities, including Ananda Village in California (Love Brown 2002), and Hawaii was a particularly fertile place for such development. Well-known spiritual communes were established, including Taylor Camp (est. 1969 on Kauai), The Source Family (est. 1973 on Maui), Kauai's Hindu Monastery (est. 1970 on Kauai), and in the Puna District, Kalani Honua (est. 1975). Concurrent with the development of these and many other intentional communities, Hawaii, Eastern religion, and yoga became fused together in popular culture as surfing legend Gerry Lopez and friends were often depicted in popular media meditating in lotus posture with surfboards in the background just before catching the next big wave at the North Shore's Bonzai Pipeline. Under such popular cultural influences, a large influx of retirees, ex-military personnel, counterculturalists, and others seeking solace from life on the American mainland began to make their way to Puna's affordable subdivisions so that they too could imaginatively live in harmony with nature (Matsuoka et al. 1996: 64). During this time, those seeking to create New Age, back-to-the-land intentional communities in paradise also purchased large parcels of agricultural land in the Puna area.

The district's Hawaiian name, Puna, or "well-spring," reflects the area's geographical capacity to attract abundant rainfall that recharges the entire island's water table (ibid.: 33). Situated in one of the state's wettest geographical regions, Puna's rainfall provides abundant year-round water supply that is harvested in private household catchment tanks and private community reservoirs to support local farming and off-grid natural living (University of Hawai'i at Mānoa 2011). Combined with increasingly accessible solar energy harvesting technology installed throughout the area, the more affluent among Puna's residents and intentional communities can afford to live the "simple life" that has for long remained part of the wider American dream (cf. Shi 2007) and was also a key feature of Yogananda's call for "simple living and high thinking," the inspiration for which he took from William Wordsworth (Miller 2020a). By the mid-1990s, approximately 200,000 of Puna's 320,000 acres remained zoned for agriculture, though only 50,000 were used for such purposes and the land has since been further subdivided for the sale of more residential parcels (Matsuoka et al. 1996: 65). The ongoing subdivision of land has led to what one scholar has deemed the complete gentrification of Puna (Ivester 2010), an undeniable material reality which has enabled the establishment of the prominent "White Utopias," to borrow a fitting term from Lucia, which persist there into the present (Lucia 2020).

For whatever personal reasons people decide to visit Puna, most SBNRs who come to the area do so on account of the area being a "healing," "spiritual," and "magical" place where they can get back in touch with nature, live more sustainably, and experiment with alternative ways of living and relating to others within intentional community settings. A long-time member of the Polestar community summed up the attraction of Puna quite succinctly when he said, "the draw of this area is its cheap land, abundant water, sunshine, the world's cleanest air, and its openness to higher levels of consciousness."[21] For these and other similar reasons, mobile, middle-class visitors come to Puna – and Polestar in particular – for months, perhaps stay for years, while some never leave. A principal draw of Polestar in particular is its *kīrtan* music, which unfailingly draws participants to the tropical island community from near and far. Polestar's participatory *kīrtan* is indeed well known in the Puna area and a favorite (if not *the* favorite) activity among its residents and visitors alike.

Kīrtan at Polestar Gardens: Harmoniums and Ukuleles Transport us to the Internal Sound

It is 8 AM on a sunny Hawaiian April morning, and members and participants of the Polestar Gardens community have just finished their breakfast and are scrambling to find a seat in the community house's meeting space.[22] Folding chairs, recliners, couches, and stools form a large circle for approximately 30 participants, some old, some young, and many from international destinations all over the world. As is typical, as the group settles in, Jack Roberts, the community's maintenance manager, plays an upbeat, happy Hawaiian song on the ukulele and everyone starts to sing along:

E malama i ka he-i'au
E malama i ka he-i'au
E malama pono i ka he-i'au
Ehh (2x)
Earth and Sky
Sea and stone
Hold this land in sacredness

When the song concludes, everyone shares a moment of laughter, interrupted a few seconds later by Michael Gornik, the community's co-founder, who interjects, "OK, let's calm down and sing a *sāttvik* song now." Following Yogananda's basic yoga philosophy, Michael is suggesting here, as he often did, that the first song was *rājasik* (passionate, active, and energizing; Sanskrit:

rājasika) and that it is now necessary to play a *sāttvik* (light, uplifting, and calming; Sanskrit: *sāttvika*) song more conducive to meditation. The laughter quickly dissipates and the group tangibly shifts into a mood of devotion. With guitar in hand, Michael leads the community into one of Yogananda's songs:

I am the sky, Mother
I am the sky
I am the sky, Mother
I am the sky
I am the vast blue ocean of sky
I am a little drop of the sky
Frozen sky[23]

After several minutes, the song ends in a long silence as participants close their eyes in quiet meditation, broken minutes later when the community's Intern Intake Coordinator and hobby-musician Lauren Quinn officially starts the morning meeting by sharing an article she read on the internet: "So I read this really cool article this morning about music's capacity to harmonize our heartbeats and at the same time our community. There is scientific evidence that our inner and outer environments are harmonizing when we sing together!"[24] A passionate discussion ensues as participants share their experiences with the power of sacred music.

Before this daily morning meeting, Polestar's daily schedule begins at 6 AM at which time the entire community is expected to assemble on the back lawn of the property overlooking the Pacific Ocean. As participants congregate and observe the rising morning sun one April morning,[25] they are told by the morning leader – on this particular day Michael Gornik – to shut their eyes, repeat a prayer, and complete Yogananda's "Energization Exercises." For 15 minutes, breath and bodily movements are coordinated using 39 calisthenic exercises in total. Following the yoga teachings Yogananda brought to the United States in the early 1920s, the Energization Exercises mark the preliminary stage in his four-part *rāja-yoga* system.

Following the completion of the Energization Exercises, the community collectively gathers in Polestar's meditation temple. It is here that participants undertake their first sacred music practice each day, and today Michael starts by playing a song on his harmonium:

I am a bubble, make me the sea, (2X)
So do Thou my Lord, (2X)
Thou and I, never apart, (2X)
Wave of the sea, dissolve in the sea, (2X)
I am the bubble, make me the sea, (2X)
Make me the sea, oh, make me the sea, (2X)
Wave of the sea, dissolve in the sea (2X)

The community sings this tune together for a few minutes as bodies move to and fro and – in some cases – tears flow. Michael eventually slows the pace down, bringing the group into silence. Following a brief prayer, he commences an additional devotional song with his harmonium:

I have made Thee Polestar of my life (2X)
Though my sea is dark, and my stars are gone (2X)
Still I see the path through Thy mercy (2X)

After several minutes of this second song, Michael gently directs the group to, "Take the sound and emotions of your devotional chanting deep into your meditation," next adding the epiclesis,[26] "Reveal thyself, oh Lord, Reveal thyself to us in our meditation," eventually leaving the group in silence. The group then begins a silent 45-minute meditation.

Participants commence their individual meditation practice using the "Hong Sau" technique, the second stage in Yogananda's *rāja-yoga.* "Hong Sau" is Yogananda's Anglicized version of the "*haṃsa*" mantra, a breathing technique achieved by inhaling as one internally chants "hong" (i.e., *haṃ*) and exhaling as one internally chants "sau" (i.e., *sa*). In doing so, individuals pneumatically reaffirm the ontological unity between their own higher Self (*ātman*) and the Absolute (*brahman*). Following Hong Sau practice, participants possessing advanced training begin Yogananda's "Aum Technique," marking the third stage of Yogananda's *rāja-yoga.* Here, both elbows are placed in a rested position on an "Aum Board" in order that the hands can cover the ears and eyes and one can listen carefully for the internal sound of "*aum*".

Following a month of practicing the Energization Exercises and the Hong Sau technique, a member of the community invited me to start this practice. Like other participants, I covered my ears, mouth, nostrils, and eyes with my fingers and thumbs using what is called *yoni mudrā* (womb seal) or *jyoti mudrā* (light seal), silently sitting and listening for signs of the *auṃ* sound inside of me. As I continued to listen, those participants who were initiated into the practice of *kriyā-yoga* undertook the fourth stage in Yogananda's *rāja-yoga,* aiming to unite with the internal sound while raising the *kuṇḍalinī* from the base of their spine and into their cranial vault.[27]

Not initiated, I continued to practice the Aum Technique for some time, listening carefully for the internal sound. After what seemed like only a short period of time (the meditation had lasted for 45 minutes), my practice ended as the sound of the harmonium steadily entered my awareness. Shortly thereafter, Michael chanted three long, drawn out *auṃ* chants followed by three "Amens":

Auuuuuuum, Auuuuuuum, Auuuuuuum,
Aaaaaa-men, Aaaaaa-men, Aaaaaa-men.

He then guided us as we sent out healing prayers and the meditation session ended with three roaring group *auṃ* chants:

Auuuuuuum, Auuuuuuum, Auuuuuuum.

Participants undertake the devotional music and meditation practices described here three times every day, using either the harmonium or the ukulele to initiate their practice. Morning and evening sessions are initiated by

Energization Exercises, while a 30-minute meditation prior to lunch only involves chanting and sitting meditation.

Weekly Public Kīrtan at Polestar Gardens

In addition to the community's daily music practice used in meditation sessions, Polestar also hosts a weekly public *kīrtan* every Wednesday evening. During this popular event, Puna's predominantly White SBNRs assemble with Polestar in the community temple to collectively chant and sing sacred music. This weekly event is structured like the aforementioned meditation session, though less time is given to meditation and more is reserved for singing.

One particular *kīrtan* hosted in May 2017 gives us a sense of the typical flow of activities at each weekly event.[28] After practicing the Energization Exercises on Polestar's front lawn, community members and visitors silently enter the temple together for a short meditation. Soon thereafter, Michael's harmonium breaks the silence, which is then followed by a series of three *auṃ* chants. Along with the harmonium, several other instruments enter the soundscape including simple percussion, an auto-harp, and, most prominently and frequently, the community's popular ukulele. During this particular week, Jack Roberts, Polestar's maintenance manager, plays the ukulele while another long-time member of the community, Charlotte Hamilton, adds some simple percussion. A friend of the community who often visits for the event has brought her violin this week and eventually joins the ensemble.

After the initial chanting of "*auṃ*," Jack, Charlotte, and Michael encourage the group to start the evening's first community chant, "O God Beautiful," the same song Yogananda sang at Carnegie Hall in 1926. Another member of the community, David Zuhars, projects the song lyrics onto the wall above the *kīrtan* leaders for all to follow along:

O God beautiful, O God beautiful, (2X)
At Thy feet, oh, I do bow! (2x)
O God beautiful, O God beautiful, (2x)
In the forest Thou art green; (2x)
In the mountain Thou art high; (2x)
In the river Thou art restless; (2x)
In the ocean Thou art grave. (2x)
O God beautiful, O God beautiful, (2x)
At Thy feet, O I do bow! (2x)
O God beautiful, O God beautiful, (2x)
To the serviceful Thou art service; (2x)
To the lover Thou art love; (2x)
To the sorrowful Thou art sympathy; (2x)
To the yogi Thou art bliss (2x)

A brief silence intervenes between every song of the evening as the group sings "Jai Ma Durga," followed by "God of Beauty," moving then into "Om Kali," and finally "Jai Guru Omkara" over the course of the next 45 minutes.[29] Each of these songs contain what Srinivas, who is drawing from sociolinguistics, has referred to as "code-blending" as a form of lyrical and musical multilingualism. That is to say, English lyrics are paired to Indian melodies, or alternatively Indian language utterances (here Sanskrit) are paired to Euro-American tunes (Srinivas 2008: 309).

With each successive song, the emotionality in the room increases. Participants' bodies start to sway to and fro as the voices and music become increasingly louder and involved in the singing. A local male architect and prominent weekly participant is in his usual position up front in the center of the room in an upright position on his meditation pillow. His singing transforms into what starts to sound like rapturous shouting. Other group participants seated in chairs around him follow his cue as some laugh and others cry uncontrollably.

At almost the same moment each week, the singing stops and Michael directs all who are present to bring all of the sounds and emotions inward for meditation just as he does during the community's daily meditations. After what was a rather dramatic episode of sonic catharsis, the group observes 15 minutes of silent meditation. During this period of silence, a more docile ambiance begins to fill the room. The session is brought to an end with one final, relatively subdued performance of a song titled, "Desire, My Great Enemy."[30] As the *kīrtan* finishes, all begin to slowly exit the temple and enter Polestar's main house where they enjoy socializing and a potluck vegetarian dinner.

The Harmonium's Unexpected Accompaniment: Madeira's Machete, a.k.a. the Ukulele

Yogananda's beloved harmonium, as we have seen, is a mainstay in Polestar's ongoing *kīrtan* practice. While this instrument has also become definitive of contemporary *kīrtan* practice, I was surprised to find that not all community members and participants expressed the same ideas about it when I asked them how they experience it in their meditation practice. For example, while speaking with a woman who was a community intern one day, she half-jokingly replied, referring to the drone sound of the instrument, that, "The harmonium sounds like a ghost and it makes it feel like the meditation temple is haunted sometimes!"[31] On another occasion a couple of months later, a male resident community member told me in confidence, "It is too *rājasik* for me and I can't stand when it always sounds like they are banging on the harmonium."[32] Many others privately expressed ambivalence toward the instrument, suggesting that the harmonium has in fact retained its ambiguous and multivalent social character into the present. Many others including myself, of course, found the harmonium delightful.

In addition to the harmonium, I frequently encountered the ukulele, as we have here on multiple occasions, accompanying Yogananda's musical practices in both formal and informal settings. The ukulele's acceptance at Polestar arises, no doubt, on account of the fact that it is popularly understood to produce an entertaining and traditional Hawaiian Island sound. But while I was not surprised to encounter the harmonium, I was surprised that the seemingly paradigmatic Hawaiian ukulele was being used for something beyond entertainment, often serving as the musical bridge into the community's meditation practice.

As I would discover later, however, the ukulele is an instrument that has found its meaning redefined and renewed in a variety of social contexts, much like the harmonium, and is therefore quite suited to join Polestar's *kīrtan* ensemble. Furthermore, Yogananda's universal directive to use audible sacred music of any kind as the bridge to meditate upon the unstruck, internal sound (*anāhata-nāda*) turned out to be the seamless conceptual juncture where the sound of tropical Island nostalgia produced by the ukulele could effortlessly combine with his *kriyā-yoga* system. In other words, if the harmonium could produce the necessary effects to prepare one for meditation, why not the ukulele?

The effectiveness of the ukulele also depended, of course, on whether it was being used for fun (*rājasik*, as Michael described it), which, as we saw in the morning meeting, was often the case. And indeed, in a number of routine circumstances the ukulele found itself at the center of play and entertainment. During the community's annual Sacred Music Festival, for example, we were all sitting in a circle out on the lawn when community member Jack started playing the ukulele to slowly cajole the group into singing playful Hawaiian songs. Everyone joined into the singing, which was very entertaining amidst the ocean breeze, sun, and the spectacular view of the Pacific. One of the community's interns even leaned over to me and said, "now that's how you play the ukulele, in the sun and for fun in Hawaii!"[33]

Although the small, guitar-shaped ukulele is apparently Hawaiian and made for fun in the sun, its rich history as an instrument of European origins and its subsequent colonial encounters have, like the harmonium, been mostly forgotten. The ukulele's social history in fact begins on the colonized British tropical island of Madeira (off the Moroccan coast, first colonized by the Portuguese and then later returned to them by the British) from which it eventually made its long voyage to the colonized American tropical island of Hawaii. Though popularly understood to be the paradigmatic tropical instrument of the Hawaiian Islands, it arrived to Hawaii in 1879 in the hands of sugar cane contract workers fleeing food shortages in Madeira. These contract workers called the compact four-stringed instrument resembling a small guitar the "machete" (Tranquada and King 2012: 2–6, 18). The exact origins of the machete are unknown, though some suggest that it was brought to Madeira from Portugal in the fifteenth century and may indeed be a descendant of a guitar from Renaissance Europe (ibid.: 10–11). Eventually arriving to the islands, the machete entered into the broader colonial history of Hawaiian music.

When White American Christian missionaries encountered Hawaiian music, their reaction was in many ways comparable to the British civilizing attitude in India that sought to reform or erase what were considered to be "primitive" indigenous cultural practices. From the missionary perspective, Hawaiian music and its associated hula were "connected with idolatry and licentiousness, and wholly incompatible with Christianity" (ibid.: 20, 23). It was not until after the United States took Hawaii from its native inhabitants that Hawaiian music became not only tolerable, but in fact "a powerful form of marketing for the Islands" for the White men who sought to sell a tropical experience to White tourists on the mainland (ibid.: 72). The machete performed an important role in this colonial project, and along with the guitar reified "Americans' view of Hawaiians as sensuous savages" (ibid.: 78).

Due to its portability and easy tuning, the machete, like the harmonium, was a convenient instrument for Madeiran travelers to take to Hawaii (ibid.: 27, 46–47). Machetes were also easy to construct, and it was Madeiran cabinet makers in Hawaii who became the first to build and sell them in consumable quantities (ibid.: 38). The machete likely first took the Hawaiian name "pila liilii" ("little fiddle") but eventually became known as the "ukulele" (ibid.: 43). The name ukulele was itself a preexisting Hawaiian word that came to mean "bouncing flea" (first used to describe the cat flea that had come to the islands on European ships in the nineteenth century) to refer to how, as musician Ernest Kaai once wrote, "Hawaiians have a way of playing all over the strings at the same time, strumming and skipping their fingers from one side of the instrument to the other" (Ernest Kaai as cited in Tranquada and King 2012: 41–43).

As Tranquada and King emphasize, "… by the turn of the [nineteenth] century the name 'ukulele' had taken firm hold – as had the instrument itself on the musical culture of the Islands… Just as quickly, the ukulele became an indispensable element of island iconography" (Tranquada and King 2012: 45). In this regard, the ukulele was appropriated as a key object in the construction of native Hawaiian cultural identity and political discourse in the late nineteenth century, providing the main accompaniment for the newly emerging genre of music known as "hula kui" (ibid.: 52). Not long after, the sound of the ukulele was also marketed to the American middle class to mediate the sound of a tropical vacation paradise, sometimes by a number of racially exoticized bands performing on the American mainland (ibid.: 76, 80).[34] The instrument eventually ended up back in Europe – albeit as a fully transformed social object – by way of World War I's traveling soldiers, and by the 1950s the ukulele was gradually adopted into more culturally diverse ensembles including for Jazz and Latin music (ibid.: 108, 149).

In sum, like the harmonium, the ukulele has today become many (often contradictory) things to many people, "operating on several different levels simultaneously" (ibid.: 166). Tranquada and King, whose fascinating and comprehensive social history of the ukulele I have drawn upon here extensively, conclude that the ukulele is,

> An instantly recognizable symbol of Hawaii, a promise of an island paradise, a tourist souvenir, an instrument central to a rich and celebrated

> musical culture, a tool of political protest, a highly sought-after collectible, a remarkable synthesis of Western and Pacific cultures, the butt of jokes – the ukulele is all these things.
>
> (ibid.)

This small "jumping flea," brought to Hawaii from Madeira, used in both nationalist struggles against racist Americans and Europeans but then for entertaining their White middle-class desires for the exotic, now fittingly finds itself alongside the harmonium as one of the primary tools for achieving the meditative goal of Yogananda's *kriyā-yoga* meditation at Polestar. Putting the ukulele to such a task may seem like a curious and perhaps even questionable undertaking. But for ethnomusicologists and those writing about contemporary sacred musical practices more broadly, Polestar's new ensemble addition represents yet another cultural transformation enabled by the community's flexible musicology as well as the ukulele's protean social history.[35] In total, the ukulele is simultaneously Hawaiian, tropical, entertaining, relaxing, exotic, and now also a bridge to *kriyā-yoga*'s internal, unstruck sound.

Polestar's Sacred Music Festival: Contextualizing and Debating "Universal" Sacred Sound

In addition to daily and weekly devotional music events, the ukulele joins the harmonium and many other instruments when Polestar hosts its annual Sacred Music Festival to celebrate the universality of sacred world music (see Figure 2.3). For ten days, the entire community journeys around the Big Island and the immediate Puna district in order to provide *kīrtan* performances in private and public locations. The climax of the festival takes place in the "Maha Kirtan," a six-hour event during which guests from around the Big Island are joined by international visitors in Polestar's Community Center. A day before the performance, Michael Gornik explains Polestar's vision for the Sacred Music Festival and the Maha Kirtan to his audience at one of the preliminary events:

> You're probably aware of all that research they've done about people who sing together? In a very short period of time heartbeats sync up, breath rates sync up. It's a wonderful way to have a visceral experience of our connection with each other and with the divine that is flowing through us and all around us all the time… Our Maha Kirtan… the concept of this celebration is that music is a universal language. It's a way we can all remember our connections. You see throughout the world all of these well-developed approaches to spirit, to the divine through sacred music. We are trying to celebrate, appreciate, and tune into all the different expressions from various paths, various traditions and thereby appreciate and empathize with and understand our humanity more fully.[36]

Figure 2.3 Scenes from Polestar's annual Sacred Music Festival. Top Left: Members of a hula group, most White retired transplants from the United States mainland, perform a hula and Hawaiian chant in Polestar's temple. Top Right: "Maha Kirtan" stage. To the right of the stage we also see the altar, featuring gurus from a number of traditions, as well as Pele, the volcano goddess, atop them all. Bottom Left: Polestar musicians prepare for *kīrtan* in Kalani Honua's EMAX performing arts center. Bottom Right: Opening *kīrtan* of Sacred Music Festival at Beach 69 in Kona.

Source: Author.

While universalizing statements like these are not attuned to the cultural specificities of much of transnational *kīrtan* practice, they also clearly show us Michael's commitment to Yogananda's musicological understanding that all sacred world music is a "universal language" that can serve as a pathway to the sacred. Furthermore, the notions of human interconnectedness, clearly influenced by the article Lauren Quinn had mentioned in the morning meeting regarding music's capability to biologically harmonize communities that regularly sing together, reveal sacred music's *biocultural* capacity to induce psychosomatic experience that nevertheless also plays an important role in maintaining social order.

During the Maha Kirtan on the following day, each of the features of Michael's theory of universal sacred music coalesced. At the event, participants and musicians assembled around the stage on the Polestar property where they shared six hours of devotional music. First, Polestar's musicians led the group through 108 repetitions of the Gayatri Mantra which included an interchange between the harmonium and ukulele, followed then by 2 local *kīrtan* performers, Robinette and Aim, who took to the stage to lead participants through several Sanskrit call and response chants such as the popular mantras "Aum Nama Shivaya" and ISKCON's "Hare Krishna." As the crowd grew, the volume of the voices and music followed, eventually culminating in a performance by the popular "Unity and the Band of Angels." Unity, a woman from Vietnam, played sacred songs from international locales for a few hours using a variety of stringed instruments. During the entire event, audience members danced ecstatically, some sang along or responded to basic lyrics in a variety of foreign languages, whereas some others meditated at a decorated altar containing a picture of Yogananda, Hindu goddesses and gods, portraits of several gurus, and a picture of the well-known resident volcano goddess, Pele. Following close to six hours of singing and chanting, the music slowly wound down and the Maha Kirtan was brought to an end with participants being led into a silent meditation lasting until 9 PM.

Both the Maha Kirtan and the Sacred Music Festival more broadly assert Polestar as a significant musical meditation community within the Big Island spiritual landscape. Many individuals who meet the community at the festival are encouraged to partake in Polestar's weekly *kīrtan* where they learn more about Yogananda's devotional music and meditation practices. Many of these people are then inspired to join in Polestar's daily *kīrtan* and meditation, where the community offers a supportive atmosphere for developing ongoing awareness of the relationship between what Yogananda referred to as effortful and joyful "chanting aloud" and effortless "superconscious chanting" achieved through concentration on the internal sound (Yogananda 1974 [1938]: xi).

Not all who practiced *kīrtan* in the community or at the Sacred Music Festival understood or adhered to Yogananda's theology of internal sound, of course, and described instead their own experiences and interpretations of the practice from their own spiritual perspectives. The day after one of the weekly community *kīrtans*, for example, one long-term community participant who was not initiated in *kriyā-yoga* named Vivian said that "It was amazing! I felt my *kuṇḍalinī* rising and after I had to go sit by myself blissed out and watch the sunset. I couldn't be around the crowd at the potluck after, I just had to go enjoy it by myself."[37] Similarly and on another occasion, a guest named Rachael visiting from Oregon shared during a morning circle, "I saw my *kuṇḍalinī* spiral upward and out of my head!"[38] Finally, during the community potluck after *kīrtan* one week, a guest named Jesse, who frequently visited the community from the mainland, said to me, "All the singing brings us to an elevated state and then we bring that down into our little embodied lives and try to live it out, however imperfectly."[39] Theological and experiential commitments thus varied, depending on who one spoke with, and were often divergent from the predominant discourse espoused by Polestar's primary *kriyā-yoga* disseminators.

Jesse's interpretations here fell closest to one of the other predominant internal community discourses surrounding the purpose of *kīrtan* and meditation which indicated the importance of using the practice to overcome difficult emotions in the intentional community environment. During the six months that I lived and worked at Polestar in 2017, I certainly experienced the "harmonizing," psychophysiological benefits of communal singing frequently attested to by community voices, an experience I can only describe as relaxing and tranquilizing. And while there were certainly plenty of opportunities for conflict, Michael Gornik's ongoing directive to take emotionality into meditation after cathartic *kīrtan* sessions along with his concurrent teaching of Yogananda's prescription to develop an ongoing disposition of imperturbability (*titikṣā*) in weekly philosophy discussion sessions resulted in a carefully scheduled cycle for emotional regulation.

While discussing the community's challenges with dealing with internal conflict, a long-term resident once admitted to me in confidence that they were indeed "not good at dealing with negative communication, emotions, or conflict." Instead of worrying about it, she said, "Whenever we experience conflict we should all go in the temple and meditate and take the experience inward."[40] In another conversation, the community's permaculturalist similarly conveyed to me a widely held community opinion indicating that she and others found relief from such issues through singing and meditation, simply stating, "Since we can't do drugs here, we sing and meditate!"[41] Polestar was by policy drug-free, intending to demonstrate to members and visitors alike how meditation can serve as an alternative practice for emotional wellness.

On several occasions during my stay at Polestar Gardens, interns who began to express behaviors deviating from community norms were reprimanded because they were in fact not attending the community's daily chanting and meditation sessions. "I just got reprimanded," an intern told me in confidence one day. "For what?," I asked, to which she replied, "For not going to meditation."[42] I was actually not surprised to receive this news from this intern, as I had noticed (and written in my journal) in the days preceding our conversation that she had been slacking in her assigned tasks, leaving community work early, and had a very poor emotional disposition overall. Thus, while the reasons for reprimanding such community participants for not showing up to meditation were for the spiritual benefit of the participants, it was clear that these reprimands were also intended to indirectly point out that their arising emotional issues were a direct result of their absence from the community's calming daily meditation and chanting sessions.

While chanting and meditation certainly aided emotional regulation in the community, an email I received at the very end of my stay from Ann Gornik about another one of the interns who was in a similar situation reflected the community's actual prioritization of chanting and meditation over community work:

> [Anonymous intern] meditated with us regularly in the beginning but it seem[ed] to fall off a little as time went on. To us, energizing and meditating together are the most important things we do here at Polestar. It's

> why we do Polestar… So often the conversation is "I work so hard that I'm exhausted and don't have the energy to meditate"… we would so much rather have the conversation be "because I am meditating all the time, I'm not quite having time to get all my hours in."[43]

We can see here that community chanting and meditation are not merely tools for emotional regulation, but the community's *top* priority, and a welcome distraction from community work.

Therefore, while existing academic literature variously suggests how the practice of *kīrtan* produces a sense of *communitas* (Turner 1967: 29), "collective effervescence" (Durkheim 1964 [1915]: 218; Kapchan 2008; Wilke and Moebus 2011; Brown 2014) or an emotional sonic body among participants (Lorea 2023; cf. Henriques 2011), I would like to offer two other ways of interpreting the purpose of these musical practices.[44] That is to say, in the intentional community setting at Polestar, *kīrtan* plays a particularly critical role in aiding community members and participants in the regulation of their emotional challenges that naturally arise when living and working in such close quarters on an ongoing basis. But also, following Yogananda's musicological assumptions, *kīrtan* is intended to lead some willing participants toward a meditative experience of an internal, unstruck sound that allows them to momentarily transcend these very real challenges altogether.

Conclusion: Yogananda's Multilingualism and the Yogic Specificity of Universal Sacred Music

The late P.B. Pandit (1923–1975), a respected scholar of sociolinguistics, challenged Western notions which suggested that monolingualism and linguistic homogeneity ought to be the normal and proper condition of humanity. Rather than interpreting linguistic difference as an obstacle to effective communication, he suggested that multilingualism was a *precondition* for a form of unity in diversity – a higher, pluralistic linguistic unity that was counter to Western imperialist projects aimed at cultural homogeneity and dominance (Uberoi and Uberoi 1976: 638–639). According to Pandit, language maintains difference in multilingual and bilingual settings while productively developing new expressions through ongoing acts of negotiation during acts of communication (Pandit 1969: 114). Reflecting on the legacy of Pandit's work, Uberoi and Uberoi write, "The switch from one form of speech to another, like that from one domain of activity or social role to another, is done efficiently and smoothly for the simple reason that all is in the service of a higher unity" (Uberoi and Uberoi 1976: 642). Central to Pandit's theory is the observation that during the act of what linguists refer to as "code-switching," or changing from one language to another during a speech act, creativity is enabled and effective cross-cultural communication is accomplished while neither party loses their unique linguistic and cultural independence. And even more, something novel and useful for both parties emerges from such forms of multilingual communication.

Being from South Asia, Yogananda was no doubt accustomed to a multilingual culture and the ongoing negotiations such a social environment required. Furthermore, his training in Christian theology in college had supplied him with the requisite knowledge to be able to negotiate the United States' racist, White, and Protestant social landscape in creative ways (Williamson 2010). Thus, as I bring this chapter to a close, I would like to suggest that Yogananda's musical practices both in the early twentieth-century United States and at Polestar Gardens today constitute a form of musical multilingualism. This multilingualism constitutes Yogananda's "ability to use two or more languages with different degrees of proficiency and in various contexts" (Srinivas 2008: 308), which he accomplished through his creative adaptations of lyrics, music, and ensembles.

In making this suggestion, I draw from the earlier work of Srinivas, who has already suggested that Yogananda's collection of music in *Cosmic Chants* (Yogananda 1974 [1938]) set an early precedent for a transnational "guru language" (Srinivas 2008: 313). Borrowing from sociolinguistic theory, Srinivas demonstrates how Yogananda's *Cosmic Chants* deployed not only "code-switching" but also "code-blending" (ibid.: 309) to effectively communicate with an American audience much in the same way that other religious traditions have historically done so in South Asia (ibid.: 313–314).[45] Srinivas defines "code-blending" as the occasion,

> ...when the tune of one composition is paired with the words of a different clearly recognizable composition, when Indian melodies are paired with English-language utterances, or when Euro-American tunes are paired with Indian-language utterances.
>
> (ibid.: 309)

Yogananda's popular chant "O God Beautiful," a Sikh chant translated into English that is as popular today among his devotees as it was among early twentieth-century Americans, is one among the types of musical compositions to which Srinivas refers.[46] Following something akin to his contemporary Rabindranath Tagore's internationalist ambition for mature Indian minds to assimilate other cultures into one's own home culture (van der Linden 2013: 128), Yogananda's "guru language," mediated through his musical multilingualism, communicated the soteriological promise of his *kriyā-yoga* tradition to soul-seeking Americans with lyrics and ensembles they could welcome and appreciate.[47] The transnational, Christian-European derived harmonium played with the Anglicized and simple Sanskrit lyrics of his *Cosmic Chants* met his Western audiences at a crucial sonic juncture, where sacred struck sound (*āhata-nāda*) of any kind could, at least according to the practical and musicological foundations of Yogananda's initiatory *kriyā-yoga* tradition, serve as an appealing bridge to an unstruck, divine sound (*anāhata-nāda*) within.

The ukulele, the harmonium, and the other instruments we saw joining the ensemble at Polestar Gardens augment Yogananda's initial musical offerings to create a soundscape capable of attracting a transnational SBNR audience living in or visiting the Puna area. In this way, Polestar and the guest musicians with whom the community performs have certainly gone beyond Yogananda's own sacred music collection and ensemble, though theoretically without sacrificing their guru's underlying sonic theology and thereby theoretically leading practitioners to *kriyā-yoga*'s unstruck sound.

As we have seen, however, not all community members, visitors, and participants necessarily understood the ukulele, the harmonium, and *kīrtan* practice as conveying such a clear theological message or as primarily useful for meditation or even a spiritual setting. Perhaps that might be because only some of these meditators were initiated into the more secretive practices of *kriyā-yoga*. Thus, in general, lyrical code-blending combined with island instrumentation and the iconic harmonium have created a social setting where multiple interpretations, whether they are theological, psychological, touristic, entertainment-focused, or all of the above and more, can converge.

Finally, it is worth noting that the Polestar community recently decided to sell its Hawaii property on account of, quite sadly, the destruction caused by the 2018 Kilauea volcanic eruption in Puna. They have nevertheless already moved to a new location in Fort Collins, Colorado, where their community continues as "Polestar Village" (polestarvillage.com). The way Polestar's *kīrtan* ensemble will change in Colorado according to their new social environment is yet to be seen, and will be an interesting development to follow. One thing is certain, however, which is that they will definitely be taking their universal *kīrtan* and *kriyā-yoga* practice into new social terrain. So too, apparently, will the ukulele follow. As the community was preparing for the big move, Michael emailed to let me know that within the context of his *kīrtan* practice, "My ukulele has overtaken my harmonium as my favorite instrument which has been really fun for me."[48]

For those wishing to learn to meditate, Polestar Village and the ukulele are waiting for your visit. The community's new location in Fort Collins offers many of the same opportunities to chant, meditate, and perform selfless service amidst a beautiful and clean natural environment. As long as Polestar can manage to avoid nearby Denver's "Brown Cloud" of polluted city air that we encountered in the introduction to this book, leaving Puna's famously clean air behind will not be such a sacrifice. In the chapter that follows, the sacrifice-performing yoga practitioners near Pune, Maharashtra, do not have this same privilege.

Notes

1 Laack defines the role of the scholar of religion undertaking a secular transdisciplinary study of music as follows:

> …claims regarding a divine source of music or the explanation of music's power by reference to its divine quality may be *described* by a secular study and analyzed in their social, cultural and historical context; however, their truth claim should not be discussed in such studies.
>
> (Laack 2015: 231)

In this chapter I draw broadly and liberally from the insights and methods of Ethnomusicology, Musicology, Organology, Sound Studies, and other allied fields in order to study *kīrtan* as "music in culture" (cf. Nettl 2015: 16). I follow some of the most recent trends found in cultural studies of world music which most prominently feature special attention to the categories of materiality, race, religion, well-being, and political economy (Clayton et al. 2012: 10), as well as cultural imperialism, hybridity, and authenticity (Stokes 2012: 108).

2 Laack acknowledges that there was early interest in music in the study of religion that has since evaporated:

> Rudolf Otto (2004) and Gerardus van der Leeuw (1957)… Both authors concluded that music, given its ability to arouse strong, irrational feelings, points toward a reality that is wholly other, but it never manages to capture and express the Numinous. Notwithstanding, it appears that these questions did not appeal to religious scholars following Otto and van der Leeuw.
>
> (Laack 2015: 223)

3 As Wilke and Moebus suggest, "sound is one of the key media of cultural representation and reproduction, and thus a key to Indian culture and to Sanskrit Hinduism in particular" (Wilke and Moebus 2011: 13).

4 For example, Schultz does an excellent job explaining the broader nationalist and political context in contemporary India, though in doing so reveals a "bewildering, contested landscape of Indian nationalism" where *rāṣṭrīya kīrtankārs* nevertheless produce "regional idioms in local contexts" in spite of hegemonic nationalist narratives (Schultz 2013: 4–5). Another example is the work of Rees, who illustrates the creative musical agency of ethnic minority musicians of Dongjing despite their being dominated by the Chinese government in the twentieth century (Rees 2000).

5 Rasmussen has traced, for example, how Islamic music is performed around the Indian Ocean basin, writing, "my discoveries of similarities in musical instruments, styles, and approaches to musical organization around the Indian Ocean have been a productive way to confirm a musical connection between regions that are known to have cultural connections that date back half a millennium" (Rasmussen 2016: 315).

6 See, for example, Bohlman's *The Land Where Two Streams Flow: Music in the German-Jewish Community of Israel* which considers how some German Jewish migrant composers created a new style of music influenced by their new Mediterranean environment in Palestine (Bohlman 1989), as well as Brinkmann and Wolff's *Driven into Paradise: The Musical Migration from Nazi Germany to the United States* regarding how migrant European composers fleeing Nazi Germany and who came to America adapted (and in some cases did not adapt) their music to the new musical landscape (Brinkmann and Wolff 1999). Also of relevance is Turino's *Moving Away from Silence*, which tracks how the panpipe moves from the rural Andes into the city of Peru where it becomes an imagined musical symbol of cultural identity for the urban middle class (Turino 1999), as well as Turino's *Nationalists, Cosmopolitans, and Popular Music in Zimbabwe* where the indigenous music produced on the guitar takes center stage in youth-driven, cosmopolitan African nationalism (Turino 2000). See also Olsen's work on Japanese music in South America (Olsen 2004) and Silverman's study of the global patronization influences on diasporic Balkan "Gypsy" music in *Romani Routes* (Silverman 2012). Perhaps most interesting and relevant for understanding musical change with respect to this chapter are Myers' *Music in Hindu Trinidad: Songs from the Indian Diaspora* (Meyers 1999) and Manuel's *East Indian Music in the West Indies* (Manuel 2000), both of which consider musical continuity, syncretism, and innovation with regard to diasporic Indian music among Afro-Creole cultures in the Caribbean.

7 As Dawe also importantly notes, musical instruments are

> ... sites of meaning construction... embodiments of culturally based belief and value systems, an artistic and scientific legacy, a part of the political economy attuned by, or the outcome of, a range of associated ideas, concepts and practical skills: they are one way in which cultural and social identity (a sense of self in relation to others, making sense of one's place in the order of things) is constructed and maintained... The fact is that a musical instrument is much more than the thing itself.
>
> (Dawe 2012: 195)

8 This is, of course, not the only thing that happened during India's colonial period with the cultural arts. As many scholars have shown, a more nation-facing attitude toward cultural preservation within India – as opposed to sharing Indian culture with the world – was a major project taken up by another large segment of the Indian population. In her study of nationalist *kīrtan* in *Singing a Hindu Nation*, for example, Anna Schultz makes it clear that her "...experience with *rāṣṭrīya kīrtan* suggests a nationalist world beyond middle-class reform that is vast, variegated, and shaped by local leaders who sang for the nation without worrying about whether it was homologous with other nations. They left that up to the cosmopolitan elite" (Schultz 2013: 51). That being said, the nation-facing and global-facing imperatives also often times intersected in interesting and contradictory ways, and continue to do so into the present (cf. Miller 2020b).

9 Other yoga gurus also famously popularized *nām-kīrtan* and other similar forms of sonic devotion in America and around the globe, including ISKCON's A.C. Bhaktivedanta Prabhupada, Sai Baba, and Swami Sivananda.

10 Perhaps foremost among the religious influences with which Yogananda had to contend in the early twentieth century were the American Protestant ethos as well as the proliferation of metaphysical religions. Regarding both of these influences Foxen writes: "The focus on 'miraculous' healing forms a curious point of intersection between American metaphysical and Evangelical spiritual currents" (Foxen 2017: 151).

11 It is also important to note that Yogananda included Jesus as a central guru figure in his yoga lineage, a practice which continues into the present. Doing so provided White Christian Americans some comfort in knowing they would not have to sacrifice their beloved savior.

12 As we will see, Yogananda was not unique in this way. As Wilke and Moebus remind us, among other things, throughout Hindu forms of devotional music, "acoustic piety is very widely spread, comprising religious forms in which the act of recitation itself or the devotional attitude range first, whereas the semantic meaning is not necessarily important or known" (Wilke and Moebus 2011: 12). In other words, in many social settings, sound and devotional intention are what count first, rather than the actual meaning of the devotional lyrics themselves.

13 Note that I am using the term "authentic" in this chapter as an emic term debated among music reformers and traditionalists, and do not wish to suggest that one instrument or form of musical practice is authentic while the other is not. As Lucia shows, "Anxieties over Authenticity" in contemporary yoga cultures have a historically identifiable provenance and are tightly connected with contesting yogic authority (Lucia 2020: 69–98).

14 See, for example, Brown's ethnography of *kīrtan* within Utah's Hare Krishna community, where, "Traditional kirtan, as Hare Krishnas describe it, is commonly accompanied by the harmonium and an array of Indian folk percussion instruments..." (Brown 2014: 459).

15 As Dawe writes regarding the appropriation of instruments, "In general, we consume objects and give them meaning, and in doing so, reproduce them, so to speak, in our own image – we colonize them" (Dawe 2012: 204).

16 More recently, scholars of Sikh music have begun to call into question the harmonium's inclusion in Sikh ensembles (cf. Cassio 2019: 24–25).

17 It is also interesting to note that as India neared independence in 1938, All India Radio forbid the use of the harmonium during broadcasts under the influence of both Indian and non-Indian voices. This ban would remain in place until 1972 when some restrictions were eased, though it was not until 1980 that restrictions were fully lifted (van der Linden 2013: 102–103).
18 Swami Kriyananda was a direct disciple of Yogananda. After being unanimously voted off the board of directors of the Self-Realization Fellowship in 1962, he established Ananda Village a few short years later in 1968. Kriyananda made it his life mission to create "World Brotherhood Colonies," a name coined by Yogananda for intentional spiritual communities he had envisioned as early as 1932 to create communities for "plain living and high thinking." In my experience, the colonies founded in Yogananda's name are not aware of the origins of the phrase "simple/plain living and high thinking," which Yogananda actually adopted from William Wordsworth's romantic notion of "plain living and high thinking" (1802). For more details regarding the founding of World Brotherhood Colonies including both Polestar Gardens and Ananda Village, see: Miller 2020a, where I also discuss Swami Kriyananda's legal woes with the Self-Realization Fellowship and the lawsuits against Kriyananda for rape and assault.
19 Ann Gornik, in discussion with the author, South Kona, Hawaii, June 23, 2017.
20 Ann Gornik, in discussion with the author, Puna, Hawaii, April 10, 2017.
21 James Blackman, in discussion with the author, Puna, Hawaii, April 8, 2017.
22 The events and quotes that follow took place in Puna, Hawaii, April 25, 2017.
23 Both of these songs are recorded on Polestar's music website: http://www.polestarmusic.net/music/.
24 The article to which Lauren Quinn was referring can be read here (Morelle 2013), and reinforces the notion that somatic regimens including those of the yogic variety have distinct biological effects: http://www.bbc.com/news/science-environment-23230411
25 The following musical practices and meditation took place on April 10, 2017.
26 For more on the use of the meta-category of epiclesis in the analysis of contemporary sacred music, see Beck 2012: 24–25.
27 Roughly translated as "the coiled one," "*kuṇḍalinī*" is a Sanskrit term used to describe a female-gendered serpentine goddess energy coiled at the base of the yogic body that can be released or "forced" (*haṭha*, see Birch 2011) up along the spine and through the cranium of the yogic body to produce metaphysical experiences. For a detailed outline of these *kriyā-yoga* practices, see Foxen's *Biography of a Yogi: Paramahansa Yogananda and the Origins of Modern Yoga* (Foxen 2017).
28 This *kīrtan* took place on May 3, 2017.
29 Here are the lyrics corresponding to each song:

"Jai Guru Omkara":
Jai Guru Omkara, Jaya, Jaya, Satguru Omkara (2x)
Bramha, Vishnu, Sadhashiva, Hara Hara Hara Hara Mahadeva (2x)

"God of Beauty":
God of beauty (peace, love, joy) is now reigning
In the temple of my heart (2x)
In my heart, in my heart
In the temple of my heart (2x)

"Om Kali":
Om Kali, Om Kali, Om Kali, Om
Om Kali, Om Kali, Om

"Jai Ma Durga":
Jai Ma Durga

30 Here are the lyrics for "Desire, My Great Enemy":

> Desire, my great enemy, with his soldiers surrounded me;
> Is giving me lots of trouble, oh, my Lord! (2x)
> That enemy I will deceive, remaining in the castle of peace,
> Night and day in Thy joy, oh, my Lord! (2x)
> What will be my fate? O Lord, tell me!
> "Pranayam be thy religion, pranayam will give thee salvation,
> Pranayam is the wishing tree. (2x)
> "Pranayam is beloved God, Pranayam is Creator–Lord,
> Pranayam is the Cosmic World. (2x)v"Control the little pranayam, become All-Pervading Pranayam.
> You won't have to fear anything anymore.

31 Anonymous in conversation with the author, Puna, Hawaii, July 23, 2017.
32 Anonymous in conversation with the author, Puna, Hawaii, September 7, 2017.
33 Anonymous in conversation with the author, Puna, Hawaii, April 24, 2017.
34 In this regard, one example provided by Tranquada and King from the Washington Post says, "Thousands in the Capitol during the last six months have been charmed by the melody of a group of dark-hued visitors, the melody of far-off Hawaii… One uses a flute, two employ guitars, and three play upon the peculiar little string instrument called 'ukelele,' which in native Hawaiian means 'the flea.'" (Tranquada and King 2012: 80).
35 Consider, for example, how Krishnacore represents an intersection with the genre of straightedge punk, which uses "Guitars, drums and vocals," and is now being "used as a means of expressing devotion – whether via frustration, surrender or anger – towards Krishna" rather than protesting capitalist society as is typical of the straightedge punk genre (Dines 2013: 152).
36 Michael Gornik in public lecture before a *kīrtan* at Kalani Honua Oceanside Retreat Center, April 28, 2017. The "Maha Kirtan" took place a few miles away the next day in Polestar Gardens' Community Center.
37 Vivian, in discussion with the author, Puna, Hawaii, May 11, 2017.
38 Jaime, in discussion with the community, Puna, Hawaii, April 27, 2017.
39 Jesse, in discussion with the author, Puna, Hawaii, June 14, 2017.
40 Anonymous, in discussion with the author, Puna, Hawaii, August 25, 2017.
41 Anonymous, in discussion with the author, Puna, Hawaii, September 11, 2017.
42 Anonymous in discussion with the author, Puna, Hawaii, July 7, 2017.
43 Ann Gornik, in email message to the author, September 12, 2017.
44 Victor Turner's "*communitas*" pertains to the periodic, dialectical, and revitalizing release of members from community structure. Turner writes, "There is a dialectic here, for the immediacy of *communitas* gives way to the mediacy of structure, while, in *rites de passage*, men [sic] are released from structure into *communitas* only to return to structure revitalized by their experience of *communitas*" (Turner 1967: 29, 129). In addition to *communitas*, Durkheim's, "collective effervescence," is the well-known observation that through religious practice fellow community members "…feel themselves transformed in the same way and express this sentiment by their cries, their gestures and their general attitude" (Durkheim: 1964 [1915]: 218). For the religious practitioner experiencing collective effervescence, "everything is just as though he really were transported into a special world, entirely different from the one where he ordinarily lives, and into an environment filled with exceptionally intense forces that take hold of him and metamorphose him" (ibid.). As Wilke and Moebus observe regarding *kīrtan* specifically, "This group dynamic that Durkheim termed 'social effervescence' was known to bhakti theoreticians and they therefore particularly recommended communal singing. Singing in groups and singing the

name and deeds of God (*kīrtana*) loudly became the religious centerpiece of whole movements, and in many institutionalized bhakti traditions such activities play a vast role" (Wilke and Moebus 2011: 884).

45 For example, Srinivas emphasizes how, "Shrivaishnava religious literature from the mid-twelfth century onwards was indebted to both Sanskrit and Tamil and this linguistic blurring acquired a new dimension as it came to be embodied in the manipravala language" (Srinivas 2008: 313). She also reminds us that, "It has been argued that the language of the Adi Granth, the sacred scripture of Sikhism that was edited, collated and reduced to writing in the vernacular in 1604, is not one language" (ibid.: 314).

46 Brown has since made similar observations of Hare Krishna *kīrtan* in Mormon Utah, "particularly the use of hybrid musical styles that combine elements of popular music with traditional Indian sounds." Brown suggests "that the cultivation of hybrid, synergistic musical forms is crucial to the performers' ability to effectively invite their audience into musical and kinesthetic participation in the process of kirtan" (Brown 2014: 457). Interestingly, Brown further observes, "hybrid styles of kirtan based in rock, reggae, reggaeton, hip hop, dubstep, and other styles of popular music have gained traction among American Hare Krishnas" (ibid.: 459).

47 Similarly, Weidman suggests, in the twentieth century music came to function as a language of its own in Tamil Nadu, albeit in nationalist political discourse (Weidman 2006: 152).

48 Michael Gornik, in email message to the author, February 14, 2021.

References

Affonso, Dyanne D., June Y. Shibuya, and B. Christopher Frueh. 2007. "Talk-Story: Perspectives of Children, Parents, and Community Leaders on Community Violence in Rural Hawaii." *Public Health Nursing* 24, no. 5: 400–408.

Alpers, Edward A. 2018. "Islands Connect: People, Things, and Ideas Among the Small Islands of the Western Indian Ocean," in Burkhard Schnepel and Edward A. Alpers (eds.), *Connectivity in Motion: Island Hubs in the Indian Ocean World*. Cham: Palgrave Macmillan.

Ananda. 2016. "Chanting is Half the Battle." Ananda.org. Accessed July 30, 2022. https://www.ananda.org/blog/chanting-is-half-the-battle-2/

Bakhtin, Mikhail Mikhailovich. 1981. *The Dialogic Imagination: Four Essays by M.M. Bakhtin*. Translated by Caryl Emerson and Michael Holquist. Edited by Michael Holquist. Austin: University of Texas Press.

Bates, Eliot. 2012. "The Social Life of Instruments." *Ethnomusicology* 56, no. 3: 363–395.

Beck, Guy L. 1993. *Sonic Theology: Hinduism and Sacred Sound*. Columbia: University of South Carolina Press.

Beck, Guy L. 2012. *Sonic Liturgy: Ritual and Music in Hindu Tradition*. Columbia: University of South Carolina Press.

Berendt, Joachim-Ernst. 1991 [1985]. *The World Is Sound: Nada Brahma: Music and the Landscape of Consciousness*. Rochester: Inner Traditions.

Bhabha, Homi. 1994. *The Location of Culture*. London: Routledge.

Birch, Jason. 2011. "The Meaning of Haṭha in Early Haṭhayoga." *Journal of the American Oriental Society* 131, no. 4: 527–554.

Bohlman, Philip V. 1989. *The Land Where Two Streams Flow*. Urbana: University of Illinois Press.

Brinkmann, Reinhold, and Christoph Wolff, eds. 1999. *Driven into Paradise*. Berkeley: University of California Press.

Brown, Sara. 2014. "Krishna, Christians, and Colors: The Socially Binding Influence of Kirtan Singing at a Utah Hare Krishna Festival." *Ethnomusicology* 58, no. 3: 454–480.

Byl, Julia. 2023. "Squinting at Greater India," in *Sounding the Indian Ocean: Musical Circulations in the Afro-Asiatic Seascape*. Berkeley: University of California Press.

Byl, Julia and Jim Sykes. 2020. "Ethnomusicology and the Indian Ocean: On the Politics of Area Studies." *Ethnomusicology* 64, no. 3: 394–421.

Campbell, Susan M. and Patricia M. Ogburn. 1992. "Puna Sugar Company History." Hawaiian Sugar Planters' Association Plantation Archives. Last modified August 2004. http://www2.hawaii.edu/~speccoll/p_puna.html.

Cassio, Francesca. 2019. "The Sonic Pilgrimage. Exploring kīrtan and Sacred Journeying in Sikh Culture." *Sikh Formations* 15, nos. 1–2: 152–182.

Chatterjee, Partha. 1986. *Nationalist Thought and the Colonial World: A Derivative Discourse?* Minneapolis: University of Minnesota Press.

Clayton, Martin, Trevor Herbert, and Richard Middleton, eds. 2012. *The Cultural Study of Music: A Critical Introduction*. 2nd Edition. New York: Routledge.

Consillio, Kristin. 2018. "Poverty, illness compound problems for Puna community." *Honolulu Star Advertiser*, May 22, 2018. http://www.staradvertiser.com/2018/05/22/hawaii-news/poverty-illness-compound-problems-for-puna-community/.

Cooper, George and Gavan Daws. 1985. *Land and Power in Hawai'i*. Honolulu: Benchmark Books.

Damon Tucker. 2017. "Community Forum on Crime and Drug Abuse in Puna." Accessed August 22, 2018. https://damontucker.com/2017/12/14/community-forum-on-crime-drug-abuse-in-puna/.

Dawe, Kevin. 2012. "The Cultural Study of Musical Instruments," in Martin Clayton, Trevor Herbert, and Richard Middleton (eds.), *The Cultural Study of Music: A Critical Introduction*. 2nd Edition. New York: Routledge: 195–205.

Dines, Mike. 2013. "The Sacralization of Straightedge Punk: Bhakti-yoga, Nada Brahma and the Divine Received: Embodiment of Krishnacore." *Muzikoloski Zbornik* 50, no. 2: 147–156.

Durkheim, Emile. 1964 [1915]. *The Elementary Forms of Religious Life*. London: George Allen and Unwin Ltd.

Engelhardt, Jeffers. 2012. "Music, Sound, and Religion," in Martin Clayton, Trevor Herbert, and Richard Middleton (eds.), *The Cultural Study of Music: A Critical Introduction*. 2nd Edition. New York: Routledge: 299–307.

Erlmann, Veit. 1999. *Music, Modernity, and the Global Imagination: South Africa and the West*. New York: Oxford University Press.

Foxen, Anya P. 2017. *Biography of a Yogi: Paramahansa Yogananda and the Origins of Modern Yoga*. New York: Oxford University Press.

Gerety, Finnian M. M. 2021. "Sound and Yoga," in Suzanne Newcombe and Karen O'Brien-Kop (eds.), *Routledge Handbook of Yoga and Meditation Studies*. New York: Routledge: 502–521.

Giri, Swami Satyananda. 2004. *A Collection of Biographies of 4 Kriya Yoga Gurus*. Battle Creek: Yoga Niketan.

Goldberg, Philip. 2018. *The Life of Yogananda: The Story of the Yogi Who Became the First Modern Guru*. New York: Hay House.

Gough, Ellen. 2021. *Making a Mantra: Tantric Ritual and Renunciation on the Jain Path to Liberation*. Chicago: University of Chicago Press.

Hancock, Mary and Smriti Srinivas. 2018. "Roundtable on Spirited Topographies: Religion and Urban Place-Making: Ordinary Cities and Milieus of Innovation." *Journal of the American Academy of Religion* 86, no. 2: 454–472.

Healthcare Association of Hawaii. 2015. *Hawaii County Community Health Needs Assessment*. Berkeley: Healthy Communities Institute.

Henriques, Julian. 2011. *Sonic Bodies: Reggae Sound Systems, Performance Techniques, and Ways of Knowing*. New York: Continuum.

Ivester, Sukari. 2010. "Gentrification Hawaii Style." Paper presented at *the meeting of the American Sociological Association Annual Meeting*, Hilton Atlanta and Atlanta Marriott Marquis, Atlanta, Georgia.

Juergensmeyer, Mark. 1991. *Radhasoami Reality: The Logic of a Modern Faith*. Princeton: Princeton University Press.

Kapchan, Deborah. 2008. "The Promise of Sonic Translation: Performing the Festive Sacred in Morocco." *American Anthropologist* 110, no. 4: 467–483.

Kurt, Ronald. 2009. *Indien und Europa: Ein kultur-und musiksoziologischer Verstehensversuch*. Bielefeld: Transcript.

Laack, Isabel. 2015. "Sound, Music and Religion: A Preliminary Cartography of a Transdisciplinary Research Field." *Method and Theory in the Study of Religion* 27: 220–246.

Lallie, Harjinder Singh. 2016. "The Harmonium in Sikh Music." *Sikh Formations* 12, no. 1: 53–66.

Lorea, Carola Erika. 2023. "An Untouchable Kīrtan: Sonic Liberation in the Andaman Islands," in Jim Sykes and Julia Byl (eds.), *Sounding the Indian Ocean: Musical Circulations in the Afro-Asiatic Seascape*. Berkeley: University of California Press.

Love Brown, Susan, ed. 2002. *Intentional Community: An Anthropological Perspective*. New York: State University of New York.

Lucia, Amanda J. 2020. *White Utopias: The Religious Exoticism of Transformational Festivals*. Oakland: University of California Press.

Manuel, Peter. 2000. *East Indian Music in the West Indies*. Philadelphia: Temple University Press.

Matsuoka, Jon K., Luciano Minerbi, Pualani Kanahele, Marion Kelly, Noenoe Barney-Campbell, James W. Saulsbury, and Lillian D. Trettin. 1996. *Native Hawaiian Ethnographic Study For the Hawai'i Geothermal Project Proposed for Puna and Southeast Maui*. Oak Ridge: Oak Ridge National Laboratory. http://hdl.handle.net/10524/19366.

Merriam, Alan P. 1964. *The Anthropology of Music*. Evanston: Northwestern University Press.

Meyers, Helen. 1999. *Music of Hindu Trinidad: Songs from the India Diaspora*. Chicago: University of Chicago Press.

Miller, Christopher Patrick. 2020a. "Paramahansa Yogananda's World Brotherhood Colonies: Models for Environmentally Sustainable and Socially Responsible Living," in Christopher Patrick Miller, Michael Reading, and Jeffery Long (eds.), *Beacons of Dharma: Spiritual Exemplars for the Modern Age*. New York: Lexington Books: 163–180.

Miller, Christopher Patrick. 2020b. "Softpower and Biopower: Narendra Modi's 'Double Discourse' Concerning Yoga for Climate Change and Self-Care." *Journal of Dharma Studies*, Special Issue on Yoga Studies. 3, no. 1: 93–106.

Morelle, Rebecca. 2013. "Choir singers 'synchronise their heartbeats'." *BBC News*, July 9, 2013. Accessed March 10, 2023. https://www.bbc.com/news/science-environment-23230411

Nettl, Bruno. 2015. *The Study of Ethnomusicology: Thirty-three Discussions*. Urbana: University of Chicago Press.

Neumann, David. 2019. *Finding God through Yoga: Paramahansa Yogananda and Modern American Religion in a Global Age*. Chapel Hill: University of North Carolina Press.

Ogasapian, John. 2007. *Church Music in America, 1620–2000*. Macon: Mercer University Press.

Olsen, Dale A. 2004. *The Chrysanthemum and the Song: Music, Memory, and Identity in the South American Japanese Diaspora*. Gainesville: University Press of Florida.

Pandit, Prabodh B. 1969. "Logistics of Language Development," in Arabinda Poddar (ed.), *Language and Society in India*. Simla: Indian Institute of Advanced Study.

Pandit, Prabodh B. 1988. "Prospects in Sociolinguistics," in Lachman M. Khubchandani (ed.), *Language in a Plural Society*. New Delhi: Motilal Banarsidass: 3–7.

Pinch, William R. 2006. *Warrior Ascetics and Indian Empires*. Cambridge: Cambridge University Press.

Purohit, Vinayak. 1988. *Arts of Transitional India: 20th Century*. Mumbai: Popular Prakashan.

Rahaim, Matt. 2011. "That Ban(e) of Indian Music: Hearing Politics in the Harmonium." *The Journal of Asian Studies* 70, no. 3: 657–682.

Rasmussen, Anne K. 2016. "Performing Islam around the Indian Ocean," in Karin van Nieuwkerk, Mark Levine, and Martin Stokes (eds.), *Islam and Popular Culture*. Austin: University of Texas Press: 300–322.

Rees, Helen. 2000. *Echoes of History: Naxi Music in Modern China*. New York: Oxford University Press.

Reyes, Adelaida. 1999. *Songs of the Caged, Songs of the Free: Music and the Vietnamese Refugee Experience*. Philadelphia: Temple University Press.

Schmidt, Leigh Eric. 2005 *Restless Souls: The Making of American Spirituality*. San Francisco: HarperCollins.

Schultz, Anna. 2013. *Singing a Hindu Nation: Marathi Devotional Performance and Nationalism*. New York: Oxford University Press.

Shi, David E. 2007. *The Simple Life: Plain Living and High Thinking in American Culture*. Athens: University of Georgia Press.

Silverman, Carol. 2012. *Romani Routes: Cultural Politics and Balkan Music in Diaspora*. New York: Oxford University Press.

Singh, Roopa Bala. 2020. "Yoga's Entry Into American Popular Music Is Racialized (1941–67): A Critical Yoga Studies Analysis of Race, Othering, and 'Belonging'." *Resonance: The Journal of Sound and Culture* 1, no. 2: 132–162.

Singleton, Mark. 2008. "The Classical Reveries of Modern Yoga: Patañjali and Constructive Orientalism," in Mark Singleton and Jean Byrne (eds.), *Yoga in the Modern World: Contemporary Perspectives*. New York: Routledge: 77–99.

Singleton, Mark. 2010. *Yoga Body: The Origins of Modern Posture Practice*. New York: Oxford University Press.

Srinivas, Smriti. 2008. *In the Presence of Sai Baba: Body, City, and Memory in a Global Religious Movement*. Boston: Brill.

Stokes, Martin. 2012. "Globalization and the Politics of World Music," in Martin Clayton, Trevor Herbert, and Richard Middleton (eds.), *The Cultural Study of Music: A Critical Introduction*. 2nd Edition. New York: Routledge: 107–116.

Tranquada, Jim and John King. 2012. *The ukulele: A History*. Honolulu: University of Hawai'i Press.
Tsing, Anna Lowenhaupt. 2005. *Friction: An Ethnography of Global Connection*. Princeton: Princeton University Press.
Turino, Thomas. 1999. "Signs of Imagination, Identity, Experience: A Peircian Semiotic Theory for Music." *Ethnomusicology* 43, no. 2: 221–255.
Turino, Thomas 2000. *Nationalists, Cosmopolitans, and Popular Music in Zimbabwe*. Chicago: University of Chicago Press.
Turner, Victor 1967. *The Ritual Process: Structure and Anti-Structure*. Chicago: Aldine.
Uberoi, Patricia and J.P.S. Uberoi. 1976. "Towards a New Sociolinguistics: A Memoir of P B Pandit." *Economic and Political Weekly* 11, no. 17: 637–643.
University of Hawai'i at Mānoa. 2011. "Rainfall Atlas of Hawai'i: Hawai'i's Rainfall Patterns." Accessed August 22, 2018. http://rainfall.geography.hawaii.edu/rainfall.html
Urban, Hugh. 2003. *Tantra: Sex, Secrecy, Politics, and Power in the Study of Religion*. Berkeley: University of California Press.
van der Linden, Bob. 2013. *Music and Empire in Britain and India: Identity, Internationalism, and Cross-Cultural Communication*. New York: Palgrave Macmillan
van der Veer, Peter. 2001. *Imperial Encounters: Religion and Modernity in India and Britain*. Princeton: Princeton University Press.
Wallace, Anthony. 1956. "Revitalization Movements." *American Anthropologist* 58, no. 2: 264–281.
Weidman, Amanda J. 2006. *Singing the Classical, Voicing the Modern: The Post-Colonial Politics of Music in South India*. Durham: Duke University Press.
Weiss, Richard S. 2019. *The Emergence of Modern Hinduism: Religion on the Margins of Colonialism*. Oakland: University of California Press.
White, David Gordon. 2009. *Sinister Yogis*. Chicago: University of Chicago Press.
Wilke, Annette and Oliver Moebus. 2011. *Sound and Communication: An Aesthetic Cultural History of Sanskrit Hinduism*. Berlin: Walter de Gruyter GmbH and Co. KG.
Williamson, Lola. 2010. *Transcendent in America: Hindu-Inspired Meditation Movements as New Religion*. New York: New York University Press.
Yogananda, Paramahansa. 1946. *Autobiography of a Yogi*. New York: The Philosophical Library.
Yogananda, Paramahansa. 1974 [1938]. *Cosmic Chants: Spiritualized Songs for Divine Communion*. Los Angeles: Self-Realization Fellowship.
Yogananda, Paramahansa. 1999. *God Talks with Arjuna: The Bhagavad Gita. Royal Science of God-Realization. The immortal dialogue between soul and Spirit. A new translation and commentary*. Los Angeles: Self Realization Fellowship.
Zapart, Jarosław. 2020. "The Rādhāsoāmī Theory of Subtle Body as an Expression of Religious Inclusivism." *International Journal of Hindu Studies* 24: 61–86.
Zennie, Michael. 2012. "'This is the Grand Finale': Creeping Lava from 30-Year-Old Eruption Finally Consumes the Last, Lonely House in a Hawaiian Subdivision." *Daily Mail*, March 6, 2012. http://www.dailymail.co.uk/news/article-2110798/Last-house-Royal-Gardens-Hawaii-consumed-lava-1983-volcanic-eruption.html.

3 Internalizing the Sacrifice in a Sacrifice Zone

Situating Purifying Prāṇāyāma in Pollution at Kaivalyadhama Yoga Institute, Lonavala

One December evening I had just completed yet another session of Kaivalyadhama's twice-daily *prāṇāyāma* (breath control) class in Lonavala, Maharashtra, just outside of Mumbai. Here, my classmates and I had implicated our bodies into the institution's health-enhancing, therapeutic *kriyā-yoga* practice which was aimed at purifying our bodies of accumulated air pollution and toxins. In addition to improving our health, this process of self-purification was ultimately intended to prepare us to perform an internalized, embodied yogic sacrifice with soteriological implications. Along with the rest of the class, I had followed my teacher's instructions to deeply inhale and exhale for an hour straight, stoking an internal, purifying fire.

Following this evening *prāṇāyāma* session, I was walking with a student visiting from Europe who conveyed to me a common discomfort shared among visiting students from Western countries. She asked, "How can anyone practice *prāṇāyāma* here? The air is so filthy!"[1] Her shock was a common response from privileged, mobile students who visit from outside India to practice yoga for the first time. I admittedly shared my friend's discomfort, and several years before had a similar reaction when, for the first time, I palpably inhaled polluted air during a therapeutic *prāṇāyāma* session in urban Delhi.

As a young scholar of Yoga Studies, the transformative, embodied yogic sacrifice into which Kaivalyadhama's *kriyā-yoga* was intended to implicate *prāṇāyāma* practitioners' bodies captivated me. I found such cultural logics undergirding the practice of *prāṇāyāma* in yoga texts and taught in India's many urban yoga institutions like Kaivalyadhama fascinating to learn, practice, and somatically experience. However, every whiff of exhaust, smoke from burning trash, and steady inhale of polluted city air I experienced during these spiritually liberating, health-enhancing sessions continued to confound me. Thus, in this chapter I explore a conundrum that has long puzzled many, including anthropologist Joseph Alter, who observes the perplexing irony of treating conditions such as asthma in yoga centers with "*prāṇāyāmi*cally breathed inner-city air" (Alter 2004: 141).

It is, however, important to keep in mind, as Pollution Studies scholar Timothy Choy conveys regarding similar encounters with Westerners in Hong

DOI: 10.4324/9781003414032-4

Kong, that only those irritating, mobile minority who have the privilege of being on the advantageous side of uneven development can afford to complain about air pollution as I and my European counterpart had at Kaivalyadhama. Choy writes "…the people I met in my first months in Hong Kong who were most vocally critical of the air quality were almost without exception expatriate businesspeople from the United States. I did not want to be associated with them" (Choy 2012: 123). Taking into consideration Choy's humbling rebuke, we might thus also read this chapter as an interrogation of my (and my classmate's) privileged access to clean air, mobility, and my own culturally conditioned response to air pollution in India and the Global South.

To elucidate the relationship between *prāṇāyāma*, privilege, and pollution, in this chapter I engage scholarship from the fields of Pollution Studies, Breath Studies, and allied fields of inquiry. Combining ethnographic data with this critical scholarship reveals that there are two distinct models of the body at work at Kaivalyadhama. First, from the emic perspective, we encounter a self-purifying *haṭha-yoga* body. And second, from an etic perspective, an environmentally and socially *entangled* yoga body. What becomes clear, then, is that Kaivalyadhama's "closed"[2] (White 2006), self-purifying *haṭha-yoga* model of the body sits irreconcilably – and perhaps precariously – alongside social-scientific models of the entangled yoga body. It was precisely this precarity that I, my classmate, and a handful of other visitors from the United States, Europe, and Australia had the luxury of complaining about – and eventually escaping. And it is the frictions between these two models of the body that produce our third and final instantiation of engaged alchemy.

Studying Air, Breathers, and Breathing

In the last 150 years or so, posture (*āsana*) has become the defining practice of yoga (Singleton 2010). Prior to this, *prāṇāyāma* had held this esteemed position. The term *prāṇāyāma* comes from the Sanskrit nouns *prāṇa* (√*prāṇ*, "to breathe"), meaning "breath," and *āyāma* (√*āyam*, "to extend, restrain"), meaning "control." As a Sanskrit compound, *prāṇā-āyāma* usually translates, therefore, as "breath control" or "control of the breath." The word *prāṇa* is also sometimes referred to as the "life force" or "energy" and thus we sometimes encounter *prāṇāyāma* translated as something like "control of the life force" in contemporary yoga practice. The types and purposes of *prāṇāyāma* used in yoga to control the breath have evolved over thousands of years and have been explained in various yoga texts to produce a variety of effects. Though *prāṇāyāma* does not have one single definition or purpose, it was often historically understood to be a difficult, purifying, ascetic (*tapas*) practice intended to promote success in yoga (Mallinson and Singleton 2017: 127–170). In Kaivalyadhama's *kriyā-yoga* system, *prāṇāyāma* occupies a prominent place where it serves this principal purpose of purification (*tapas*) for both therapeutic and soteriological purposes.

In 2017, I spent several months at Kaivalyadhama Yoga Institute where I had the time to practice *prāṇāyāma* in Lonavala, just outside of Mumbai. Here, among other things, I took a close look at the institution's *prāṇāyāma* practices while participating in daily postural (*āsana*) yoga classes, daily *prāṇāyāma* sessions, and an ongoing weekly yoga therapy regimen in the Institute's yoga hospital that also included dietary modification, *āyurveda* treatments, and lectures on how to cultivate good health and wellbeing. During this time I also conducted a number of formal and informal interviews, collected institutional reading material and publications, and spoke with many participants and students who visited the campus for both long-term and short-term stays and who were suffering from a variety of ailments, many of which were related to Mumbai's air pollution. Since leaving Kaivalyadhama and during the COVID-19 pandemic, I have maintained communication with the institution and have followed their publications (both popular and peer-reviewed) and online programming via their website and social media, particularly as they relate to the institution's discourse surrounding *prāṇāyāma*.

Delhi air pollution ethnographers Negi and Srigyan implore us to use an interdisciplinary approach to the study of urban air pollution, insisting that "the blindspots of air's present demand many voices and contributions" (Negi and Srigyan 2021: 17). In this regard, as my project developed, I realized that my own field of Modern Yoga Studies could be quite helpful for explaining to Pollution Studies and Breath Studies scholars the cultural logics undergirding contemporary *prāṇāyāma* practices in geographically polluted regions. I could also share with these fields of study the history of how *prāṇāyāma* practices were deeply transformed during India's colonial encounters with the British and other transnational spiritual movements, including the Theosophical Society, in ways that made today's *prāṇāyāma* practices both popular and possible. I share many of these cultural and historical facts in this chapter for the benefit of colleagues in the fields of Pollution and Breath Studies so that they might better understand how religious aspirations directly influence human outlooks on the material reality of polluted city air. As we will see, Kaivalyadhama's therapeutic *prāṇāyāma* practices and their accompanying yogic ideologies challenge the suggestion put forth by Pollution Studies scholar Liboiron who says that, "Science, rather than religion, is our contemporary arbitrator of matter out of place" (Liboiron 2016: 7; cf. Douglas 1984 [1966]). This chapter shows how religious outlooks, and in this case the self-purifying practice of yoga, significantly shape human perspectives on the matter of air pollution in Mumbai and its environs in ways that defy the hard realities presented by air pollution science, albeit in precarious ways. Still, my own academic field has its limits and in order to better understand the contemporary polluted situation I found myself breathing in at Kaivalyadhama, I had to reach into some new and uncomfortable disciplinary territory which nevertheless lent me some theoretical fresh air.[3]

More specifically for this chapter, the approach I am using is undergirded by the fundamental assertion that our bodies and the air that they breathe are not only indissolubly linked to one another, but also mutually co-constituted and shaped by particular social and environmental contexts. Thus, while I will relate to my readers some of the universal claims relating to *prāṇāyāma* according to Kaivalyadhama's yogic ideology, I will also situate the practice of *prāṇāyāma* in its particular social and historical contexts. Like other ethnographers who have considered air pollution in India, I am doing so within a globalizing nation whose poor air quality is at least in major part caused by the flow of transnational capital and distinct geopolitical and economic pressures (Fortun 2001: 18), as well as the lack of regulatory strength to enforce its abundant air quality legislation (Negi and Srigyan 2021: 2).[4]

Rather than viewing "air" as inanimate or homogenous, I consider Mumbai's polluted[5] city air as a central and influential "substance" (Choy 2012: 140, 157) both shaped by and capable of shaping specific forms of human behavior and attendant cultural practices – in this case *prāṇāyāma* practices (cf. Chen 2012: 2–3).[6] An ethnography of air and the atmosphere, as Choy and Zee write,

> … looks up and around, at plumes, clouds, and sky. It looks inward through the vital interiors that render bodies channels, containers, and filters for airs and the things they hold… The wrong air of the Anthropocene trains our attention to the mechanics of suspension, to how things lift and settle in mediums, to how things exist in atmospheres.
>
> (Choy and Zee 2015: 210)

An ethnography of air in the Anthropocene requires careful attention to particular changes in the air and atmosphere as well as to the human body's "suspension" in "air spaces filled with danger" (ibid.: 210–211).

The fluid, protean yoga bodies who regularly breathe Mumbai's polluted urban city air and who I follow through my field site comprise what Choy calls "breathers." The term "breathers… refers to those who accrue the unaccounted-for costs that attend the production and consumption of goods and services, such as the injuries, medical expenses, and changes in climate and ecosystems" and who must, despite the pollution around them, continue to breathe (Choy 2012: 145–146; cf. Kenner 2018: 6). Rather than considering the bodies of these "breathers" to be static, fixed, and unchanging, I consider them to be fluid in so far as they are biologically "processual, indeterminate" and dynamic (Blackman 2010: 6–7). Critically, these bodies are "biosocial" to the extent that their biological state is indissolubly linked to and shaped by their social environments (ibid.: 6–7). They are, furthermore, ensnared in a mutually co-constitutive "environment/human entanglement" (Niewöhner and Lock 2018: 687; see also Cohen 2009: 271) due to the fact that their individual health issues are a direct result of their bodies' epigenetic entanglements with the inescapable air pollution within which they are situated. As Niewöhner and Lock explain,

> … epigenetic findings suggest that humans and social/material environments develop in relation to each other in the same way that genes relate to their respective environments at different spatial and temporal levels of analysis…. organism and environment always penetrate each other in several ways or co-construct each other… Hence, we speak of environment/human entanglement to demonstrate that a ceaseless process of relating is going on through which environment and human become defined as such.
> (Niewöhner and Lock 2018: 692)

In sum, our social and material environments directly affect our body's genetic expression (ibid.: 681, 685) and our bodies and the world around us are in a permanent, co-constitutive relationship (ibid.: 692, cf. Landecker 2011). Also informed by related fields of inquiry including "new materialisms" (Coole and Frost 2010; cf. Gamble et al. 2019), the ethnographic study in this chapter thus analyzes yogic bodies as inseparable from their social and ecological environments, and thus permanently entangled and relational.

The social and ecological entanglements at my field site resulted in a number of bodily ailments. Many of those I met traveling to Kaivalyadhama for relief complained of suffering from breathing issues from air pollution, particularly asthma, while others also attributed their various illnesses to the poor air quality in Mumbai. Following Kenner, who encourages us to study global somatic epidemics like asthma and their accompanying remedies within the particular "carescapes" where they are treated (Kenner 2018: 6, 16), Kaivalyadhama provides one particularly interesting case study in so far as it shows us how yoga therapy and seemingly universal spiritual aspirations intersect with neoliberalism, biopolitics, class/caste privilege, nationalist aspirations, and as I will show, necropolitics (Mbembe 2003, 2019). When undertaking ethnography in such carescapes, Kenner advises, we must therefore pay attention to "who cares, how do we care…" and also to how power affords "different modes of care, where, and for whom" (Kenner 2018: 20). These questions require us to pay particular attention to the class privilege that allows one to seek care for disease that is related to air pollution in the first place, and to perform, as Choy encourages, "an emic analysis of [air's] presence and distinction in acts" (Choy 2012: 161).

The particular distinguishing "class acts" with which I am concerned in this chapter and that I study within their particular social context are yogic breathing practices known as *prāṇāyāma*. These breathing techniques are touted as "universal" in most every yoga center that teaches them. Nevertheless, the field of Modern Yoga Studies has already begun to consider *prāṇāyāma* as a category of practice worthy of historical contextualization. As several authors have demonstrated, breath practices found in the modern yoga landscape were, like postural practices (*āsana*), significantly re-invented in a transnational dialogue between Indian and Western innovators during the late nineteenth and early twentieth centuries (Green 2008; Singleton 2010; Foxen 2020). Surprisingly, these historical studies have yet to prompt a critical ethnographic study of *prāṇāyāma* in practice, and it is this lacuna in current Modern Yoga Studies scholarship that this chapter seeks to address.

Though critical ethnographies of *prāṇāyāma* are currently lacking in scholarship concerned with modern yoga, Górska underscores how breathing techniques and the contemporary act of breathing more generally are not homogenous social phenomena and thus give us an opportunity to study these material practices within specific social contexts (Górska 2016: 29). Indeed, as Górska shows, breathing "can inspire diverse analyses of relational natural and cultural, material and social scapes that are oxygenated across diverse spaces, times, geopolitical relations, ecosystems, industries and urbanization while being situated in their phenomenal specificities" (ibid.: 30). Within these "phenomenal specificities" we can ask,

> … questions about political, social and economic distribution and maintenance of privilege and lack thereof, and power that materializes not only in (un)breathable and (non)toxic air but also in political, social and ethical matters such as whose lives are breathable and whose loss of breath is grievable.
>
> (ibid.)

It is to the latter "grievable" lives that we now turn, as we enter Kaivalyadhama Yoga Institute to take a close look at the substance of air, its breathers, and the inescapable material act of breathing.

Prāṇāyāma at Kaivalyadhama

When Swami Kuvalayananda founded Kaivalyadhama in 1924, he institutionalized the *kriyā-yoga* practice from his own guru, Swami Madhavadas,[7] into the organization's various therapeutic yoga regimens where its basic structure was nevertheless maintained even as its practices were expanded and elaborated. Kuvalayananda is well known for using the universal language of science in order to translate his universal message of yoga for dissemination in transnational discourse, a process which enabled, as Alter suggests, yoga to eventually "colonize the West" (Alter 2004: 106). A quote from the end of Kuvalayananda's introduction to *Yogic Therapy* is particularly illustrative of this scientific yoga discourse:

> … the stress laid on regulation of diet, respiration and cultivation of positive attitudes goes to show that the aim is primarily to bring about a beneficial change in the metabolism of the body as a whole. These metabolic changes, through the body fluids, may act on different systems, such as glandular, circulatory, nervous, excretory, etc., and bring about a complete change in the total personality of the individual, before he takes to the higher practices of yoga. Thus, Yogic Therapy does not consist of mere lavages and exercise treatment but lays great stress on control of diet, social attitudes and personal habits so as to bring about beneficial changes in the whole of the metabolic process.
>
> (Kuvalayananda and Vinekar 2017 [1963]: xv)

As Alter's work suggests, Kuvalayananda had a tendency to conflate yogic terminology with scientific and biomedical language in order to translate yogic ideology into a language his global audiences could understand (Alter 2004). Following Alter's earlier work, we can see, for example, how Kuvalayananda's use of biomedical language here, such as his mention of the body's "metabolic process" and his emphasis on phenomena like "metabolic changes, through the body fluids" that "may act on different systems," was intended to encrypt a particular logic of embodied yogic transformation within the language of biological science. Today at Kaivalyadhama, participants initiate and tend to this transformative process during their participation in the institution's therapeutic programming, where the daily regimen includes a significant amount of *prāṇāyāma* practice that takes place, uncomfortable as it is, amidst polluted city air.

Kaivalyadhama advertises and promotes the practice of *prāṇāyāma* as a panacea for seemingly all potential ailments that could afflict its visitors, including asthma. Repeating many of the therapeutic claims found in *haṭha-yoga* texts and combining them with contemporary biomedical concerns, a recent post on Kaivalyadhama's website titled "The Power of Prāṇāyama" conveys the institution's discourse in this regard quite well:

> There is no doubt that by practicing pranayama one acquires complete control over one's body. It cures the diseases of Vata (air), Pitta (bile), Kapha (cough) and enhances the gastric fire in one's body. *One who regularly practices Pranayama is able to develop* a lustrous face, clarity of voice, brightness of eyes, slimness of the body, *freedom from diseases like Asthma*, Sinusitis, Hypertension, Ischemic Heart Diseases, Indigestion, and many more. It helps in the management of reproductive disorders, degenerative diseases like Fibromyalgia, reduces the metabolic strain on kidneys and most importantly increases the blood supply to the cortex in the Brain. It improves one's mental health and cures many personality disorders. Pranayama has a tremendous power to revert back the aging process. It has an inherent power to boost the immune system. It increases one's confidence and self-esteem and helps in channelizing positive energy.
>
> (Kaivalyadhama 2021, emphasis added)

These and other similar claims aimed at demonstrating the efficacy of *prāṇāyāma* also appear in Kaivalyadhama's journal titled *Yoga-Mīmāṃsā* ("Investigation of Yoga"). For example, a 2021 peer-reviewed article concerned with how "Ambient air pollutants such as ozone, oxides of nitrogen, SO_2 and particulate matter are also associated with adverse health effects" concludes that "the limited available evidence on effects of yogic breathing on [the] respiratory system indicates a positive trend of change in the respiratory physiology" (Vaid and Verma 2021: 72). *Prāṇāyāma*, in other words, is believed to be able to address contemporary health ailments caused by polluted air. Citing the

Haṭha-Yoga-Pradīpikā's verse 2.17 on breathing practices directly, a more recent peer-reviewed review article in the same journal writes regarding the importance of *prāṇāyāma* in asthma treatment that "Hiccups, *asthma*, coughs, headache, ear pain, eye pain, and various other diseases are caused due to disturbances of the vital air" (Chetry et al. 2022, emphasis added).

After practicing *prāṇāyāma* amidst the Anthropocene's "air spaces filled with danger" (Choy and Zee 2015: 211), I often found these and other similar claims hard to take in and perhaps important to contextualize, with public health in mind. As an ethnographer, my primary concern here is to try to explain why Kaivalyadhama can confidently make these claims so often in the many places where *prāṇāyāma* is practiced, theorized, and published just outside of Mumbai.

Lonavala: Mumbai's getaway

Kaivalyadhama is located in Lonavala, a rather small (15 square miles, population 57,698) (Census2011 2015) but busy tourist hill station approximately 2,000 feet above sea level, in the Pune District among the Western Ghats. The small town serves as a tourist getaway for city dwellers seeking some reprieve from their urban lifestyles. Known as "Mumbaikars," as one enormous sign along the highway passing next to the Kaivalyadhama campus also advertises, these individuals flood the streets, restaurants, bars, chikki storefronts, and shops of Lonavala every weekend as they make their way out of coastal Mumbai and up the Mumbai-Pune Expressway in taxis, private automobiles, or even piled on the back of motorcycles.

The Expressway is a rather massive, six-lane construction project that was completed by the Maharashtra State Road Development Corporation in 2002. It was intended to connect coastal Mumbai with inland Pune approximately 100 kilometers away, and Lonavala happened to be one of several major interchanges along the Expressway's path. As a result, by the time of the Expressway's completion in 2002, the Kaivalyadhama campus found itself wedged between the old, rather modest National Highway 48 just outside the southern walls of the campus and the new, exhaust-laden six-lane Expressway which today still cuts across the campus's northern border (see Figure 3.1) (Times of India 2018). While the presence of the Expressway has made Kaivalyadhama more accessible from urban Mumbai, it has also provided "new frontiers of domesticity and mobility" (Srinivas 2018: 478) that have transformed the institution's once-rural paradise into a busy, polluted tourist destination extending from the city. Overcrowded streets are now filled with the noise of horns and engines and the air is full of automobile exhaust and the fumes of burning trash as enthusiastic holidaymakers consume one experience after another. Together these conditions create an unhealthy average Air Quality Index (AQI) of 144 in the geographic regions of Mumbai approaching Lonavala for the late months of the year during which I performed my fieldwork.[8]

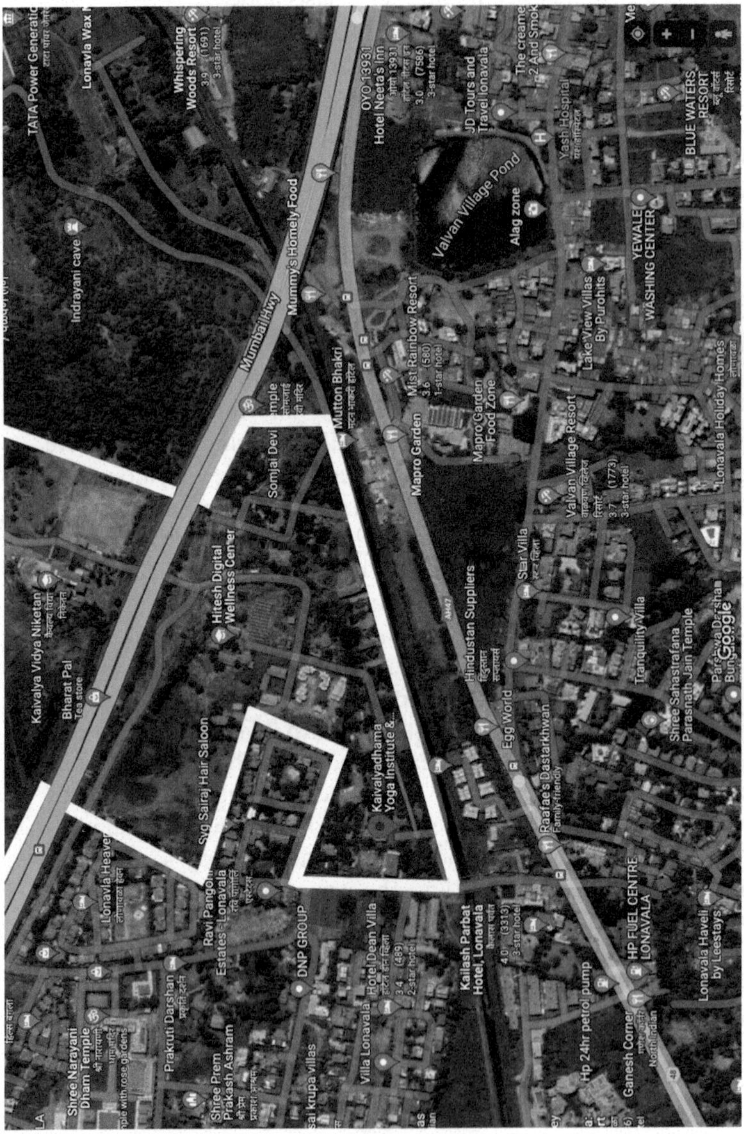

Figure 3.1 Aerial map of the main Kaivalyadhama campus, outlined in white. Note old Highway 48 ("48"/"AH47") at the campus's southern border and the new six-lane Expressway ("Mumbai Hwy") to the north. Also note the aqueduct at the southern border, which delivers water from the nearby TATA dam to urban Mumbai.

Source: Imagery ©2022 Airbus, CNES/Airbus, Maxar Technologies, Map data © 2022; Google Maps 2022.

Combined with the other religious institutions in town, Kaivalyadhama comprises one of the central features of the city's "religious monumentality" (Srinivas 2018: 481) catering to middle-class tourists and those with vacation homes in the area. What is unique about Kaivalyadhama, however, is that those seeking an alternative Lonavala tourism experience will encounter a yoga therapy hospital and ongoing yoga trainings and workshops not offered anywhere else in the area. Many of these individuals arrive sick from Mumbai city life in search of healing, while those who are healthy periodically visit to "detoxify" their bodies of the polluted city atmosphere. When they arrive, they meet a handful of short-term international guests who have come with similar motivations, but also long-term residential students from all over India, and perhaps a few students from other parts of the world, who are completing one of Kaivalyadhama's highly prized degree or certificate courses with the hopes of obtaining a yoga teacher or physical education position in India or, in some cases, abroad. Though the air is polluted in Lonavala and despite the inconveniences car exhaust, burning trash, cigarette smoke, highways, and industry-borne hazardous air pollutants might create, the therapeutic space at Kaivalyadhama provides a relatively more privileged "safe space" (Murphy 2006: 159) for middle-class Indian *prāṇāyāma* practitioners visiting from heavily polluted Mumbai just two hours away on the coast. A number of visitors conveyed this to me, including Maya, a middle-aged woman from Mumbai suffering from asthma-related breathing issues, who said, "I know the air is polluted. But in Mumbai it is much worse. Here it is much easier for me to breathe."[9]

All of these short-term and long-term visitors are trained and supported by a small full-time staff of yoga therapists, naturopaths, and *āyurvedic* practitioners who have already graduated from Kaivalyadhama, a full-time research staff, a resident doctor, and a supporting administrative staff, most of whom live on the campus grounds and all of whom are Indian. Furthermore, visitors find themselves on a clean and well-manicured campus maintained by members of lower castes living in the village of Pangoli adjacent to the campus. These social groups converge on the campus to offer year-round opportunities for middle-class yoga retreats, yoga therapy, and/or yoga education along with multiple activities, lodging, and dining options on Kaivalyadhama's 180-acre campus.

Swami Madhavadas' Kriyā-Yoga

Kaivalyadhama disseminates and structures its yoga practices throughout the organization according to Swami Madhavadas' *kriyā-yoga*. This *kriyā-yoga* is comprised of a three-part sequence inspired by Patanjali's *Yoga-Sūtra* that consists of the practices of *tapas* (purification), *svādhyāya* (mantra repetition), and *īśvarapraṇidhāna* (devotion to god).[10] Many practices of later *haṭha-yoga* texts, including a number of *prāṇāyāmas*, are also grafted onto this regimen. Most often, these practices include those undertaken in the yoga hospital for therapy and those taught in the college and to other certificate students, as well as in the twice-daily *agni-hotra* ceremony performed at the institution.[11]

In its most basic form, Kaivalyadhama's *kriyā-yoga* proceeds as follows (see Bhogal 2016). One commences the practice of *tapas* (purification) with ten rounds of purifying alternate nostril *prāṇāyāma* breathing (*anuloma-viloma prāṇāyāma*). According to Dr. R.S. Bhogal, both nostrils must be clear so that uniform amounts of air are taken in and breathed out through each nostril. Dr. Bhogal suggests that when undertaken correctly, *anuloma-viloma* not only purifies but also "extends your energy [*prāṇa*],"[12] preparing the practitioner to undertake the second and third stages of *kriyā-yoga*. These final two stages of practice, *svādhyāya* (mantra repetition) and *īśvarapraṇidhāna* (devotion to god), involve, at the most basic level, the practice of *auṃ* chanting (*oṃkāra*) and the recitation of the Gayatri Mantra, respectively. Here, one begins by practicing *auṃ* chanting for ten rounds, reciting the sacred syllable "*auṃ*" by vocalizing the "*au*" syllable for three seconds, and then tapering to the nasalized *anusvāra* "*ṃ*" sound. In this stage, instructs Dr. Bhogal, *auṃ* chanting *disseminates* one's energy/*prāṇa* to wherever it is needed in the body in specific measures and quantities. Having completed this process, the practitioner then enters the final stage wherein ten rounds of the Gayatri Mantra[13] are chanted to *protect* one's energy/*prāṇa*, which, Dr. Bhogal tells us, is the meaning of *gāyatrī*, namely, "one who protects your energy." As Dr. Bhogal also informs us, "This is a *sādhana* [spiritual practice], by which we salute the god sun so that we are energized" (Bhogal 2016). Thus ends Kaivalyadhama's *kriyā-yoga* sequence, which, in the most basic version presented here, takes approximately ten to 12 minutes to complete. The soteriological goal of *kriyā-yoga* is to experience *samādhi* (meditative absorption) and some encounter with the divine, though, as we can see in Kaivalyadhama's instantiation of the practice, therapeutic effects are also understood to result.

This system of *kriyā-yoga* is elaborated and expanded upon in the organization's many courses and therapeutic formats. It combines closely related breathing and sacred sound practices. Prior to and concurrent with the undertaking of yoga practices based upon this *kriyā-yoga* at Kaivalyadhama, students and visitors are further advised to assume preliminary body-purifying practices (*ṣaṭ-karma*) cited directly from *haṭha-yoga* texts (see Figure 3.2) to prepare their bodies for yoga and are also encouraged to abstain from drugs, alcohol, and smoking. To prepare for *prāṇāyāma*, Kaivalyadhama also constantly advises the adoption of a pure (*sāttvik*; Sanskrit: *sāttvika*) vegetarian diet consisting of food prepared in multiple locations within the campus limits, and in fact the cultural logic undergirding Kaivalyadhama's *prāṇāyāma* practices cannot be fully appreciated without understanding the institution's dissemination of yogic diet.

Stoking the internal sacrifice: mitāhāra *and* prāṇāyāma

Along with the practice of *prāṇāyāma*, the food served at Kaivalyadhama is intended to support the practice of *kriyā-yoga* by assisting in the purification of the subtle channels (*nāḍīs*) of the yogic subtle body. For both therapeutic and soteriological purposes, it is critical that yoga practitioners keep these subtle channels running throughout the yoga body and through which *prāṇa* travels, pure. If they do not, diseases are said to manifest and their ability to

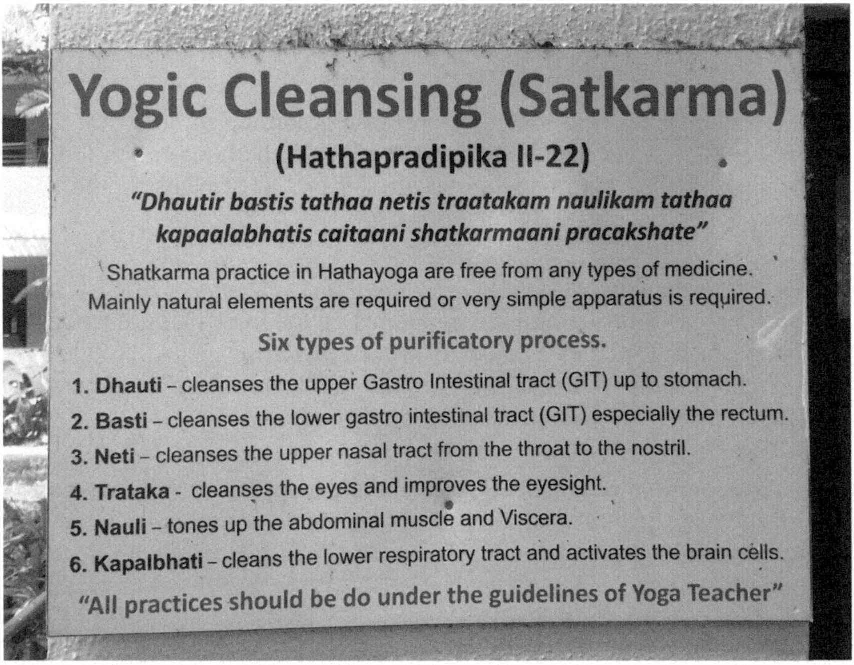
Yogic Cleansing (Satkarma)
(Hathapradipika II-22)
"Dhautir bastis tathaa netis traatakam naulikam tathaa kapaalabhatis caitaani shatkarmaani pracakshate"
Shatkarma practice in Hathayoga are free from any types of medicine.
Mainly natural elements are required or very simple apparatus is required.
Six types of purificatory process.
1. Dhauti - cleanses the upper Gastro Intestinal tract (GIT) up to stomach.
2. Basti - cleanses the lower gastro intestinal tract (GIT) especially the rectum.
3. Neti - cleanses the upper nasal tract from the throat to the nostril.
4. Trataka - cleanses the eyes and improves the eyesight.
5. Nauli - tones up the abdominal muscle and Viscera.
6. Kapalbhati - cleans the lower respiratory tract and activates the brain cells.
"All practices should be do under the guidelines of Yoga Teacher"

Figure 3.2 "Yogic Cleansing (Satkarma)" practices posted outside yoga hospital *ṣaṭ-karma* room at Kaivalyadhama.

Source: Author.

experience god will be hindered. *Prāṇāyāma* and yogic diet work together to facilitate this necessary purificatory process.

Much of the information I learned about yogic diet and its relationship to *prāṇāyāma* occurred in one of the two main dining halls on the Kaivalyadhama campus, Annapurna and Sadapurna. For example, Tanu Singh, one of the staff of the Annapurna kitchen where students and faculty regularly dine, explained to me some of the organization's dietary habits during lunch one day:

> Eating creates a *havan* like the *agni-hotra* and sacred substances are poured in. Our bodies are a sacrificial pit and should be treated that way. We should only put pure, *sāttvik* vegetarian food in our bodies. It is transformed into the five *vāyus* or *prāṇas* or energies that sustain us.[14]

Following Mr. Singh's explanation, Dr. Akshaya Khetan, a research officer, added,

> Another thing to consider is the concept of *mitāhāra*. This means moderate food. Food should be taken in moderation. At each meal one-third of our stomach should be filled with food, one-third with water, and the other one third left empty.[15]

A few days later, Madav Talwar, the Registrar of the yoga college, added the following:

> We should eat three to four times per day according to need, not for pleasure. The stomach should be filled with one-half vegetarian food, one-quarter water, and one-quarter air. All of the elements should be present and offered to the Almighty.[16]

Finally, according to *Essence of Prāṇāyāma* (Krishna 2012 [1985]), Kaivalyadhama's most recent book published on the topic that is intended to explain the intricacies and methods of *prāṇāyāma* disseminated both on the campus and also at its annual "Pranayama Sadhana Shibir" ("Pranayama Practice Camp") (Kaivalyadhama 2017: 56–57),

> … it is recommended that [diet] should be clean, appetizing and balanced with adequate quantities of all the ingredients… moderation is the Key-rule, to be observed for the maximum and risk-free benefits from the Prānāyāma.
>
> (Krishna 2012 [1985]: 88)

The common features I wish to emphasize here are my informants' intention to convey the notion that measured yogic diet, or *mitāhāra*,[17] not only maintains a healthy body, but also lays the kindling for an embodied sacrificial process reflective of the *agni-hotra* ceremony, where the yoga body is the *havan* (Sanskrit: *havana*; sacrificial pyre) itself. The word *mitāhāra* is used in the *Haṭha-Yoga-Pradīpikā* and the *Gheraṇḍa-Saṃhitā*, two medieval yoga texts used to instruct students and visitors at Kaivalyadhama on a regular basis, to describe how one should consume precise proportions of food conducive to supporting the preparation of this internalized, embodied sacrifice that is performed in *haṭha-yoga* practice. The food that is consumed to fuel this sacrificial process must be "pure" and "*sāttvik*," as Singh himself put it, since it also in effect becomes the energy by which the body is sustained. Furthermore, though the exact proportions Mr. Talwar suggests are different from those that were suggested by Dr. Khetan, both share a concern for the sacrificial, soteriological nature of the yogic meal as something to be "offered to the Almighty."

The notion of internalizing the sacrifice within one's own body is not unique to Kaivalyadhama and has its origins in religious texts that were produced in the first millennium BCE known as the *Āraṇyakas* and *Upaniṣads* (Flood 1996). The Vedic fire sacrifice, which was originally an external ritual intended to produce auspicious material outcomes, was in these texts and later yogic scriptures re-envisioned as finding its highest meaning as an internal ritual aimed at producing spiritual knowledge and experience (ibid.: 75). Flood writes,

> The internalization of the ritual means that the real purpose of the rite is not its external performance, but knowledge of its deeper meaning, a meaning which points to an underlying foundation or being, supporting the ritual and even the cosmos itself.
>
> (ibid.: 84)

This internalized sacrifice would later inspire what would become *haṭha-yoga* practices developed in medieval India which were, at least in great part, intended to facilitate the sacrificial process in the body of the yogin in order to induce a liberating experience.

Though interpretations of both *mitāhāra* and *sāttvik* diet changed as multiple social groups converged on the campus; students, patients, faculty, and other visitors' bodies became implicated, to varying degrees, in a process intended to purify and reform their urban diets, which were presumed to be unhealthy and indulgent, practiced as these urban diets were by the urban middle and upper classes. This process was then intended to ignite an embodied sacrifice wherein the food that was consumed in the digestive fire could be offered up to god within the yogic body. This process, as I came to learn, would be stimulated by applying the breath practices of *prāṇāyāma*.

Prāṇāyāma as a preliminary form of purification

Drawn from the instructions found in a number of yoga texts used, published, and sold at the institution, *prāṇāyāma* is taught in several contexts on the Kaivalyadhama campus to fulfill the first purificatory stage in Madhavadas's *kriyā-yoga*. These texts include, most prominently, the *Yoga-Sūtra*, *Haṭha-Yoga-Pradīpikā*, and *Gheraṇḍa-Saṃhitā*. The somatic practices gleaned from each text reflect, as Green writes, how through re-enacting *prāṇāyāma* practices found in mass-published yoga texts since India's late colonial period, "… practitioners were to be transformed into the physical embodiment of textually-mediated religious ideals" (Green 2008: 315). These ideals are, as Mallinson has more recently demonstrated through painstaking philological research, often re-constructed in the *Haṭha-Yoga-Pradīpikā* and other yoga texts from a somewhat inconsistent bricolage of yoga practices and goals that were haphazardly compiled from a multiplicity of textual sources in medieval India (Mallinson 2014).[18]

Alternate nostril breathing, or *anuloma-viloma prāṇāyāma*, is one among the many breath practices gleaned from yoga texts at Kaivalyadhama. It comprises the first stage of *kriyā-yoga*, which is classified as purification (*tapas*). Very often, *anuloma-viloma* is preceded by the practice of "skull-shining," or *kapālabhāti*, which, though involving a forceful exhale followed by a passive inhale, is not considered a *prāṇāyāma* practice, but, rather, one of several purifying practices (*śuddhi-kriyās* / *ṣaṭ-kriyās* / *ṣaṭ-karmas*; see Figure 3.2) intended to be used, along with yogic diet, as a preliminary to *prāṇāyāma* practice to purify the subtle channels (*nāḍīs*) of the yogic body. Diet, purifying practices, and *prāṇāyāma* continue to be used at Kaivalyadhama both in the yoga college and the yoga hospital to prepare participants for more advanced stages of yogic experience.

As Kuvalayananda's classic publication *Prāṇāyāma* (Kuvalayananda 2016 [1931]) conveys, the deployment of *kapālabhāti* at Kaivalyadhama is intended to be consistent with *haṭha-yoga* texts, which, as interpreted therein, indicate that *kapālabhāti* is a purification technique to be followed by one or several *prāṇāyāma* practices. By self-purifying the subtle body and practicing *prāṇāyāma*, the yoga practitioner is said to achieve optimum health and, eventually, metaphysical experiences. Kuvalayananda writes,

> Kapālabhāti is one of the six cleansing processes, known in Haṭha Yoga as Shat Kriyās and is intended to clear the nasal passages *contained in the skull*, along with the remaining parts of the respiratory system… Although Kapālabhāti is not a Prāṇāyāma in the strictly technical sense of the word, it is surely a breathing exercise…
>
> (Kuvalayananda 2016 [1931]: 83–84)

> We are studying the physiology of Kapālabhāti in our laboratory… the little work that has been done in this connection, has led us to think that the exercise is capable of cleansing not only the respiratory system but also the different parts of the human anatomy connected with the skull. We have also reason to believe that [Kapālabhāti] is capable of cleansing even the capillaries of the remotest parts of the human body.
>
> (ibid.: 83 fn 2)

As we already observed regarding the body's "metabolic process," we can similarly observe here how Kuvalayananda's theories around breathing practices craftily conflate the "capillaries" with the subtle channels (*nāḍīs*) of the yoga body which are said to be purified through the practice of *kapālabhāti* breathing in *haṭha-yoga*. These conflations continue to manifest in institutional discourse throughout the campus and in online media publications. One evening during a lecture, for example, resident instructor Ms. Lakshmi told one of the audience members, "Swami Kuvalayananda has taught that *kapālabhāti* is not a *prāṇāyāma*, it is a *ṣaṭ-kriyā* that we do to purify our blood and the *nāḍīs*."[19]

In his later book, *Yogic Therapy: Basic Principles and Methods*, Kuvalayananda goes so far as to say that *prāṇāyāma, in and of itself*, is sufficient for accomplishing the self-purification required for the higher stages of yoga. He writes, "Prāṇāyāmas are of primary importance in Yoga. So much so that the authorities on the subject, as can be deduced from the traditional texts of Yoga, felt that no other practice was necessary for attaining purification of body and mind" (Kuvalayananda and Vinekar 2017 [1963]: 74). Quoting the *Haṭha-Yoga-Pradīpikā*, he continues in parentheses, "…Prāṇāyāma, by itself, is sufficient for the eradication of all 'mala's [sic] or toxins'. So opine some authorities who feel that no other practice is necessary" (ibid.). "Mala" is a Sanskrit term used to describe the impurities in the subtle channels (*nāḍīs*) of the yogic body that must be purified through yoga practice. Here, we can see that Kuvalayananda translates "mala" as "toxin," thereby once again conflating concepts of the yogic body found in Sanskrit texts with a seemingly English equivalent. This is significant because "mala" is still translated to the English term "toxin" along with other similar *haṭha-yoga* references and Kaivalyadhama's English translations remain a central feature in the institution's *prāṇāyāma* discourse concerning self-purification from air pollution. Heavily grounded in the authority of popular *haṭha-yoga* texts and Kuvalayananda's interpretation of those texts, the organization's lectures and *prāṇāyāma* classes repeatedly disseminate this ideology of self-purification through breath practice into the present.

This self-purifying *prāṇāyāma* discourse also intersects with the institution's use of Nature Cure as part of its overall therapeutic regimen which also includes *āyurvedic* treatments, organic food grown on campus, and other seemingly natural remedies.[20] In two repeating lectures titled "Fasting Therapy" and "Diet Therapy" delivered at the hospital every week to a large gathered audience, for example, Kaivalyadhama's Dr. Mitra begins her lecture each time by stating that the therapies she is describing constitute the "purification of the mind-body of accumulated waste matter, toxins, and poisons through the use of Naturopathy and Nature Cure."[21] In her weekly lectures, Dr. Mitra repeatedly links these accumulated toxins, first and foremost, to air pollution as well as to other factors including poor diet, which then result in disease. Nature Cure, she then tells the audience, is used to expel accumulated toxins from the body and is accomplished by using, as she instructs, "the *pañcamahābhūtas* [five great elements – earth, water, fire, air, and space] alone to cure ourselves. But how so?" Dr. Mitra proceeds to detail how each element can be used for its specific healing properties. When she reaches the air element, she tells the audience that "in *prāṇāyāma* we use the whole part of the lungs and more oxygen enters to remove toxins." In her "Diet Therapy" lecture we are further told that through a process of detoxification,

> We take the elements in their most natural form for healing… air is used in *prāṇāyāma*. We get increased immunity and that is what they are doing at the yoga hospital, eliminating toxins from the body and then rebuilding intake of certain things.[22]

Following the logic of Nature Cure as it has been understood in India, each natural element including air can be used to heal the body of disease. Thus arises the apparent irony, however, of treating asthma and other air-pollution related diseases by "rebuilding intake" of the very air that caused these conditions in the first place.

Similarly, in another lecture titled "Yoga for Total Health," yoga therapist Ms. Lakshmi frames health maintenance as an individual responsibility according to the popular yoga therapy model of the five sheaths (*pañca-kośa*). From the *manomaya-kośa* (mind sheath), we are told, disease manifests when we cannot control our mind. "If we are sick or have disease," she asserts,

> …then it is our fault, because we don't have control of our mind… Negative thoughts create breathing problems in *prāṇomaya-kośa* (breath sheath) and all diseases are psychosomatic… we therefore control the mind with *prāṇāyāma*.[23]

Ms. Lakshmi was drawing inspiration from the *Haṭha-Yoga-Pradīpikā*, which suggests that we can control the mind if we can control the breath. Following this alternative logic, asthma and other breathing problems are conditions caused by a disturbed mind and can only be fixed by yogic breathing exercises, though without reference to the quality of air that is actually being inhaled.

For all of Kaivalyadhama's concern with curing participants' bodies through nature using only nature's elements, it seems important to mention here how surprised I was one day when I saw that a small encampment that had been set up near the border of the Kaivalyadhama campus since we had arrived, and which had been inhabited by ecological refugees (Gadgil and Guha 1995: 14) in search of water and timber, had been torn down and the inhabitants evicted (see Figure 3.3). When I asked an official from Kaivalyadhama why they were evicted when they seemed to be harmlessly living a subsistence lifestyle in harmony with nature, he angrily replied, "They might be dangerous. We contacted the forest ministry to come have them removed. They steal electricity and other things and must go now."[24] I had not seen electricity anywhere near the area, nor had I perceived any threat when I would occasionally play games with the kids from the encampment on the dirt path leading to the main part of the campus. I had, however, taken notes in my field journal expressing

Figure 3.3 Left: Constructed ecological refugee camp on border of Kaivalyadhama campus. Right: Ecological refugee camp following eviction and deconstruction.

Source: Author.

my respect for these ecological refugees who were truly living the simple, natural lifestyle Kaivalyadhama so often espoused to its middle-class participants. This experience, which took place fairly early on during my fieldwork, foregrounded for me the class/caste disparities at the institution and the country's neoliberal, post-colonial approach to environmentalism and scientific forestry. Perhaps more importantly, it augmented Alter's insights regarding the "'farcical simplicity' of institutionalized Nature Cure/Yoga" in India (Alter 2004: 112).

In sum, in Kaivalyadhama's weekly discourse and ongoing programming, *prāṇāyāma* is situated within the framework of Nature Cure and is purported to both purge the body of accumulated air-borne toxins and eliminate diseases manifesting from the unwieldy mind itself. I noted during one of these ongoing evening lectures that the external systemic sources of these "accumulated toxins" and patients' mental instability are never discussed in any significant way. This is certainly not to say that Kaivalyadhama's visitors, the majority of whom are from Mumbai's middle class, are duped and unaware of the external causes of their ailments (cf. Negi and Srigyan 2021: 18). Many often asked during these evening lectures how they could perform such breathing exercises in a place like polluted Mumbai. Rather, it is to say that they have little to no control over the uneven economic development dynamics and environmental injustices that pollute their air – and, in many ways, financially benefit from them – and therefore the solutions proposed to these problems are necessarily neoliberal and technocratic in nature.

Similarly, the individualistic forms of asthma intervention that we see at Kaivalyadhama might also be understood as agency operating, "in a system that has already been identified as acutely constraining and harmful," wherein "actions are not necessarily about changing the system (though they can be) so much as existing in it…" (Liboiron et al. 2018: 342). Just as "cleaning when there is no chance for cleanliness" performs a particularly important social and political function in toxic politics (ibid.: 343), performing self-purifying *prāṇāyāma* exercises when there is no chance for self-purification in Lonavala and Mumbai signals neoliberal aspirations as well as, given the purported soteriological potential of such practices, participants' aspirations for salvation from the inescapable material realities they incessantly face.

Provoking liberating experiences with prāṇāyāma

In addition to therapeutic bodily purification, as one makes one's way through Kaivalyadhama's numerous teachings pertaining to *prāṇāyāma* in publications and on-site lectures, they will find that a number of potentially liberating experiences are possible as a result of undertaking the practice. In *Prāṇāyāma*, for example, Kuvalayananda concludes the final chapter as follows:

> Again we are hypothetically satisfied that the practice of Prāṇāyāma introduces high pressures both in the central canal of the spinal cord and the ventricles of the brain. These pressures centrally stimulate the whole

> nervous system. Owing to these central and peripheral stimuli, the human consciousness begins to be internalized and supersensuous perceptions begin to be possible. Worlds subtler and still subtler begin to be opened out in proportion to the consciousness itself getting more and more refined, till at last the individual consciousness merges with the cosmic and the individual becomes one with the Infinite.
>
> (Kuvalayananda 2016 [1931]: 152)

Other more recent institutional publications make similar suggestions such as the following found in *Essence of Prāṇāyāma* which creatively embeds the practice of *prāṇāyāma* within the context of the popular soteriological theory of the five body sheaths (*pañca-kośa*) of the yogic body:

> While practicing *Prāṇāyāma*, therefore, it is strongly advocated that the mind should be applied to the practice itself, making the internal awareness as an integral and obligatory part of the *Prāṇāyāmic* technique. In other words, it means that our inner awareness which otherwise remains occupied with the *Annamaya Kosha* should open out itself through the practices of *Prāṇāyāma*, to more and more subtle activities taking place in the *Prāṇāyāma Kosha*,[25] *Manomaya Kosha*, and *Vijnānamaya Kosha* and then should learn to regulate all these activities with an aim to reach to [sic] state to [sic] *Ānandamaya Kosha*.
>
> (Krishna 2012 [1985]: 28)

In short, *prāṇāyāma* delivers one from one's worldly psychosomatic experience ("*Annamaya*" through "*Vijnānamaya Kosha*") to an internal sense of metaphysical bliss ("*Ānandamaya Kosha*").

Finally, to add one more relevant example from a lecture titled "Stress Management" which also takes place weekly in the yoga hospital, resident teacher Dr. Lakit informed us, "Regular *prāṇāyāma* preserves the *prāṇa* and leads to *kuṇḍalinī* preservation. The *kuṇḍalinī* then gets redirected to the brain and recharges the brain."[26] As we can see from each of these examples, the heteroglossia espousing reasons for undertaking *prāṇāyāma* suggest both therapeutic and soteriological consequences, however different each of the popular closed yogic models of the body described here may be. In practice, such dual objectives also work concurrently in Kaivalyadhama's twice-daily *prāṇāyāma* class.

Prāṇāyāma in practice at Kaivalyadhama

The twice-daily public *prāṇāyāma* class held in Kaivalyadhama's yoga hospital illustrates the institution's breath control in practice quite succinctly, while also providing a reminder of the importance of paying close attention to the hard material realities of the institution's surrounding air quality. The evening class takes place daily after the *āsana* class (5:00 PM to 6:00 PM) on Monday through Thursday from 6:15 PM to 7:15 PM. What follows here is a detailed description of the evening *prāṇāyāma* class that took place on October 25, 2017.

After the postural (*āsana*) class preceding it, the yoga therapy room in the yoga hospital accommodates participants who will continue with the *prāṇāyāma* class after a 15-minute break (see Figure 3.4). Approximately 40 men and women gather on yoga mats and sit quietly waiting for the instructor to arrive. For those with serious health conditions, a series of hospital beds are provided along the perimeter of the room which quickly fill up.

A red digital clock hangs on the wall, and just after it reaches 6:15 PM, the class begins when resident yoga instructor Mr. Sahas Bhat walks in and immediately instructs everyone in a gentle voice, "Get ready for session. Sit in any meditative cross-legged posture with your spine erect."[27] As bodies begin to sit up straight and follow Mr. Bhat's instructions, he continues,

> Hands in *jñāna mudrā* on your knees, and gently close your eyes. Drop your shoulders down and relax your facial muscles. Now follow the natural pattern of your breath. Now be aware of the movement of your abdomen and your chest while you are inhaling and while you are exhaling.[28]

Figure 3.4 Students prepare for class in Kaivalyadhama's yoga therapy room.

Source: Author.

A few minutes of silence ensue as we all focus on our breath. As we do so, I cannot help but notice how, as I so often experienced during this class, fumes from burning trash and car exhaust from the nearby Highway 48 seep in through the screens of the open windows and into my lungs.

Following some brief instruction in *kapālabhāti* breathing, the class is then instructed to lay in corpse posture (*śavāsana*). Mr. Bhat informs the class, "Now this is the time to release the tension of your back… be aware of your back muscles and relax them."[29] While we lay in corpse posture, the scent of cigarette smoke fills the room. Two participants from Germany who were regularly found to be smoking during their yoga therapy week were now smoking just outside the hospital walls where they habitually snuck away from *prāṇāyāma* class throughout the week. As I pull my shirt over my face to filter the smoke out, the class continues as we begin to practice *kriyā-yoga*'s fundamental *anuloma-viloma prāṇāyāma* (alternate nostril breathing), followed then by the buzzing *brāhmarī prāṇāyāma* (bee breath) which involves making a humming sound on exhalation that rattles the skull.

What follows these *prāṇāyāma* techniques is the practice of *auṃ* chanting (*oṃkāra*), the beginning of the second of three aspects of Madhavadas's *kriyā-yoga*, which involves mantra recitation (*svādhyāya*) of the sacred syllable *auṃ* in rhythmic fashion with our inhale and exhale. I note during the class the rather fluid boundaries between the practice of *prāṇāyāma* and sacred sound practices, as even this sonic practice involves careful regulation of the breath. In the end, the class was indeed quite tranquilizing and I always felt, despite the ongoing intrusion of air pollution, extremely relaxed and rejuvenated afterward.

Concurrent with this *prāṇāyāma* class, Madhavadas's *kriyā-yoga* finds its fullest expression in the twice-daily fire sacrifice (*agni-hotra*) ceremony held on the campus in the morning and evening. Here, the evening chill does not discourage Kaivalyadhama's most dedicated from attending the evening fire ceremony conducted by the organization's resident Swami Maheshananda[30] and his resident German assistant. Performed at 7:00 AM and 6:30 PM every day, this event attracts a dozen or so resident students, local visitors, and international participants to a small room in Maheshananda's living quarters where we also find the burial sites (*samādhis*) of his two predecessors, Swami Digambar (1903–1990) as well as Kaivalyadhama's original founder, Swami Kuvalayananda (1883–1966). Some evenings I chose, in lieu of the therapeutic *prāṇāyāma* session, to join the group as they crammed into Maheshananda's room.[31]

As the ceremony commences, Maheshananda recites opening Vedic chants while his German assistant carefully piles dried cow dung and wood in a small earthen vessel. We are then told to perform three rounds of alternate nostril breathing (*anuloma-viloma prāṇāyāma*), followed by the chanting of the sacred *oṃkāra* mantra, or *auṃ*, several times aloud together and, afterwards, mentally on our own. After a minute or so of chanting *auṃ* mentally, Maheshananda commences chanting from the *Ṛg Veda*, starting with the Gayatri Mantra, and thus the final stage of *kriyā-yoga* – *īśvarapraṇidhāna* (devotion to god) – as his assistant ignites the cow dung and wood with fire. As Maheshananda's chanting continues, the square base of the sacrificial altar is dressed in the four cardinal directions with wooden sticks, fresh flowers, and sprinkles of water. Milk and ghee from Kaivalyadhama's cow-shed (*gośāla*) are warmed in a small ladle and roasted over the fire for some time, after which Maheshananda offers ghee into the flame. As the ghee is poured into the fire, the substance evaporates and fills the room with a distinct smell that lingers long afterward. Maheshananda's assistant continues to make these offerings to the fire, also adding grains of organic brown rice.

Once these offerings have been made, Maheshananda leads us through an extended period of chanting the Mahamrtyumjaya Mantra.[32] After we chant this mantra aloud for approximately ten minutes, he instructs us to recite it ten times mentally, after which he chants closing mantras as the fire slowly dies down while he continues to offer ghee to the vanishing flame. His assistant undresses the altar of flowers and twigs, dries the water with a brush, and with perfect timing, the chanting ends as the flame disappears, leaving only ashes below. Following a period of silence, another assistant walks around and offers honeyed milk into the right palm of each participant, as well as a small piece of the food offering consecrated during the ceremony. After consuming both, all bow in reverence to the burning embers and depart for the evening.

With the comments Tanu Singh had conveyed to me earlier in mind, it was clear that the *agni-hotra* served to reflect the internalized sacrifice taking place within the yogic body as systematic offerings of sacred material substances, including water, milk, rice, and ghee, were made to the purifying force of fire. As the flames digest and carry the material substances upward into empty space, participants concurrently practice the three stages of Madhavadas's *kriyā-yoga* signaling the co-implication of their bodies in the sacrificial process through their *prāṇāyāma* practice.

My alternating participation in the *agni-hotra* ceremony and *prāṇāyāma* classes at Kaivalyadhama developed into a habit that I came to enjoy very much as a welcome reprieve from thinking, researching, keeping notes, and writing. That being said, my ongoing experience of the intersection between air pollution and the ostensibly therapeutic and soteriological techniques I was learning compelled me to take the materiality and agency of Mumbai and Lonavala's air seriously (Choy 2012). This task became particularly important because, as Shapiro highlights, regulating the effects of toxicity "at the molecular register will almost always fail to address toxics' larger relations" (Shapiro 2019: 154). In other words, I eventually realized that I needed to situate Kaivalyadhama's *prāṇāyāma* breathers within their seemingly intangible, and yet very real, atmospheric context that was comprised of concrete social, historical, environmental, and political influences.

Situating Kaivalyadhama's Purifying Prāṇāyāma in Pollution

It will now be helpful to telescope out to take a look at some of the broader contexts which give shape to, and also enable, Kaivalyadhama's self-purifying *prāṇāyāma* discourse. Today, air-pollution-related ailments are too common in India[33] and other areas in the Global South, where the "toxic unevenness" of global development has led to environmental disasters in so-called "sacrifice zones" (cf. Lerner 2010; Liboiron et al. 2018: 332, 339) where labor is cheap and development projects are largely unregulated. Perhaps the most unforgettable of these disasters was the unfortunate "late industrial" (Fortun 2014: 312) accident at Union Carbide's pesticide plant in Bhopal in 1984 that left thousands dead and countless injured on account of the toxic pollution released into the atmosphere (Fortun 2001: xiii–xviii), but also more recently the incalculable number of COVID-19 deaths that have occurred due to the concomitant health complications caused by India's urban air pollution. These major disasters are enabled by the fact that the environment is sacrificed in the name of economic development in India, while the implementation of air-quality regulation and clean technology are seen as important – and yet necessary to defer – until some imagined economic development threshold is reached (Negi and Srigyan 2021: 2).

Though not a single catastrophic event like Bhopal, the persistent unhealthy air pollution in India is a disaster of its own. An overabundance of monitoring and data demonstrates that the consistently high levels of toxic urban air in India "have a proven link with increased rates of asthma attacks, breathlessness, persistent cough, and frequent chest infections in the short term, and with incidence of lung cancer with prolonged exposure" (Negi and Srigyan 2021: 9; see also 33–35). Women and children are particularly vulnerable, while the elderly suffer from dementia and Alzheimer's as a result of the effects of air pollution on the brain (ibid.: 9, 65). The country's high levels of toxic air pollution occur despite the nation's glut of legislation governing air quality and pollution that stretches all the way back to the Air Act of 1981 and its largely impotent regulatory arm that was later added in 1987 to penalize those who violate the Central Pollution Control Board's standards for air pollution (Sharan 2013: 81).

Like in many global mega-cities in India and elsewhere, citizens in Mumbai and its surrounding environs regularly face dangerous levels of air pollution. As a result, in 2023 doctors in Mumbai reported a five-fold, "'exponential rise' in the number of chronic cough, wheezing, upper-respiratory infections" and related hospitalizations compared to previous years (Ramesh 2023). The online news outlet *the Quint* even reported that in February 2023, "Mumbai overtook Delhi as the second-most polluted city in the world, as per global Air Quality Index" (ibid.), and for Mumbai's medical professionals, this was clearly the reason for the increased infections and hospitalizations. "The top pulmonologists," reported *the Quint*, "point all fingers at pollution, and the relentless construction that is happening all across the city" (ibid.).

Mumbai's increasingly unbreathable urban air did not develop overnight, however, and has a long colonial history that has contributed to its current state. By the late nineteenth century in the colonial Indian Ocean port of Bombay, air pollution had already become a central concern as "dense smoke belching from factories and workshops, railway yards, munitions factories, printing works and steamships docked in Bombay harbor" materialized atmospheric pollution in unprecedented ways (Arnold 2016: 192–193). And by the early twentieth century, pollution from automobile exhaust was already recognized as a serious health risk (ibid.: 195–196), and continues to be recognized as such today. With these early red flags signaling the detrimental health effects of air pollution, Bombay and other cities, including Kolkata, characterized the "'contaminated city' of the colonial era" and served, as Arnold writes, "as a precursor and proxy for toxicity in the post-colony" (ibid.: 176).

Indeed today, Mumbai has become one of several "mega-cities of India's postindustrial aspirations" (Rademacher and Sivaramakrishnan 2013: 18) that has grown exponentially since India's economic liberalization policies of the 1990s as a result of, among several primary factors, a "new demand for urban land among the local middle and upper classes and transnational elites" (Doshi 2013: 228). With the highest car density of any Indian city during the time I performed my fieldwork (Sen 2016) and a heavy concentration of air-polluting industrial emissions (Press Trust of India 2019), Mumbai's urban population as well as those living in the city's environs persistently breathe a toxic atmospheric cocktail of exhaust and other industry-borne Hazardous Air Pollutants (HAPs) (cf. Srivastava and Som 2007). These populations face, as Kenner conveys, "the slow and uneven violence that makes the world increasingly unbreathable" (Kenner 2018: 28), and it is important to note that the negative health effects become even more uneven when we consider that it is the urban poor who suffer disproportionately as a result of Mumbai's polluted air (cf. Tankha et al. 2019). How, then, to manage the demand for unrestrained economic development in major cities like Mumbai on the one hand, and the resultant air-pollution-induced breathing infirmities this development necessarily entails, on the other?

The answer to this question often comes in the form of privileged, individual, technocratic solutions. There is no lack of home air filtering technology available from "Airprenuers" (Negi and Srigyan 2021: 79), for example, who sell air purifiers to middle-class consumers who can afford such necessary and protective safety devices for their homes and automobiles in major Indian cities (ibid.: 88).[34] Within this context, Kaivalyadhama's individualistic, self-purifying *prāṇāyāma* practices present another tempting solution that many of Mumbai's middle-class breathers are willing to consider to find some relief for their burdened lungs and bodies. In this regard, Kenner has demonstrated in *Breathtaking*, an ethnographic study of asthma and other related breathing ailments, how,

> ...asthma care has been individualized in neoliberal ways; even public health responses have tended to emphasize the responsibility of individuals – taking medication, cleaning home environments, and monitoring pulmonary performance – over collective responsibility.
>
> (Kenner 2018: 8)

Among these neoliberal solutions, Kenner shows how Buteyko breathing (a therapeutic Russian breathing technique) has played a special role in transnational therapeutic asthma treatment (ibid.: 25, 85) in a manner similar to that which we have encountered with the use of *prāṇāyāma* at Kaivalyadhama. Such individualized, neoliberal approaches to treating asthma and other breathing difficulties that result from air pollution do not challenge the political and economic systems that produce air pollution in the first place. In fact, they leave these systems intact while placing the burden of responsibility for healing on the individual who often cannot escape, as we have seen at Kaivalyadhama, the toxic air that burdens their lungs day in and day out (cf. Godrej 2016; Jain 2020).

Conclusion: From Biopolitical to Necropolitical Individualism

Cohen, who studies the history of biological immunity in Western cultures, describes the predominant self-responsibilizing approach to global health we have encountered here as "biopolitical individualism," a rather recent phenomenon that developed in the middle of the nineteenth century wherein individual immune systems were conceived as the principal boundary and defense system between the human body and the countless external toxic forces that could potentially wreak havoc within it (Cohen 2009: 239). As Chen elaborates, such a conception of the human being amounted to "the abandonment of humans' integral relation to their environments and the insistence on a radical segregation of self and world fueled by a bellicose antagonism" (Chen 2012: 194–195). Consequently, we now often encounter in popular media discourse an imperative to *fight* asthma and other illnesses such as cancer, heart disease, and diabetes by our own individual means, for example, rather than calling into question the structural injustices that cause toxicity to permeate human bodies and create illnesses like asthma in the first place.

Kaivalyadhama's self-purifying *prāṇāyāma* regimens appear to constitute nothing more than another instantiation of Cohen's biopolitical individualism, though it is important to keep in mind that India also has its own entangled histories of immunity, pollution, and toxicity that challenge, coincide with, and also influence those of Western cultures and which attempt to provide solutions to the issues posed to human health by environmental pollution in the Global South on their own terms. In this regard, during its dialogical encounter with the West in the late nineteenth and early twentieth centuries in and around Mumbai (cf. Alter 2000, 2004), Indian understandings of pollution and toxicity became entangled and experienced friction with British colonial perspectives (Arnold 2016: 10). Pre-existing religious notions of purity and danger (Douglas 1984 [1966]) concerned with caste and occupational boundaries, ritual purity, and human and animal waste intermingled, and were often irreconcilable, with British scientific understandings of what constituted urban pollution and hygiene as the environmental footprint of colonial imperialism began to make its increasingly deleterious mark on the city and its environs (Arnold 2016: 184–186; cf. Alley 2002).

One particularly important development that took place in colonial India is how, as Arnold has shown, Indian forms of medicine became at various points of time "an important element in the unfolding ideology of empire and, later, in the emergence of anticolonial discourse and an aspirant counterhegemony" as well as a tool that was used against the scientific, biomedical practices of the imperial British (Arnold 1993: 15). Significantly, this Indian repertoire of alternative medicine included *prāṇāyāma* practices that had previously been kept secret and that were transmitted only from guru to disciple. Through mass publication during India's late colonial period, these *prāṇāyāma* practices were made widely accessible to the Indian middle class in popular yoga texts.[35] Furthermore, these newly democratized forms of breath practice, which were both therapeutic but also potentially liberating from a yogic perspective, eventually became a key form of somatic nationalism for developing "homegrown alternatives to [the British] imperial culture of the body" (Green 2008: 285–287, 292). "In this version of Indian breath as Indian empowerment," Green writes, "we see meditation as a form of *politics*" (ibid.: 304, emphasis added).

Among the yoga texts popularized during this time were the *Yoga-Sūtra*, *Haṭha-Yoga-Pradīpikā*, *Gheraṇḍa-Saṃhitā*, and *Śiva-Saṃhitā* (cf. Alter 2004, x; Singleton 2010: 44–49), all of which contain a number of *prāṇāyāma* practices that are, as we have seen, today widely instructed at Kaivalyadhama. Importantly, and as we have seen in my fieldwork, these texts, often grafted onto the German system of Nature Cure (Alter 2000), propose models of the yoga body as a self-purifying instrument capable of eradicating most any disease or illness through the practice of *prāṇāyāma* and other yoga techniques. Subramaniam characterizes the contemporary outcome of India's encounter with British governmentality and biopolitical rule that have enabled techniques such as these breath practices to emerge at Kaivalyadhama and elsewhere as constituting "new formations of contemporary biopolitics" (Subramaniam 2019: 13). As Subramaniam writes in full:

> There was no easy alliance, and anticolonial struggles and the independence movement at times contested and at times colluded with the British, helping shape a new biopolitical order that has in turn strongly shaped postcolonial biopolitical governance. This postcolonial biopolitics has given us new formations of contemporary biopolitics in India.
>
> (ibid.)

Individualistic, self-responsible models of the yoga body have certainly enabled yogic ideology to effortlessly unite with neoliberal, biopolitical conceptions of health in a distinctly Indian way that might potentially produce a "neoliberal yogi" who is focused on health and self-optimization in competitive economic markets (Godrej 2016).

I would like, however, to suggest that the notion of neoliberal biopolitics seems to lack the necessary analytical depth to describe the fact that at Kaivalyadhama, even those deadly ailments – the etiologies of which are air pollution – are said to be curable by the very act of breathing the inescapable polluted air that created them in the first place. Indeed, given its yogic ideology of self-purification that is precariously disseminated amidst polluted urban air, Kaivalyadhama's discourse evades being categorized simply as promoting yet another "biopolitical individualism" (Cohen 2009: 239).

Rather, to the extent that the air-polluted material realities in which Kaivalyadhama's yoga practitioners regularly breathe might be considered environmental "sacrifice zones," I suggest that it would be more accurate – and deeply tragic, sad, and humbling, given the context provided in this chapter – to describe Kaivalyadhama's *prāṇāyāma* discourse as encouraging a distinctly *necropolitical* individualism (Mbembe 2003, 2019). Mbembe's notion of necropolitics, or the "subjugation of life to the power of death" (Mbembe 2003: 39), notably accounts for those bodies deemed *expendable* under global neocolonial, neoliberal ideologies and therefore implicated in specific "*death-worlds*" which comprise "new and unique forms of social existence in which vast populations are subjected to conditions of life conferring upon them the status of *living dead*" (ibid.: 40, emphases in original). At its roots, necropolitics is grounded in racism, which, according to Mbembe,

> … is the driver of the necropolitical principle insofar as it stands for organized destruction, for a *sacrificial* economy, the functioning of which requires, on the one hand, a generalized cheapening of the price of life and, on the other, a habituation to loss.
>
> (Mbembe 2019: 38, emphasis added)

As the recent work of geographers engaging Mbembe's notion of necropolitics suggests, we can conceive of entire air-polluted geographic regions as what Mbembe would describe as "death-worlds," subject as the populations in these regions are to specific, lamentable manifestations of "nonspectacular and more quotidian understandings of necropolitical pollution" (Davies 2018: 1543). In this regard, Davies, who is particularly concerned with the Louisiana–Mississippi Chemical Corridor – the population of which is predominantly Black – calls us to pay close attention to, "the necropolitics of place, how certain places, polluted through the slow violence of environmental denigration, are rendered death worlds, exposing some inhabitants to violent experiences of pollution and the denigration of living conditions" (ibid.: 1542). From the perspective of environmental racism and growing calls for environmental justice, we should, as I have in this chapter, extend Davies' call to consider air-polluted regions in the post-colonial Global South as necropolitical "*death-worlds*" (Mbembe 2003: 40).

Therefore, though a number of scholars of modern yoga, myself included, have discussed yoga's intersections with neoliberal ideology and biopolitics in

India and elsewhere at great length (Godrej 2016, 2022; Miller 2020; Jain 2020), we need to begin to consider how yoga might also promote the slow loss (rather than the maintenance) of life. When proceeding with such projects, the analytical framework of necropolitics opens new pathways for those conducting fieldwork in sites where uneven development, racism, classism, and other social ills of late industrial capitalism are rampant. For example, might prison yoga, situated as it is within the American carceral state, and which Godrej has analyzed extensively from the perspective of neoliberal ideology (Godrej 2022), in fact be better studied as a necropolitics designed for expendable populations? Or would the BJP's Common Yoga Protocol, practiced annually amidst dense city smog at the International Day of Yoga and encouraged as a regular daily practice in India's most polluted cities, not be better understood within the context of New Delhi's disastrous air pollution?

As I have at least shown in this chapter, a necropolitical – rather than a biopolitical – approach to the study of contemporary yoga amidst the air pollution created by environmental exploitation under neoliberal capitalism can, in fact, serve as a fitting interpretive framework for the study of particular contemporary yoga cultures. At Kaivalyadhama, one of India's first and foremost yoga institutions, the emic logic of a purifying, embodied, internalized yogic sacrifice found in *haṭha-yoga* texts simultaneously implicates, from an etic perspective, seemingly expendable bodies into a slow sacrifice on the pyre of uneven post-colonial development and late industrial capitalism. Following these emic and etic logics simultaneously allows us to pay tribute to the incredible cultural legacy of yoga and *prāṇāyāma* practice at Kaivalyadhama on the one hand, but also obliges us to confront the harsh, unjust, air-polluted realities the institution routinely faces on the other. In light of the perplexing irony with which I began this chapter, we can thus conclude here by definitively declaring that there are two sacrifices taking place in Kaivalyadhama's *prāṇāyāma* practices. The first is purifying and liberating, while the second, given the necroworld in which it is taking place, is tragically noxious and pestilent.

Notes

1 Jennifer, in discussion with the author, Lonavala, Maharashtra, December 3, 2017.

2 I borrow the term "closed" from David Gordon White, who juxtaposes closed models of the yogic body with "open" models that seek forms of union or connection with phenomena outside of the yogic body itself. "Closed" models of the yogic body do not seek such external forms of union and remain concerned with the body's fortification against death as well as its internalized soteriological potential. Combining therapeutic and soteriological goals, Kaivalyadhama prioritizes and champions a closed, self-purifying yoga body that is said to be capable of simultaneously purifying itself of environmental toxins that have entered the body, fortifying itself against disease, and experiencing liberation using, among other practices, the transformative practice of *prāṇāyāma*. It is important to note here that there are other "open" models of the yogic body discussed at Kaivalyadhama that are nevertheless not accentuated or emphasized anywhere near as much as the closed models that I present in this chapter (see White 2006).

3 Special thanks to Smriti Srinivas and Tim Choy at the University of California, Davis for their help in finding relevant sources for this project during its initial phases. I would also like to acknowledge the incredible resources that I found for this article at The Asthma Files (TAF) (theasthmafiles.org). As their website states, "TAF is a collaborative ethnographic research project designed to advance understanding and efforts to address environmental public health challenges around the world."

4 Negi and Srigyan elaborate: "There seems a fundamental contradiction at the heart of Indian environmental realities: large-scale degradation coexists with stringent legal regulatory regimes and a decent record of biodiversity conservation" (Negi and Srigyan 2021: 2).

5 I interchangeably employ the language of toxicity, poison, and pollution throughout this chapter to describe the state of Mumbai's urban air quality and its effects on the human body and human behavior. I do so not as an Orientalist construction of India's current ecological situation (cf. Arnold 2016: 12), but because these terms are also, as I discovered, part of the emic discourse at my field site used to describe – in English – the tragic and lamentable post-colonial situation that creates India's poor air quality and concomitant public health challenges.

6 As Choy writes, "How similarly fruitful might an anthropology of air be, an anthropology of this stuff sensed in and through the moment of bringing breath into the body, or at the moment when wind opens the body to ailments? Air muddies the distinction between subjects and environments, and between subjects. This thickness and porosity rendered by air is part of what makes the air and the airborne such deeply felt elements" (Choy 2012: 139–140).

7 For more on the life and influence of Swami Madhavadas, see Alter's *Gandhi's Body: Sex, Diet, and the Politics of Nationalism* (Alter 2000). For a social history of Kaivalyadhama and Swami Kuvalayananda's work at the institution, see Alter's *Yoga in Modern India: The Body Between Science and Philosophy* (Alter 2004).

8 According to India's Central Pollution Control Board, an AQI measurement between 101 and 200, "May cause breathing discomfort to the people with lung disease such as asthma and discomfort to people with heart disease, children and older adults". An AQI of 144 far exceeds what is considered "Satisfactory" quality, which according to the CPCB is 50–100 (Central Pollution Control Board 2014: 36). In the words of India's Central Pollution Control Board, the AQI is "a tool for effective communication of air quality status to people in terms, which are easy to understand. It transforms complex air quality data of various pollutants into a single number (index value), nomenclature and colour" (Central Pollution Control Board n.d.: 1).

Air quality data was provided by "Air Quality Data in India" for the city of Mumbai, which provides a historical excel summary of India's Central Pollution Control Board's city-by-city daily AQI data. Historical data is not available for Lonavala itself, though the AQI as I write this chapter in April 2022 is 130 (https://www.iqair.com/india/maharashtra/lonavla). Because air pollution levels are seasonal in India, and since data for Mumbai's daily AQI did not become available until 2018, the average AQI provided here is based on the same period during 2018 during which I performed fieldwork in the previous year, 2017. My fieldwork was performed during the last quarter of 2017 during the months of October, November, and December, and thus the average AQI presented here is from the same period in 2018. For data, see: https://www.kaggle.com/datasets/rohanrao/air-quality-data-in-india?resource=download.

9 Maya, in discussion with the author, Lonavala, Maharashtra, October 25, 2017.

10 Translations of *tapas*, *svādhyāya*, and *īśvarapraṇidhāna* follow the translations often provided at Kaivalyadhama.
11 Dr. Akshaya Khetan, in discussion with the author, Lonavala, Maharashtra, December 1, 2017.
12 Dr. Bhogal uses the words "energy" and "*prāṇa*" interchangeably throughout his instruction.
13 *auṃ bhūr bhuvaḥ svaḥ*
auṃ tat saviturvareṇyaṃ
bhargo devasya dhīmahi
dhiyo yo naḥ pracodayāt
14 Tanu Singh, in discussion with the author, Lonavala, Maharashtra, November 2, 2017.
15 Dr. Akshaya Khetan, in discussion with the author, Lonavala, Maharashtra, November 2, 2017.
16 Madav Talwar, in discussion with the author, Lonavala, Maharashtra, November 7, 2017.
17 Not following Monier-Williams' colonial convention here to translate *mitāhāra* as simply "moderate diet," I translate *mitāhāra* as "measured diet" or "measured yogic diet." For a full discussion of this translational choice and its significance in *haṭha-yoga* theory and praxis, see "Preparing and Stoking the Internal Sacrifice in Hatha Yoga: Diet and Breath Control to Move beyond the Mind" (Miller 2019).
18 The canonical *Haṭha-Yoga-Pradīpikā* is a prime example of this, containing, as Mallinson shows, 173 verses from at least 15 other pre-existing yoga texts (Mallinson 2014: 239).
19 Ms. Lakshmi, in weekly hospital lecture, Lonavala, Maharashtra, November 8, 2017.
20 With origins in Germany, Nature Cure intersected with yoga in the early twentieth century in India. Nature Cure suggests that people can cure themselves using the power of the natural elements of earth, water, fire, and air alone. For a detailed history of the relationship between Nature Cure and yoga, see Alter's *Gandhi's Body: Sex, Diet, and the Politics of Nationalism* (Alter 2000).
21 Dr. Mitra, in weekly hospital lecture, Lonavala, Maharashtra, October 10, 2017.
22 Ibid.
23 Ms. Lakshmi, in weekly hospital lecture, Lonavala, Maharashtra, November 8, 2017.
24 Anonymous Kaivalyadhama official, in discussion with the author, Lonavala, Maharashtra, October 14, 2017.
25 I believe that the author was referring to the "*Prāṇāmaya*" Kosha rather than the "*Prānāyāma*" Kosha.
26 Dr. Lakit, in weekly hospital lecture, Lonavala, Maharashtra, on October 27, 2017. Roughly translated as "the coiled one," "*kuṇḍalinī*" is a Sanskrit term used to describe a female-gendered serpentine goddess energy coiled at the base of the yogic body that can be released or "forced" (*haṭha*, see Birch 2011) up along the spine and through the cranium of the yogic body to produce metaphysical experiences.
27 Mr. Sahas Bhat, in daily *prāṇāyāma* class, Lonavala, Maharashtra, October 25, 2017.
28 Ibid.
29 Ibid.
30 Swami Maheshananda took *mahāsamādhi* and left his body on June 28, 2021. I am very grateful for the time I was able to spend with him while at Kaivalyadhama and for all the insights he provided to me during my fieldwork there.
31 The following *agni-hotra* ceremony took place on November 2, 2017.

32 The Mahamrtyumjaya Mantra is chanted as follows:

> *auṃ tryambakaṃ yajāmahe*
> *sugandhiṃ puṣṭivardhanam*
> *urvārukamiva bandhanān*
> *mṛtyormukṣīya mā' 'mṛtāt*

Kaivalyadhama has translated the Mahamrtyumjaya Mantra as follows:

> Oṃ. We worship the Lord of all the three worlds, who permeates everywhere like a fragrance and gives the sustenance to it.
>
> May He detach us from the bondage of death just as the ripe cucumber gets detached from its stem, but may He not keep us away from immortality.
> (Kaivalyadhama 2016)

33 Writing about Delhi, Negi and Srigyan estimate that "Over 30 million residents of the region are forced to live with respiratory ailments, as the poison builds up inside their lungs, brain and other organs, bringing mortality ever closer" (Negi and Srigyan 2021: 3).

34 Negi and Srigyan nuance this perspective, noting that in their ethnographic study of Delhi's air pollution, they found that Delhi's "airpreneuers" saw themselves as creating change through faith in their technology. They write,

> the neoliberal impulse to seek individualised solutions to social and political concerns, such as pollution, is yet another forceful critique. However, in keeping with this book's emphasis on building concepts from ethnographic work rather than pregiven frames, we argue that the commodification of air is a complex process that far exceeds the narrow framings within which it is otherwise.
> (Negi and Srigyan 2021: 76)

We might also interpret the perceived activism-through-consumption that these types of devices enable as akin to what Jain has described as "gestural subversions," wherein consumers gesture their subversive resistance toward the pitfalls of neoliberal capitalism through consumption while their subversion is nevertheless simultaneously contained through the consumptive process itself (Jain 2020: 8, 30, 71).

35 Nevertheless, as Green emphasizes, "…there was something deeply fraudulent about the written discourse of meditation during the nineteenth and twentieth centuries, for this was less the high road to real experience than the disguised pathway to its concealment" (Green 2008: 314).

References

Alley, Kelly D. 2002. *On the Banks of the Gaṅgā: When Wastewater Meets a Sacred River*. Ann Arbor: University of Michigan Press.

Alter, Joseph S. 2000. *Gandhi's Body: Sex, Diet, and the Politics of Nationalism*. Philadelphia: University of Pennsylvania Press.

Alter, Joseph S. 2004. *Yoga in Modern India: The Body Between Science and Philosophy*. Princeton: Princeton University Press.

Arnold, David. 1993. *Colonizing the Body: State Medicine and Epidemic Disease in Nineteenth-century India*. Berkeley: University of California Press.

Arnold, David. 2016. *Toxic Histories: Poison and Pollution in Modern India*. Cambridge: Cambridge University Press.

Press Trust of India. 2019. "Delhi, Mumbai, 4 More Indian Cities Hotspots for Rising Nitrogen Oxide Levels: Report," *First Post*, July 8, 2019. https://www.firstpost.com/tech/science/delhi-mumbai-four-more-indian-cities-hotspots-for-rising-levels-of-nox-report-6953291.html

Rademacher, Anne and K. Sivaramakrishnan eds. 2013. *Ecologies of Urbanism in India: Metropolitan Civility and Sustainability*. Hong Kong: Hong Kong University Press.

Ramesh, Mythreyee. 2023. "Are More Mumbaikars Complaining About Relentless Coughing Than Before?" *the Quint*, March 4, 2023. Accessed March 11, 2023. https://www.thequint.com/fit/why-is-all-of-mumbai-coughing-relentlessly#read-more

Sen, Somit. 2016. "At 430/km, Mumbai has highest car density" *Economic Times*, June 20, 2016. https://auto.economictimes.indiatimes.com/news/industry/at-430/km-mumbai-has-highest-car-density/52826974?redirect=1

Shapiro, Nicholas. 2019. "Persistent Ephemeral Pollutants," in Marie-Pier Boucher, Stefan Helmreich, Leila W Kinney, Skylar Tibbits, Rebecca Uchill and Evan Ziporyn (eds.), *Being Material*. London: MIT Press: 154–161.

Sharan, Awadhendra. 2013. "One Air, Two Interventions: Delhi in the Age of Environment," in Anne Rademacher and K. Sivaramakrishnan (eds.), *Ecologies of Urbanism in India: Metropolitan Civility and Sustainability*. Hong Kong: Hong Kong University Press: 71–92.

Singleton, Mark. 2010. *Yoga Body: The Origins of Modern Posture Practice*. New York: Oxford University Press.

Srinivas, Smriti. 2018. "Highways for Healing: Contemporaneous 'Temples' and Religious Movements in an Indian City." *Journal of the American Academy of Religion* 86, no. 2: 473–496.

Srivastava, Anjali and Dipanjali Som. 2007. "Hazardous air pollutants in industrial area of Mumbai – India." *Chemosphere* 69: 458–468.

Subramaniam, Banu. 2019. *Holy Science: The Biopolitics of Hindu Nationalism*. Seattle: University of Washington Press.

Tankha, Ishan, Aruna Chandrasekhar and Prerna Srigyan. 2019. "Mumbai's Mahul." *The Asthma Files*. Accessed May 5, 2022. https://theasthmafiles.org/content/mumbais-mahul

Times of India. 2018. "Mumbai Pune Expressway," *Times of India*. Accessed August 23, 2018. https://timesofindia.indiatimes.com/topic/Mumbai-Pune-Expressway?_ga=2.19741178.359634436.1535132969-763796356.1527883235

Vaid, Mansi and Sanjay Verma. 2021. "Kapalabhati: A physiological healer in human physiological system." *Yoga-Mīmāṃsā* 53, no. 1: 69–74.

White, David Gordon. 2006. "'Open' and 'Closed' Models of the Human Body In Indian Medical and Yogic Traditions." *Asian Medicine* 2, no. 1: 1–13.

Conclusion

Future Directions for the Study of Yoga

I have approached the study of contemporary yoga in this book using methods that are simultaneously critical and yet sympathetic. My approach no doubt emerges from the manifold experiences I have had while embodying, but also critically studying, transnational yoga. Before being introduced to the critical study of yoga, and while living both in California and on the Big Island of Hawaii in 2012 and 2013, I immersed myself in intensive yoga techniques involving not only postural exercises but also vegetarian dietary regimens, fasting, musical practices, breathing techniques, and meditation. I supported my lifestyle by working first as a yoga studio production manager at Yoga Glo in Santa Monica, California, where I encountered a variety of yoga systems and teachers from many different places. I then moved to serve as a certified public accountant and business manager at Kalani Honua, a non-profit retreat center in the coastal jungle of Puna, Hawaii, where transformative, spiritual experience was part of everyday life for most all residents and visitors hailing primarily from the middle and upper classes of the United States mainland.

While I was in Hawaii, Jeffrey Kripal published the following:

> We need these nondual knowers, these modern gnostics, desperately.
>
> But we also need real scholars, truly sympathetic and truly critical thinkers who are not afraid to study these teachers and their communities with all the tools of the humanities and social sciences, to interact with them, to be moved, maybe even enlightened, by them, but also to argue with them and make some historical sense of the riotous and often troubling facts of their biographies and community narratives.
>
> (Kripal 2013: 218)

Not yet trained in the critical and ethnographic study of religion, the first sentence resonated deeply with me as I was surrounded by and practiced yoga with self-proclaimed sages, gurus, and spiritual teachers from all over the world. The meaning of the second, much longer sentence made much more sense when I began my graduate studies in 2014 at the University of California,

DOI: 10.4324/9781003414032-5

Davis and eventually researched and wrote this book even as I remained – and still am – immersed in yoga practice.

It is possible and necessary to study yoga in a way that is simultaneously critical and sympathetic. Yoga practices are carried out in particular times and places, often intersect with troubling social facts such as abuse, racism, sexism, colonialism, and speciesism – to name but a few – and thus critical historical and ethnographic attention to yoga's seemingly universal somatic regimens is essential (cf. Miller 2021; Deslippe 2021). At the same time, close consideration of somatic yoga regimens on their disseminators' own terms can reveal transformative yogic cultural logics with origins in Indian Ocean worlds. The culturally generative frictions between traveling yoga systems and the novel social contexts they encounter produce what I have called engaged alchemies. Studying embodied yoga regimens as expressive of engaged alchemy unveils complex social contexts but also the worlding of Indian Ocean imaginaries globally.

Following the early adaptions made by Ramakrishna (Sarkar 1997), *Embodying Transnational Yoga* has shown in great detail how the transformative cultural logics of three particular forms of yoga have become firmly situated within three specific contemporaneous worlds of yoga practice. Such transnational dissemination of yoga became possible beginning with the encounters between Ramakrishna, who had inherited North India's extant "*bhakti* sensibility" (Burchett 2019: 169), and an Indian middle class grappling with the constraints of Victorian British colonial imperialism. Ramakrishna's approach eventually became a flexible template for disseminating engaged alchemies to the global middle class. We saw this as we moved our attention beyond the study of postural (*āsana*) yoga practice alone (cf. Singleton 2010)[1] to instead consider the understudied repertoires of yogic techniques that include particular ways of eating, singing, and breathing within social contexts where these practices are presumed to produce embodied transformation.

Eating, singing, and breathing are practices that deserve much more consideration in the field of Modern Yoga Studies. Due to the limitations of space, I have not included a number of other instances during my fieldwork which also demonstrated great opportunities for further research into the overlooked cultural intersections between yoga, food, music, breathing, and other cultural phenomena. A brief exploration of some of these encounters provides some inspiration for the infinite possibilities still waiting to be researched.

Consider, for instance, that while undertaking my two-year yoga teacher training in 2012 (in-person) and 2013 (remotely from Hawaii) with Christopher Chapple we often listened to the music produced at Gurani Anjali's Yoga Anand Ashram. In 1995, Anjali's songs had been recorded and made available for purchase on a cassette tape titled "From the Silent Depth Within Me: The Songs of Gurāṇi Añjali" (Anjali 1999) and were printed in what remains an unpublished manuscript songbook bearing the same name. Anjali's music, accompanied by instruments popular to the counterculture such as, most notably, the acoustic guitar, expressed a number of interrelated themes that were deeply devotional toward nature (*prakṛti*) and the higher Self (*puruṣa*) and thereby sonically expressive of her *Sāṃkhya-Yoga* philosophy and ethics from Bengal. A sobering and grief-stricken song titled "The Earth is Burning" frequently sung in group settings in the ashram and in my own yoga teacher training is particularly illustrative:

> The earth is burning. The sky is ablaze (2X)
> Thoughts of the past haunt us every day (2X)
> We turn to the day. We go into the night (2X)
> Pollution on the land, in the waters, in the air (2X)
> Where are the fathers? Where are the mothers? (2X)
> Like little children we scream now and then (2X)
> To be heard once again. We scream now and then (2X)
> Hypocrites abound all around and around (2X)
> Taking issue everywhere (2X)
> No one cares, who will care? (2X)
> The earth is burning. The sky is ablaze (2X)
> Where is the embrace and the loving care? (2X)
> We keep looking for that place, with that embrace (2X)
> Stranded in this world, you and me all alone (2X)
> You are my hope, I am your hope (2X)
>
> (Anjali 1999, 36)

As one listens to Anjali's lyrics accompanied by simple acoustic guitar, one hears not just yoga but also the sounds and social concerns of the countercultural generation. And as I read further into the history of countercultural music, I realized that what I was hearing was at least in part what Gair describes as the "folk boom coupling political protest with a near-obsessive insistence on the use of acoustic instruments in a quest for 'authenticity'" (Gair 2007: 161). The folk music movement, I learned, was unabashedly engaged with "calls for progressive social change," produced "hostility to the excesses of the modern world," and contributed to "the emergence of environmentalism as a key tenet of countercultural ideology" (ibid.: 164–65). As we can see in the lyrics above, Anjali harnessed these folk impulses shared among her devotees into her own musical framework, though in a uniquely non-violent and yogic way. Her music thus provided a sonic environment wherein students' countercultural concerns were acknowledged, vocalized, and embedded within a framework in which a yogic lifestyle appeared to be a viable and natural solution. Just as her ashram's dietary practices we encountered in Chapter 1 were intended to do, and as many of her students often conveyed to me, Anjali's music was ultimately intended to lead students to an experience of yoga's higher Self (*puruṣa*).

In another interesting set of instances at Polestar and Kaivalyadhama, I noted a great interest in the connection between yoga and nature that was expressed through both communities' attempts to become more self-sufficient and sustainable through the practices of permaculture and organic farming. Initially developed in Australia, permaculture is a relatively novel, post-countercultural, transnational food-production practice primarily practiced by members of the

Global North that aims to achieve local sustainable food development in countries all over the world (Lockyer and Veteto 2013). For Polestar's purposes, however, the community's permaculture was specifically used as part of their wider strategy to attract visitors interested in reconnecting with nature and in search of the "simple life" (Shi 2007; Miller 2020) as well as to remain compliant with land use restrictions given their zoning status in an agricultural region in Hawaii. From a yogic perspective, the practice supplied food for Polestar's broader vegetarian diet aimed at creating a pure, light, and *sāttvik* disposition supportive of the meditation practices we encountered in Chapter 2.

Similarly, at Kaivalyadhama, on-site and local organic farming became part of the yoga institution's "Green Ashram" and "Goshala" projects intended to help the community source its own organic fruits, vegetables, and dairy. The locally grown food was also, like the institution's breathing practices we encountered in Chapter 3, intended to support the practice of *kriyā-yoga* by facilitating the purification of the subtle channels (*nāḍīs*) of the *haṭha-yoga* subtle body. Despite the efforts to grow organic produce on the campus, circumstances sometimes required, and I often witnessed, that the low caste agricultural staff from the neighboring village of Pangoli sprayed pesticides on Kaivalyadhama's crops that had just begun to grow after the monsoon season in order to ward off harmful pests. Once again, and as we also saw in Chapter 3, the yogic self-sacrifice that Kaivalyadhama's yoga practices sought to accomplish were clearly occurring in a sacrifice zone where not just the air, but also the earth was being polluted by the toxic products of global industrialized agriculture and the residues of India's Green Revolution.

Where do we go from here? Future Directions for the Study of Yoga

These are just a handful of examples from my fieldwork that are intended to inspire deeper reflection on the many opportunities we have in the field of Modern Yoga Studies for critical ethnographic research of yogic diet, music, and breathing practices. There are also of course many other understudied categories of contemporary yoga practice awaiting our consideration. These alternative categories of practice often emerge whenever I explore potential research projects with my graduate students, where I begin by asking them to think about what it is that excites them most about yoga, and then direct them to consider that topic for their final ethnographic research project. For example, in the most recent iterations of my Modern Yoga Studies graduate seminar, students have responded with interest in research topics such as "Yoga and Parenting," "Yoga and Social Justice," "Yoga and Food," and "Prison Yoga."

As should be abundantly clear, this book has been concerned as much about methodology as it has yoga itself. And thus the next task my graduate students have after deciding on topics such as these is how and where to perform their research. What undiscovered tools and methods are awaiting them? What can these tools help reveal about yoga? Following the research methodology used in this book, I routinely direct each of these students to find a field site where yoga intersects with the categories they are interested in studying and to begin by clearly articulating the discourses and practices they encounter within these communities. Many students are of course already practicing or teaching in these yoga spaces and are therefore particularly well-equipped to articulate these discourses and practices. Next, in addition to central scholarship in Modern Yoga Studies, I direct each student to look at secondary scholarship in the academic fields relating to the category of yoga practice they have chosen. Following my previous example, I instructed those who were interested in researching "Yoga and Parenting," "Yoga and Social Justice," "Yoga and Food," and "Prison Yoga" to take a close look at the fields of "Critical Family History," "Social Justice Studies," "Food Studies," and "Critical Prison Studies," respectively, to see what these fields might tell them about their yoga field sites.

Students are often amazed at the interdisciplinary insights other academic fields can bring to the ethnographic sites where they are immersing themselves in yoga practices. One student was surprised, for example, by the ways that a distinctly American notion of the idealized, and yet overworked mother was manifesting in the discourse in her family yoga studio that clearly endorsed a neoliberal self-care narrative (cf. Jain 2020). Another student discovered that calls for social justice and accessibility in her yoga community were clearly aligned with the ethos of Western social justice movements more broadly, and pondered whether India's yoga warrior asceticism (Pinch 2006), or perhaps instead Gandhian forms of non-violent resistance (Howard 2013), would be more effective in the face of the United States' multiple social ills. The student studying yoga and food discovered that the prevailing ideologies of "carnism" (Joy 2020) and speciesism, or the culturally invented beliefs that lead humans to believe that they should raise animals for food, permeated her yoga community – and were racing the planet toward climate collapse. Finally, my student who taught prison yoga (cf. Godrej 2022) had a transformative and powerful experience through the anger she experienced when she realized she was reproducing a toxic self-blame narrative central to the ideology of the carceral state among her incarcerated minority yoga students.

I share these experiences with you here to suggest that there are as many ways to research yoga as there are types of yoga and accompanying academic fields that can help us understand them. Every day, I receive a Google alert that informs me about the latest trends and practices in the world of transnational yoga where I commonly encounter cultural phenomena including the well-known practices of goat yoga, beer yoga, weed yoga, and much, much more. Understanding how goats, beer, and weed have come to intersect with the category of yoga evokes important conversations that can be serviceably put in dialogue with the fields of Critical Animal Studies, Beer Studies, and Cannabis Studies, respectively. These would be important studies in their own right, in so far as the scholarly fields I mention here can certainly illuminate the cultural entanglements that have inspired such practices to emerge in popular practice.

These Google alerts also show us that not all yoga is soteriological or focused on some form of liberating experience as the systems I have presented in this book were, which has been an exploration of the specific contributions that contemporary transnational Indian disseminators of yoga have made to global society through identifiable forms of soteriological yoga and their accompanying repertoires of somatic practice. I hope that we can now more fully appreciate the creativity and ingenuity these innovators possessed, as they embedded their yoga systems into novel worlds of social experience, while still finding opportunities to world their Indian Ocean influences nonetheless. And I hope we can also appreciate that the yogas they deployed followed very particular cultural logics which, in various ways, attempted to implicate practitioners into an experience of embodied transformation. When we approach contemporary yoga systems as I have done in this book, we can also likely therefore appreciate why many contemporary students, teachers, and gurus practicing soteriological yoga experience frustration and a sense of betrayal when academic studies of yoga neglect to emphasize the cultural contributions and logics undergirding the creative innovations and adaptations made by their yoga-disseminating predecessors.

We all have something to learn from one another's epistemological positions, whether yogic, academic, or both (cf. Lidke 2021). There are, in other words, at least two broad sources of knowledge which have the potential to work well together in the pursuit of the study of yoga, rather than in opposition to, or in isolation from, one another. That is to say, and to further complicate an old dichotomy,[2] the critical Western academic pursuit of knowledge amplifies the methods for attaining yoga's necessary requisite worldly knowledge captured by the Sanskrit term *loka-pratyakṣa* (empirical perception), which when coupled with yoga's embodied techniques might, as Mauss (1973 [1935]: 86–87) similarly hypothesized in the epigraph to this book, lead one to the prized biological experience of direct perception of the higher Self, or *para-pratyakṣa* (supreme perception). This biological experience was, after all, what Swami Kuvalayananda dedicated his life to sharing transnationally through his empirical research at Kaivalyadhama, and an experience which Paramahansa Yogananda and Gurani Anjali brought abroad in their own particular ways. It is an experience, as should now be clear, that can only be wholly understood by critically studying, but also embodying, transnational yoga.

Notes

1 Postural yoga is undoubtedly transformative in its own ways for many practitioners, and I thank my colleague Anya Foxen for the suggestion to make this social fact explicit.

2 I am inspired here by something Joseph Alter originally wrote, "Speaking strictly as an academic – and as a practitioner of *vijnana* (intellectual knowledge) rather than *jnana* (wisdom) yoga and *malla vidya* (knowledge of wrestling) rather *hatha vidya* (knowledge of *hatha* [yoga]) – yoga makes much better sense to me in terms of what is written in the medieval literature than in what appears in modern texts, either popular or scientific" (Alter 2005: 141).

References

Alter, Joseph S. 2005. "Modern Medical Yoga: Struggling with a History of Magic, Alchemy and Sex." *Asian Medicine* 1, no. 1: 119–146.

Anjali, Gurani. 1999. *Yoga Anand Ashram Bhajans: Devotional Songs*. Amityville: Vajra Printing and Publishing of Yoga Anand Ashram.

Burchett, Patton E. 2019. *A Genealogy of Devotion: Bhakti, Tantra, Yoga, and Sufism in North India*. New York: Columbia University Press.

Deslippe, Philip. 2021. "How the Model of Money Laundering Can Help Us Understand Abuse within 3HO," in Christopher Miller (ed.), "Abuse in Yoga and Beyond: Cultural Logics and Pathways for the Future." *Sacred Matters Magazine*. Accessed January 21, 2022. https://sacredmattersmagazine.com/how-the-model-of-money-laundering-can-help-us-understand-abuse-within-3ho/

Gair, Christopher. 2007. *The American Counterculture*. Edinburgh: Edinburgh University Press.

Godrej, Farah. 2022. *Freedom Inside: Yoga and Meditation in the Carceral State*. New York: Oxford University Press.

Howard, Veena R. 2013. *Gandhi's Ascetic Activism: Renunciation and Social Action*. Albany: State University of New York Press.

Jain, Andrea R. 2020. *Peace, Love, Yoga: The Politics of Global Spirituality*. New York: Oxford University Press.

Joy, Melanie. 2020. *Why We Love Dogs, Eat Pigs, and Wear Cows: An Introduction to Carnism*. Newburyport: Red Wheel.

Kripal, Jeffery J. 2013. "Conclusion: On Reason, Religion, and the Real," in Ann Gleig and Lola Williamson (eds.), *Homegrown Gurus: From Hinduism in America to American Hinduism*, Albany: State University of New York Press: 215–223.

Lidke, Jeffrey S. 2021. "Knowledge above Dogma: Being a Tantric Yogi Scholar in the Age of Being SBNR (Spiritual but Not Religious)," paper presented at the *2021 DANAM Conference at the Annual Meeting of the American Academy of Religion*, Boston, November 21, 2021.

Lockyer, Joshua and James R. Veteto, eds. 2013. *Environmental Anthropology Engaging Ecotopia: Bioregionalism, Permaculture, and Ecovillages*. New York: Berghahn.

Mauss, Marcel. 1973 [1935]. "Techniques of the Body." *Economy and Society* 2, no. 1: 70–88.

Miller, Christopher, ed. 2021. "Abuse in Yoga and Beyond: Cultural Logics and Pathways for the Future." *Sacred Matters Magazine*. Accessed January 21, 2022. https://sacredmattersmagazine.com/ya-introduction/

Miller, Christopher Patrick. 2020. "Paramahansa Yogananda's World Brotherhood Colonies: Models for Environmentally Sustainable and Socially Responsible Living," in Christopher Patrick Miller, Michael Reading, and Jeffery Long (eds.), *Beacons of Dharma: Spiritual Exemplars for the Modern Age*. New York: Lexington Books: 163–180.

Pinch, William R. 2006. *Warrior Ascetics and Indian Empires*. Cambridge: Cambridge University Press.

Sarkar, Sumit. 1997. *Writing Social History*. New York: Oxford University Press.

Shi, David E. 2007. *The Simple Life: Plain Living and High Thinking in American Culture*. Athens: University of Georgia Press.

Singleton, Mark. 2010. *Yoga Body: The Origins of Modern Posture Practice*. New York: Oxford University Press.

Index

Pages in *italics* refer to figures and pages followed by "n" refer to notes.